REFRACTIONS

REFRACTIONS

Octavio Armand

Translated by Carol Maier

SITES/Lumen Books
446 West 20 Street
New York, NY 10011
(212) 989-7944

ISBN 0-930829-21-2
Printed in the United States of America

SITES Books and Lumen Books are produced by Lumen, Inc., a tax-exempt, non-profit organization. This publication is made possible, in part, with public funds from the New York State Council on the Arts, and private contribubtions.

Contents

Translator to Reader: Five Notes

Carol Maier

I

Octavio Armand was born in Cuba on May 10, 1946, into a family that would be exiled twice: once, in 1958, under Batista, and again under Castro in 1960. For many years of the second exile he lived in New York City; at present he resides in Caracas.

Armand's first book of poems, *Horizonte no es siempre lejanía*, was published in 1970. Since that date he has published six other collections of poetry, the most recent of which is *Origami* (Caracas, 1987), and *Superficies*, a collection of essays (Caracas, 1980). He has also published translations of poems by Mark Strand (*Mark Strand: 20 poemas*, Caracas, 1979) and edited an anthology of Latin American poetry for Logbridge-Rhodes (*Toward an Image of Latin American Poetry*, Durango, Colorado, 1982). In 1978, he founded *escandalar*, a literary journal that he edited until 1984, in which he published works by writers from Spain and Latin America as well as many European and North American writers in Spanish translation. In English, in translations by Carol Maier, Armand's work has appeared in numerous literary journals and in *With Dusk* (Logbridge-Rhodes, 1984). In addition to many reviews and interviews, two full-length studies have been devoted to his work in Spanish: *Conversación con la esfinge (Una lectura de la poesía de Octavio Armand*, by Juan Antonio Vasco (Buenos Aires, 1984) and *Octavio Armand y el espejo, o América como ucronía,* by Luis Justo (Caracas, 1988).[1]

II

With one exception, the pieces for this collection were chosen by Octavio Armand. His model was "Refracciones" (Refractions), a manuscript of paired poems and essays, most of which had been published individually in Spanish. It was my suggestion to include "Lezama Lima or the Death of Narcissus." Although this essay considerably predates many of the others, I believed that—regardless of its place in the book—it would establish a point of departure without which the evocation of an absence in the other pieces might be difficult, if not impossible. The same might be said of "Penitence," the prose poem Armand selected as a companion poem for "Lezama Lima."

III

To the extent that a translator can identify the theoretical principle(s) guiding her practice, I acknowledge the "refraction" in the collection's Spanish title. That word, as I read it in Armand's work, indicates deflection or bending, a change in position—such as that observed in heavenly bodies—distortion. The suggestion of rupture at the word's center impresses me as misleading, despite its etymology. This I find confirmed by both *Webster's Third International* (where "break up," like "reflect," is listed as an obsolete meaning of "refract") and Bakhtin (a reference absent from Armand's writing, but one I have found useful and provocative for these translations, particularly Bakhtin's discussion of discourse as it differs in poetry and the novel).

The following three examples are offered as illustrations of the refractive relationship I have experienced between theory and practice.

(1) When I began to translate "Taste: Archaeology of a Sense" (the first piece I prepared from the previously unpublished material), one of my first concerns was Armand's frequent use of the first person plural. I found myself bristling each time "we" or "us" occurred in the text. In expository prose, "we" English-speaking North Americans rarely refer explicitly to either ourselves or our relationship with the reader. The repeated appearance of Armand's "we," therefore, seemed to mark the essay as foreign or translated. In order to prevent that otherness, which, I reasoned, would affect reading adversely, I decided to recast sentences and employ a more distant—and hence more familiar—third person. This substitution could be made almost effortlessly in the first paragraph: "An event like the discovery could find everyone"; "For Americans to speak . . . with respect to their history. . . ." Only in the penultimate sentence where, in addition to a different tradition, the use of the imperative reflects the essay's mixed origins as a talk half-written and half-spoken, did it seem necessary to

retain the Spanish construction.[2] Difficulty arose in the second paragraph, however, as I wrote "There in their own landscape . . . they. . . ." Perhaps "There in the Cuban landscape. . . we . . .," I jotted in the margin, thinking that even though I did not want English-language readers to find themselves included in a grouping they might resist for any number of reasons ("There in our Cuban landscape . . . we . . ."), I did want them to be aware of the specifically Cuban context of the essay.

I reflected on that sentence for a long time, roughing out alternative versions for it and for other sentences in which the first person plural appeared, recording each of the instances in my notes. Here "our" refers to literally everyone, I decided for one passage; here "our" is any modern reader; in this instance "we" are all Americans (North and South); in this instance, however, "we" are Cubans only; "we" are the readers of this essay.

"'We' are the readers of this essay." That was it, of course, although I was not fully aware just how much until I had very nearly finished the essay and written the translation for "we have had to study, contemplate it [the pineapple], like a truth greater than ambrosia, in order to see it on our own table. . . ."

Armand's Cuban reader is built here gradually, I noted then, and this is a different Cuban reader than the one who reads in Spanish, or the one who reads in Cuban. Since I suspect that English-language readers will, to varying degrees, be both willing and unwilling to share this Cubanness, Armand's shifting "our" must be rigorously maintained. Without it, readers are deprived of the ambivalence and abrasion immediately apparent to any Cuban who reads the essay.

Hence, "An event like the discovery could find all of us listening to a hundred lectures," and other analogous uses of the first person plural.

(2) "If I left, I would instantly long to return"; "Clinging to your *jabillo*"; "lightning flashing in that heavenly *tocino del cielo*": Armand's poems and essays are studded with references to Cuban literature, music, landscapes, and food, and not to translate them is to mystify the reader or to turn a familiar Caribbean tree or a typical dessert into something exotic. To add footnotes, however, is to interrupt reading and to render a

text academic. Substitution makes a text more accessible (a North American song; a large thorny bush or its pods; a dish of floating island) but strips it of the tension between the Cuban past and North American present constantly operative in Armand's work. Consequently, here and there I have written a brief explanation into the text and I have chosen not to translate various terms nor to seek "equivalents" for songs and literary allusions.

On the other hand, in a decision I find more correspondent than contradictory, I have not hesitated to play with English in ways that reflect Armand's play, at times without reflecting his Spanish. My goal in these instances has been to convey Armand's refraction itself, his verbal ruin(ation), his stride at once as restrained and determined as that in Góngora's description of the Count of Villamediana (in "Kafka's Living Room" and "Diamond of Wood").

(3) "Then, in a corner of the nave, with creamy rags, pupils narrowed, panting, like cats digging for bird bones, they were flattening a bundle of dirty sheets with a knife." Embedded in "Putting It Down: A Get-up," clearly boxed off from Armand's words but identified within them only obliquely, there is a passage from Severo Sarduy's *Maitreya*. Rereading it so as to make revisions for this collection, I realized that when I first translated Sarduy's lines I had not visualized them clearly. This meant that my revision required numerous changes, and as I made them I remembered that Suzanne Jill Levine had also translated those same words for her version of the entire novel. Her work was helpful to me, because by studying her reading of Sarduy I was better able to see the strengths and weaknesses of my own, and to see us both enacting the very same passage, struggling with the simultaneous precision and ambivalence of its images, with the complexities of Sarduy's sentences, with his punctuation. As in numerous other passages in Armand's essays, then, I consulted the work of another translator, but made my own translations according to the exigencies of a new context.[3]

"With small pieces of knife-shaped sandalwood they were scraping pox from a corpse," I thought in each instance of consultation, imaging all of us translators as seekers of the possible spark of life we might find under a skin we persist in covering over. There could not be a better representation of translation according to Armand, I decided, even for the instances in which I worked alone (on Rubén Darío's poem or Góngora's sonnet) or in the one instance I used another translator's work with no alteration at all (Frederick Morgan's translation of Mallarmé's "*Toute l'âme résumée . . .*").[4]

IV

"I find your 5 June version quite heartful, quite there. Mine, my comments, as usual, and as I have always insisted, are di/versions. Suggestions, promptings, dares. Very seldom, and only when I know something is way out of literal focus, do I object. And the ultimate choices, in the translations, must be yours. Must be yours! I'm only too glad when any of my diversions play well into your eventual, ultimate version."

As I begin to write my thanks to Octavio Armand for innumerable readings and comments throughout many versions, I am reminded of a letter he wrote to me in June of 1990 after I had sent him a set of extensive revisions. He was responding to some of my questions and alluding to several passages for which I had even suggested modifications, passages where, as I translated them, I found myself in disagreement.

If I recall that letter now, it is because I want to acknowledge the extent to which Armand and I consulted about *Refractions*. I also want to respond to the question I have asked myself about whether some pieces or sections of some pieces might not be best defined as collaborations rather than conventional "translations" or "versions."

"This is, should always be a collaboration," Armand wrote in the same letter, "but one where your freedom, you the translator, reigns supreme. I have that freedom when I face the blank page. You must have a sense, a different but hopefully not much diminished sense of freedom, when you face the scorched, tattooed, scarred page."

This may seem ironic, even contradictory, but in Armand's generous emphasis on my freedom and his allusion to the long friendship we have enjoyed as writer and translator I find, ultimately, a distinction between our roles. Armand and I have collaborated, and at times there have certainly been two translators. The pieces included here, however, were written in an English for which I take "final" responsibility, for I have been the one to decide when and how I would exercise the freedom Armand advocated. When and how I would choose not to follow his urging that I "trust the text enough to betray it" was my decision. In such instances, when I found my work grazing what might be termed the "last frontier" in a translator's practice, I explored the constraint of convictions as well as divergent linguistic structures and referents. On that frontier, I believe there were instances when I took issue with the text in ways that made full betrayal, according to Armand's definition, impossible, even when I was willing to set aside my own persuasions. I would suggest that in those instances I became the single translator or translator-author (as distinct from the author or author-in-translation or author-as-translator). This would be true despite my inability to identify all of the instances and despite the fact that even as the distinction between our roles occurred Armand and I continued to work in the closest of collaborations.

V

I am grateful to the Illinois Arts Council and to Bradley University's Board for Research and Creativity for support that made possible early versions of several of these essays, to the National Endowment for the Arts for a Translator's Fellowship that allowed me to prepare the new translations, and to the Research Council at Kent State University for a grant that enabled me to consult personally with Octavio Armand during the final stages of revision. I would also like to thank Debi Eler for her help with word processing.

Finally, I want to express my thanks to the friends and colleagues who encouraged these translations and my work with Armand over a period of many years, particularly George Chambers, Ronald Christ, Frank Graziano, Marilyn Kiss, Fred Maier, Noël Valis, and the late Gregory Kolovakos.

Notes

[1]The following poems in this collection are from *Origami*: "Nadabrahma," "Another Letter from Jonah to Thomas the Magnificent," "White on White," "Self-portrait Without Me," "Infinity and I," and "Diamond of Wood." "Penitence" was included in *Superficies* and and previously published in *Plural* 5.7 (1976): 18-24 and *Papeles de Son Armadans* 242 (1976): 195-208. "Birth Certificate" is from *Entre testigos* (Madrid, 1974). "Meditations," "Invisible Blue," and "The Tomb of Senmut" have not been published in Spanish.
Of the poems, only "Penitence," which appears here in a revised translation, has been published previously in English (*Voicing*. Ed. Don Wellman. *O.ARS* 6 (1989): 99-105.
All of the essays have been published in Spanish. Those that have been previously published in English, such as "Penitence," are reprinted with permission and they have been revised for this collection. Publication information is as follows:
"Birth Certificates as Fiction" was published in six parts in *El Universal* (Caracas) 2, 16, and 23 January; 3 April and 17 April; and 22 May 1983 and in *escandalar* 6.3/4 - 7.1 (July 1983-March 1984); *Fiction International* 16.2 (1986): 78-98.
"Lezama Lima or the Death of Narcissus" (*Lezama Lima o la muerte de Narciso*) and "Ramming the Page" (*Contra la página*): *Superficies*. "Lezama Lima" was also published in *Escolios*, 1.3 (November 1976): 64-81.
"Ramming the Page" (*Contra la página*): *escandalar* 1.2 (April-June 1978): 29-38.
"A Reading of Light" (*Una lectura de la luz*): *El Universal* 27 September, 4 and 11, October 1981, and *escandalar* 4.4 (October-December 1981); *Translations: Experiments in Reading*. *O.ARS* 4 (1983): 149-59.
"Putting It Down: A Get-up" (*Escribir es cubrir*): *escandalar* 5.1-2 (1982); *Fiction International* 18.2 (1990): 22-31.
"Robert Morris: Mirage, Reflection" (Robert Morris: *Espejismo, especulación* [*Un pequeño homenaje a la mirada*]): *Superficies* and *escandalar* 2.4 (1979); *October* 6 (Fall 1978): 75-80.
"Taste: Archaeology of a Sense" (*Arqueología del sabor*): *El Universal* 27 December 1987.
"A Mouthful of Infinity" (*El infinito en la boca*): *Paisajes 3* (Pamplona, Spain) (1985): 47-56; *El Universal* 7 and 14 July 1989.
"Essay in Smoke" (*Ensayo de humo*): *Nuevo Mundo* (Caracas, Instituto de Altos Estudios) 13. 2-3 (April-September 1990): 176-201.
"Kafka's Living Room" (*La sala de Kafka*): *Cielo Abierto* (Lima, Peru) 8.24 (1983) and *El Universal* 10 July 1983; *Tyuonyi* 2 (1986): 141-4.
"Poetry as *Eruv*" (*La poesía como eruv*): *El Universal* 22 February 1987; *Index on Censorship* 18.3 (March 1989): 19-21. Also forthcoming in *New Scholar*.

[2]An early Spanish language version of this essay was read at California State University at Los Angeles on November 9, 1987, an explicitly oral origin that

is shared by three of the other prose pieces: "A Reading of Light" was delivered at the Second Congress of Spanish-Language Writers, held in Caracas in 1981; "Kafka's Living Room" was read at "Kafka Unorthodox," a centennial celebration of artists, writers, filmmakers, and musicians held at Cooper Union in 1983; and "Poetry as *Eruv*" was presented at "The Poetry of Exile," a panel held at the Festival of New Latin American Poetry, Durango, Colorado, 1985.

[3]Those translators are, in particular: Mary Ann Caws, "Igitur," *Stéphane Mallarmé: Selected Poetry and Prose*, Mary Ann Caws, ed. (New York, 1982); J. M. Cohen, *The Adventures of Don Quijote* (New York, 1950); Ellen Fox, *Artificial Paradise: On Hashish and Wine as Means of Expanding Individuality* (New York, 1971); Jack Hirschman, *Igitur* (Los Angeles, 1974); Suzanne Jill Levine, *Maitreya* (Hanover, NH, 1987); Ron Padgett, *'The Poet Assassinated' and Other Stories* (San Francisco, 1984); Gregory Rabassa, *Paradiso* (New York, 1974); Tobias Smollett, *Don Quixote de la Mancha* (London, 1755; rpt. New York, 1986).

[4]"The Whole Soul Summed Up," translated by Frederick Morgan, in Christopher Wilmarth's *Breath* (New York, 1982). Reprinted with permission.

Nadabrahma

As the eyes close
I recover my gaze
Fleeting images
Stones of smoke
That conceal
The diamond
Of desperation
My true face
Is another mask
The eyelid
                A wound
That finally scars
"Who are you?"
"I am here"
A precise answer
You were naked
You were necessary
Knots of color explode
In a small quiet sky
Against the eyelid
White is black
Blank
            A ripening fruit
Who are you?
Neither mouth
                        Nor roof of the mouth
Mouthfooted
Mouthbreeder
Blows of enclosed blood
A slight tremor
Hollows four thousand walls
Flesh and lies
To breathe I hear myself breathe
I breathe the sound of my body
My name barely another sound

Welcome to lightning
Wood as it burns

Fire
As smoke
Smoke
Poorly carved
That survives
In the ashes
I discover the body
It is not mine
It is me
Who is me?
To be able to say always
What a beautiful woman!
What clear water!
What light we have made!
Geometry
Going astray
I turn
Slowly
On the empty axis
And again greet
The same wound
An endless hollow
Circle
Poisoned by charades of perfection
I surprise myself
In the kaleidoscope's tiny mirror
Who I am
Who I was
Who I will be
Who I have been
Who I would be
Who I could be
Who I might have been
Gather between two stars
A cluster of frauds
Tripping falling getting lost
At the center of blood
A syllable
Heaps wreckage
Of what I seem to have been
Of what I seem to be

Inventory and blank slate
You are
I speak to myself
The one who clouds the mirror
Asking for a match an address a handout
Heartily
Hardly
Petrified porous spoken
Weaving together four winds
The beam of a breath
Finally masters a growing landscape
A half moon more asleep
Than yellow
An island of breath
Surrounded
By the highest tide of silence.

Stone lizard fish scales
Being to death
Birth
Right now
I gather my name
And carry it
To my lungs like a shapeless flower
To see I see myself seeing
My eyes
Sandbars
The current sighted
Is
Sight
We seem
We see
My true face
Is my true mask
The snail
Flies
The bird crawls
At the center of blood
Blood is not mine

My own tracks
My own lines
                              A mazing hand
Traps webs labyrinths
Let things say their names
A snake crosses the path
Neither dust
                           Nor grass
Snake
Trip fall get lost
Wake with me
In the blood of Icarus
When only the chill
Of falling
                    Remains
For centuries
A boat
Has departed
Some geese
                        Fly
Recalling Euclid
Below
The sea sharpens
                                    Jumbled eyeteeth
Foam
            Has never been
So black

Constellations of crystal
I am not blind
                              I see darkness
Night
Resembles
                        My shadow
Paracelsus would say
There is a star in your body
I say
        The leopard
Dyes his spots
And fire

Launches a hundred summers
Gardens of oblivion
Remembering remembering remembering
Today you will lose one more mask
You feel your heart
In your knee
                    In your groin
In your sex
A fish
          You fly
A bird
You swim
                 Believing disbelief
Surly halves
                    Who am I?
I who weigh less than my shadow?
Whatever you say
                              The breath
Where a word
Lives
         Who am I?
I who look so like
Myself?
             Looks
Faces
          Phases
The wind
That scatters
                    My ashes

Birth Certificates as Fiction

We get born wherever we can.
—Jorge Luis Borges

The Present Past: Cuban Impossibility

1

This is the story of an absence. An essay in prenatal writing. A day like today—today is March 10, 1979—my erasure from Cuban history began. Perhaps I was always erased in that also-erased history. But I was a child once and I still have copies of a very detailed birth certificate. It's right here. I'm reading it because I want to be born again, here, now, another day, any day but this one.

His paternal grandparents are Octavio Armand Roch and Argimira Vega Vega, natives of France and Bayamo, Cuba, respectively, both deceased. His maternal grandparents are Rafael Santana González and Fermina Martín Medina, natives of the Canary Islands, Spain; the former is a resident of this city, the latter is deceased. That the aforementioned child was named OCTAVIO RAFAEL.

Astounding, the number of words required to report the birth of a child. Hyperbole, emphasis, redundance, proliferation. Isn't there the hint, or hunch, of a smudge? My name is here, the names of my parents and grandparents are here, signatures and countersignatures of judges and witnesses, seals and stamps, a whole legal world determined to affirm that I was born, that I exist, that I am I, that I belong. Why? It's as if I had been born in the rickety language of a municipality: as if I could only be born officially, with seals and stamps, slaps given by justice to get my name on its feet, like the other slaps I imagine were given to my body to get it breathing. So the body won't lack air, so the name won't lack language: slap them. But later came asthma, exile, gasps for air and language, breathing, writing with inadequacy, with what I lacked, as if everything were marked by separation and slaps.

Here there is also a first albeit weak sanction of verbal excess, of disproportion between word and thing, or separation between word and thing. Legal proliferation is a key to Cuban baroque. The exaggerated affirmation, or written proof of my existence, is my first confession—forced, reinforced—to a world that will insist tenaciously and repeatedly on all kinds of confessions; but by the same token a world that will suggest a thousand and one times—legalese against legality—how not to say what you've said and repeat it. This is how I would confess in another well-polished ritual for my first communion. Each subsequent communion was a replica of that first communion, simply because all my confessions repeated what was never said. The list of my sins was invariably adjusted to what I allowed myself to say rather than to what I was not allowed to do: father, I've had bad thoughts, I've said bad words, I've lied, I lie. . . . The confession was a verbal process that pointed stubbornly toward other verbal processes. Thanks to what was censored, I could have what was forbidden; the act was mine because of the word that hid, repeated it within me, secretly, when it pointed to me as a verbal process within another process that was also strictly verbal. I condemned myself unknowingly, absolving myself with the famous paradox of Epimenides, the Cretan.

which occurred at five-thirty in the afternoon on the tenth day of May in the year one thousand nine hundred forty-six, on Marti and Emilio Giro Streets in this city. He is the son of Luis Armand Vega and Julia Santana Martín, both natives of Yateras, of legal age; he is a businessman and she a homemaker; both are residents of this city.

I'm not as sure as my parents, judges, witnesses that I've been born. I distrust the language that affirms my existence so robustly. Do I dare trust such a poorly written document? Perhaps my entire effort to write down/drown the exact word is a way of correcting, rewriting my birth certificate, which for 32 years, 9 months, and 10 days has continued to give me birth—or light, as we say in Spanish—to confront me later with such numerous, numbing, and superbly unjust words. It's as if I'd been born in a ridiculously serious farce: the protagonist runs from the words that hide him on a lost page. But what aren't we told by a document that says so much, by such a documentary document? Procreate: propagate: propaganda: as if a book or the page of a book had been born while a child was being slapped. Or as if that child were born weighing nine books. Erase: establish: erect. Talk back, talk against, talk down. I wonder when it was that I disauthorized them to authorize me? When did I first suspect inadequacy, the excessive inadequacy of the very copulative municipal language? When did that child who perhaps had not yet been born no longer want to leave his birth, nor his birth certificate in the hands of his parents, his witnesses, or his judges? For as I read my birth certificate, as I am born, I feel like literature, like a page, a book, something destined for reading—or burning—that will live as long as it is readable, read.

2

I shut myself up to write and look at what I've written on the walls.[1] When I write I'm at the point of being born, always at the point of being born, birthed, in language, against language. But also against my mother's flesh—since I'm about to be born I take off my clothes—and against the four walls stuck to my skin; and I know that beyond, behind this verbal tissue there is another, biological tissue, I know that the very line I am writing right now is a reverse umbilical cord, which carries me through my mother to a world where I am only absence. [2]

This record is performed by virtue of the requirements in Law Decree three thousand six hundred ninety-six of last year, and

---

1. I'm concerned about walls the way most people are concerned about their clothes. I never know what clothes are becoming to me, and my friends all suggest colors, sizes, combinations, styles that I later forget or half remember. In an attempt to seam together my unseemliness, people always criticize what I wear; perversely they tell me to avoid loose-fitting trousers, striped shirts, blue socks, as if they didn't realize that I was wearing loose-fitting trousers, a striped shirt, blue socks. . . . I prefer the emperor's clothes: on my body I feel walls not clothing. Since I spend more time in my room than on the street, it's my walls that have to fit well, and I cover them with objects and paintings that are pleasing to my solitude the way silk or cotton are pleasing to the skin. My room is a shell; I always carry it with me.

2. The journey to one's source, or reverse birth: a Cuban theme, where the concealment of racial mixture, illegitimacy, incest is perhaps suggested. . . .

the appearing party Mr. Luis Armand Vega, whose personal circumstances show he is the father of the boy referred to in this record

Some fragments from Swarthmore that confirm the above.

1. I'm at Swarthmore. An immense solitude. I see the word immense and want to erase it: there is nothing immense here. The beauty of this place, its silence, and what I have called my solitude because of the life-with-labyrinth I lead here, all seem rather like details, pieces, like something seen at very close range, or something that closes in on all sides and always defers to a little spider that runs off spinning: colors, silhouettes. A landscape the eye can touch. Because of everything I've just said, I erase the word immense: ~~immense~~, and I continue. I feel alone. I realize once again that I cannot get along without my family nor the small space of my habits, where the rituals, however unimportant they may seem, or be, have at least bestowed order on discomfort, leading me by the hand to the place of hands: my room is a glove. An Oedipal case. This room, this spot, is not a uterus. I could not be born here.

2. Last week—I think it was the first time this ever happened to me—as I was walking home to my apartment, at night, I suddenly began to cry. Unexpectedly, with no reason, no warning. As if I'd been pulled from my mother's womb at that minute, and the streets, or the darkness, something, had slapped me. There was no one. There is never anyone here, which is just as well. That night one of the cats came to visit me—there are three who visit often: *Midnight, 1am, 2pm*—and I was surprised to find myself thanking him for the visit, talking to him as I would have talked to a close friend. One more detail. A few weeks ago my mother wrote me a note: I must not forget the white sweater because she wanted to have it cleaned. Well, I have that note hung on the wall as if it were a painting, a priceless family heirloom. It adds a homey touch to this room, which otherwise looks too much like the truncated, stagnant spaces I mention in my poetry: holes that fall into hollows, for example. This is like wearing a hole to hide your face.

3. Water on water: rain, ice, snow. Like the redundancy of the bucket falling in a well to reproduce the cavity. Without an

askance look. What a mirror that is, cavity pressed in cavity, like catching a stone you've been thrown and setting it in the center of a ring. Isn't that what baptism is? Another redundancy: being here, far from my room, which I miss terribly. On the walls I've written the names of my parents, of my cats, of Celeste, Luis, and Asela. I turn toward those names when I go to bed, and I don't have to sleep alone. I'll have to put names on all the walls. Adding names lessens emptiness. It also—I know this—adds emptiness.

4. There is no present in what is happening right now. Now is another time, memory, oblivion. That is how I live history. I recognize it precisely from its lack of present. Exile? Perhaps it is something more basic. If we could copy Sartre's idea about existence preceding essence, we would arrive, through a clouded mirror, at the affirmation that presence precedes essence. One thing is clear: to be is to be present no longer. Haven't you ever felt panicked, I asked a friend, about being present? The feeling of occupying too much space, of being obvious, as if you had stolen your body, your name, your words, and at any moment that could expose you, punish you? A Malthusian complex, an instinct for camouflage. Being present is always a squander of being; being present is not fitting; as if you screamed with your skin, with the clothing you don't put on for fear of drawing attention to your body, with the thought that goes out one ear and never enters the other.

OCTAVIO RAFAEL ARMAND Y SANTANA. -83. -In Guantánamo, Province of Oriente, at nine o'clock in the morning of the twenty-eighth day of February in the year one thousand nine hundred forty-eight, in the presence of Doctor Eudaldo Francisco Gallart Carcassés, Municipal Judge in charge of the Civil Registry, and Pedro Beatón Crespo, Secretary, the birth of a male is recorded.

3

Write, keep writing, but always in ordered disorder. To write as if I were Marcel Marceau in his glass box. Write against my birth certificate. Chance, not destiny. Chaos must be orderly, as they say in Cuba. Organize discipline. Remember an observation by Dardo Cúneo, an Argentine: "Disorder is, initially, the source of American possibility." Maybe that explains why the initial source of our presence, now, is a box of words, a rigorous classification. Using the registry, I want to create, textually, a source of Cuban impossibility. On my desk I pile papers, notes, drafts written other days, which can enter this March 10 in order to undo it as a date. For example, Tuesday, March 1, 1977. Today will also be other days, many days, with their nights mashed like ants in the blackness of these letters. It's necessary to collect some data to prove that my birth certificate is lying. Data of a person who is born, or will be born,

---

THE NEW YORK TIMES, MONDAY, NOVEMBER 29, 1976

›phy That Recalls the

after nine supposedly blissful months in the womb, with all our needs taken care of and nothing to do but enjoy, we were shot into a world of bright lights, strangers, noxious noises and yanked from a world of pleasure and calm to a world of pain and chaos.

up our breathing mechanism, learn that breathing is a positive, not a negative force. Most people go through life by underbreathing, not letting go, stuffing the birth trauma back into themselves," she said.

People begin unraveling the birth

"Our first breath is probably the closest we come to dying, so we don't see breathing as a pleasurable experience."

And, so they say, it has colored our view of life ever since.

Go back and relive your birth, understand it as an adult, and suddenly life will become a bit clearer, believe the rebirthers. Essentially, what it's all about is breathing. And letting go.

"Our first breath is probably the closest we ever come to dying, and so we don't see breathing as a pleasurable experience," explained Diane Hintermann, a young Californian who is a trained rebirther and has been with the rebirthing movement since its inception three and a half years ago.

"Through rebirthing, we learn to free

trauma by first attending a $10 rebirth seminar, where the rebirthing philosophy is discussed and procedures are explained. Clients then spend several individual sessions with a trained rebirther, someone who's been rebirthed probably dozens of times and has sufficiently worked out his own birth trauma to assist at another rebirth.

At these individual sessions (first "dry" and then "wet" rebirths), the rebirther takes the client through what is called the "breathing release," during which many people relive many of the subsconscious traumas associated with birth.

---

in installments. And it is also necessary to write, in order to be born, to continue being born always. "We can never be born enough," e.e. cummings wrote. And now that line is one of mine. With it I will try to erase another of my lines: "Being born is here an unmentionable feast."

Birth as Exile

The difficulty we have really understanding Whitman should not surprise us. Whitman, or Emerson, or William Carlos Williams, or . . . Here we can insert a whole litany of incomprehension, because it is not merely a question of a few authors, a few names, but the pulse of a whole literature for which our assumptive forms, our possible readings, are pathetically hindered by a lack of immediacy and circumstance. It would also be difficult, or impossible, for us to understand the stark lack of embellishment in North American documentation. There is a constitution that we can only imagine, or imitate, as a monument, as a museum of aspirations and promises belied at every step by the upheavals of our history, a text that, in spite of carbon paper, we will never manage to bring to life, which is the only way it could have meaning. And there are birth certificates even more incomprehensible to us who believe only in language because we come and go to lying. They do not offer enough verbiage for people like us to grab onto; these documents are almost as naked as the babies who gave them birth, and they are written as if to turn those babies over to the world, to life, and not to a file, to legal traps and signatures, seals and witnesses. Language anchors us, anchors us to a name, a genealogy, saddling us with a catalog of testimonies and oaths. On the one hand, it is as if being born were a majestic event worthy of odes to Niagara and speeches by Fidel. On the other, it is as if everything, as if our lives themselves, even when these lives have barely begun, were doubtful, a warning that we exist only if we document and prove that we only exist, if we speak and are heard, if someone wants to hear us, if we have enough of our papers in order each time they are requested, if we are always alert for the possible erasure or the possible fire, if we stick to life like a stamp, a seal, and stay there, paper octopi, immobile like the letters on our birth certificates, paralyzed forever, as if at birth we entered nine infinite months called language, history, lie, which will never let us be born completely.

The birth certificate of a North American does not look like a document. Since I am accustomed to leagues of language, at first glance it seems like a desert to me, a joke. But Eugene Sigel exists, I know him. His name seems like a photograph; I see his body on the page, and in some way I sense that here the relation between name and named is more direct. More direct and healthier. The name points to existence, leads to the

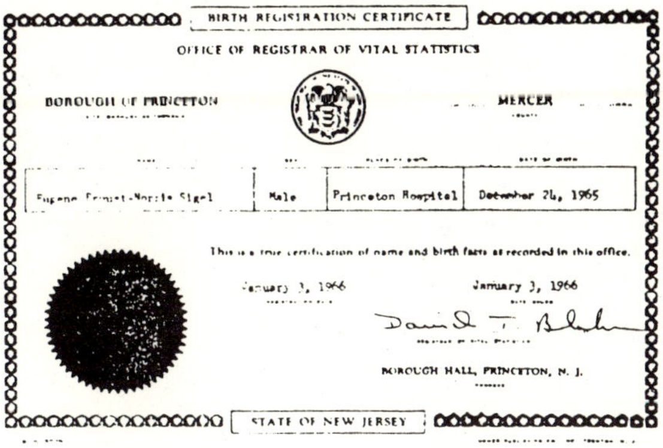

BIRTH REGISTRATION CERTIFICATE

OFFICE OF REGISTRAR OF VITAL STATISTICS

BOROUGH OF PRINCETON

MERCER

Eugene [illegible] Sigel	Male	Princeton Hospital	December 24, 1965

This is a true certification of name and birth facts as recorded in this office.

January 3, 1966

January 3, 1966

BOROUGH HALL, PRINCETON, N. J.

STATE OF NEW JERSEY

named. By desisting whenever possible, language insists on life; it quits and acquits. And it occurs to me that on birth certificates there is a relation between existence and quantity of language. An inversely proportional relation: the more language the less existence. Of course the relation between a specific quantity of language and a specific quality of existence will always be absurd. But to some, what will seem absurd is not that relation in itself but the quantity of language, or worse, existence itself. And this is what we would have to analyze. We could begin right here to discuss the incredible orality of Cubans, which has offered such splendid moments as Lezama's poetry—Seated inside my mouth I am present at the landscape, from his mouth rattled a trainload of pickled peppers—emphatic, empty gestures like that endless chorus of Fidel's speeches, capable of leaving stillborn a riotous nation, fetal as well as fatal, or the widespread shiteating of Cubans known for the swallowed S's that mark their pronunciation, who spend their lives crapping at the mouth, talking crap, eating it, and accusing everyone of perpetual coprophagia.

"Rapidly, militarily"—writes Carlos Loveira in *Generals and Doctors*—"we all get on the train, making ourselves as comfortable as possible and making a heroic effort to seem as little Cuban as we can: which is to say, quiet." Because what boarded that train was Lezama's load of pickled peppers, our loose and linguistically lewd tongue. It's not Cuban to be quiet. To be quiet is not to exist, to cease being. Only by thoroughly understanding this singularity of our racial logic can you approach the how and why of conversational poetry in recent Cuban literature. A conversational poetry where you cannot speak, at least in the case of Cuba, is not paradoxical, at least not entirely. Coprophagia, the ritual that so obsesses us, is characterized precisely by the need to invert terms, order, chronology. Once again, the reverse journey, the journey to the source. For coprophagia is the effort to begin digestion with defecation. A present past. A self-pourtrait: ingest the residue of what has already been digested. A reverse squander. Rot as premiere. Inverse consumption.

But if you eat shit, you also, and simultaneously, talk shit, which is like wanting to have your tail and eat it too, to empty yourself in reverse, perhaps because of that business about the straight way being lost. "There are no white Dominicans," I once heard a Cuban say in Miami, "nor intelligent Puerto Ricans, nor Cubans who don't talk shit." Our mouths are points of entry and exit for waste rather than language and food. Foul-mouthed, we are bad-mouthed and defined as residue, rubbish, because all we want from the world is scoria and all we return to the world is scorified. Or historified. The mouth as a world of filth. Conversational poetry passes through that mouth, is born from that translation. From not being able to speak, from censorship, from only being able to talk shit. The birth certificate, also, can be seen as part of that Cuban poetics of paradox. Its size is unwieldy precisely because of our scant birth; it identifies our names with names. Long before we can talk it talks shit for us, with our names, in our name, and it seems to want to anchor us, with its fastidious bookkeeping, to a permanent excess. Verbal usury: if I speak ten words to you, you must return twenty so I can speak a hundred back to you. Even our names, then, learn not to quit—a very Cuban civics lesson that will reduce our existence to picking pickled peppers for Lezama's rattling railroad.

and in the presence of the witnesses Jorge Gouraige Pérez, native of Guantánamo, of legal age, married, businessman, who resides on Céspedes and Estrada Palma Streets, and Félix Zenén Reyes, native of Guantánamo, of legal age, married, employed, who resides on Santa Rita and Jesús de Sol.

There is a birth certificate behind every poetics and a poetics behind every birth certificate. Eugene Sigel's birth certificate is endorsed by something right in the middle of being born, by the nation that Whitman considered a poem—"The United States themselves are essentially the greatest poem"—handmade with the strength and faith of a people who recorded family names in the Bible. A place of names and oaths, where one did not lie, where the whole family was gathered, where genealogy was a meager but necessary memory. Which is why Charles Olson can say that "the way that the Earth gets to be attained is that we are born, ourselves, with a picture of the world. That there is no world except one that we are picturers of it. And by the world here I don't mean the Earth, I mean the whole of creation. And it seems to me that I, I don't know enough, but I think that the phrase *imago mundi* is as legitimate as the better known phrase *anima mundi.* And I'd like to oppose that, really, to a condition of writing which is based on what I do or what others do, rather than what comes from the darkness on one's own initiation. Again I'm suggesting that even the overt spiritual exercise of initiation is initial in us. *We* are, *we* are, spiritual exercise, by having been born." What Olson says seems wonderful to me. A language that takes us to the source, but to the source as present, now and forever now, since the spiritual exercise of initiation is, according to Olson, "initial" in one. Being is the nascent, interminably nascent part of us. The rest is death, inertia, rhetoric. How can we not return again to that equally wonderful line of e.e. cummings: "We can never be born enough"? Compared to this—and we must not overlook the small letters in E.E. Cummings's name—just how revealing is Lezama's phrase: "Being born is here an unmentionable feast"? Being born is having or having to look for a name, an impossible, elusive, burning language: not an act, nor an initiation initial in one, but an almost mournful process, a cross of words, an infinite syntax that walks us through the land of the dead so we might be able to recognize ourselves. For this reason, instead of guiding us, Lezama, who tried to be, and was, our Dante, leaves us stranded in his own origin, in the obscure language he made for our obscurity. Why? Lezama instinctively presupposes the hidden, the obscure, the reverse of everything that is ours. He knows instinctively that Whitman's language—"simplicity, simplicity, less style, I will have nothing hang in the way, not the richest curtains"—is inexpressible from within our reality and that our irreality cannot be captured in that language. He knows that if for some creation is a natural, organic response to what is lacking, for us who are fragmentary, broken, dispersed, what is lacking is always a ruin, embers that suggest too much absence, to such an extent that we have constructed the ruin itself, step by step, and we have done it so astonishingly well that it can be defined in absolute terms: the only thing there is what we lack. Such is our republic, such is our revolution, such is our being. And such is our birth certificate. A reverse mummification. A copulative language for avoiding birth. The unborn is mummified, an absence is ritualized and perpetuated, a pyramid is built so there will be no pharaoh. We appear to be apparitions, shady shadows, tons of tongue, sights seen, romping rumps, bombed shelters, cheesy cakes, woozy wolves, chattering boxes, dribbled drivel, fired squads. We are this, we are that. Everything, nothing. Listen to my son, my sound, my song, light out, La Maya burns, gaze at the blaze, a queer song, neither pagan nor Paganini. "My neighbor's smoke makes me fume and he fumes over mine;" smoking together, we are fused, we are fumes. "It has not been proved that the salamander lived in fire," said Enrique José Varona, "but it is obvious that we can live and re-create ourselves in smoke. . . ." Right out of a movie, a cinema qua non. Cubans from Circe, from heresay, from sayings. A mouthful of nothing. To say it's Cuban is just a saying.

Having read this document before the subscribers, and after having invited them to read it if desired, the stamp of the Municipal Court was affixed and the signature of the Judge, the witnesses and the father of the boy were recorded.

Like Ulysses as he listened to the tale of Demodocus, I am moved by my birth certificate. There I am, they say. There, I know, is death. I see my name ignited almost exactly in the center of the pyramid, and I would like to think that it is the center of my mother, her womb, that there I was, am, that this is what all those empty words are really trying to say. But I can't believe it. It seems too absurd a tale to me, as if they parodied Flaubert's *mot juste* with the creaking words of justice. Names, codices, law, genealogies, toponyms, they all say everything is in order. The mother tongue is midwife, stepmother, godmother. There's a daddy and a mommy. There's an original and a copy, a collator, everything is certified, in order. On the copy, toward the end, they affirm "Faithful to the original," and it's easy to glimpse, on the papers, the obsession of a people marked by half-breeds, incest, illegitimacy, the unspeakable. Zero, Xerox. The copy is faithful to its original like the baby will be faithful to his daddy, like the son will be faithful to his father. The copy must be exact, the son must be exact, because blood must be proved pure; the name, the good name, must be preserved. There is also exile, a lot of exile, all of which demands documentation, conformity to the original, which is an erasure. Because this excess of language, a version and perversion of writing, which tries to be exact, suggests it is possible to conceal a boatload of slaves if they are declared as sacks of coal; it suggests that the sons of those sacks of coal can conceal their origins if they exaggerate the pronunciation of their S's. The solution is, always, to exaggerate language, to outdo it. To speak with Joyce's S. Words born of words. Verbal magma. A Cuban would have to remember, for example, his *con's cubaine*. His grand S. A snaky S, like his sentences, like his English. But our S's are even grander. We can set the uniformed Cuban SS, our academic Uncle Toms, against Joyce's S. We are full of S's. Our birth certificates welcome us, affirm that we exist, that we belong, that we are protected by the law. In reality, however, it's a question of an initial denunciation before a world of banter and gossip, coarse Catholicism and witchcraft, *embó*; in truth it's a question of a first

---

To complicate matters, the Cuban authorities at Mariel, the port from which refugees embark for Key West, Fla., are said to confiscate and routinely destroy any documents the refugees try to take with them: diplomas, certificates and the precious pieces of paper on which the names and addresses of American cousins, brothers and aunts have been hoarded for years.

—Iver Peterson, *The New York Times*, 26 May 1980

---

confession before a world of betrayal and torture, slander and defense committees. What's more, implicitly, we depend on papers that can be lost, burned, erased, ruined by inexact copies or bad translations. That can be seized or altered. Documents for an eventual undocumentation, history for a probable exile. Being born is here an unmentionable feast: we can never be born enough.

Cuban Poetry as Birth Certificate

"A new kind of exiles, since no one has formulated the law that bans us, we bear a collective stigma, more difficult to endure than any single mark: we bear the small scrap of yellow cloth, apparently invisible but baked into our flesh, that in dark ages marked the accursed races for reprobation and excommunication."

When I first read them, I was greatly impressed by these words of Enrique José Varona. In "Cubans in Cuba," Varona feared we were condemned to be a *wandering nation.* Irony: it happens that I, one of more than a million Cubans outside of Cuba read his lecture in exile, where I have spent more than half my life. Irony: it happens that, outside, I recognized the warning he made to those inside. Now the ones inside are the ones outside. Inside, they are outside; outside, they are inside. Vulnerability, distance, separation, impotence, four cardinal points cornering us in hollow convex landscapes that absorb, deform, destroy. Cubans in Cuba outside of Cuba and Cubans outside of Cuba in Cuba. Cuba outside of Cuba. A history for being outside inside, for being inside outside A Möbius strip, blood coursing in the distance, distance that scrapes our veins. A curse.

It's invisible, but baked into our flesh we wear that small scrap of yellow cloth. That's for sure. The paper of my birth certificate has yellowed, like the scab on a bite that's been tormenting me for years. It's the leper's little bell, the skin that rings so everyone keeps their distance, the skin that casts us off, the name they chew but never pronounce. And the voice of the Cuban poets comes to mind, then, the voice that announces enormous distances, doors slammed in one's blood, darkness where one's father raises a window but one's name raises another. "As I spoke with my father, in the darkened doorway," writes Vitier, "it seemed at times/that a dreadful cloth was about to be drawn back." It is the yellow cloth, the curse. The

---

Two days later, I hear my youngest son talking in the next room. When daddy brought me the box of paints. . .," he says. I am inside him, in his heart and his innocent mouth. I feel that I was born for this: to exist, not in my flesh and my soul, but in the voice that pierces them; not to be moored to myself like a wild man, but to have presence, to be and be born in others, in the prayer of an unknown woman, in the crystalline voice of my son, in the mysterious community of my fellow men.

—Cintio Vitier, *In Others*

---

poet does not want to exist in flesh and blood, he wants to evaporate, hide in the porousness of a voice that pierces him, that confirms his inexistence, that births him toward nothingness. It is the voice needed by Cubans, a voice that erases us, quiets us. It is the voice of Marti when he is already dead: "It's a voice we need, friends," says the sad old song, "yes, a voice, the voice of that Cuban mockingbird, the voice of that martyred brother, oh Martí was his name, yes, Martí." A voice that erases, silences itself, and thus erases, silences us. It is the voice of Eduardo Chibás, who killed himself at the end of the radio program. His very voice killed so that death could touch the blood of every Cuban. An entire nation bled, drained: insular stoicism. A speech that ended in a gunshot. The speech of a suicide and a suicidal speech: when Chibás shot himself the program was already over. Another symbol of our nobility and our absurdity. Another Martian Martí, another suicide. A voice, a name, a death. And the poet wants to evaporate in the voice of Martí, of Chibás, in the death of everyone, he wants to be pierced by a voice that confirms his inexistence, that kills itself, that kills him. But that voice is also "the entranced voice of a dark, hidden man who has had extraordinary ambitions." It is a question of "a poor accursed man who cannot believe in his innocence." It is the small scrap of yellow cloth, the paper where he writes his poem, the yellowed birth certificate. It is the yellow canary with such black eyes. It is exile starting from scratch, the inner wrench felt by anyone who experiences the irreconcilable.

There is no innocence. We cannot believe in innocence. Certainly Cuban poetry shows that we live chin over shoulder, frightened, guilty, hidden. For example, Eliseo Diego draws and withdraws his self-poortrait: an about-face. Names belong on skin. As if the body itself were a birth certificate, it's there so the name that announces and empties it can resound. The face, he says, "is afraid to admit I am darkness covered/with naked skin, the uncertain instrument/where my name sounds silently." The body: a hollow, a darkness. The name, however, seems leaden. "How heavy my name is," we read in "The First Address," "what solid patience to play out its days/on this small island surrounded by God on all sides . . ." A consecutive, uninterrupted, throbbing document, our poetry reveals a collective stigma quite adequately; it is the most explicit birth certificate of our race, where the irreconcilable figures as progenitor and its descendents are separation, distance. Blood: discontinuity. Body: cessation. The body is disposable, dispensible. It comes, we fear, from a stain, an absurdity: it is born from a statue and a ghost, from what cannot or should not have reproduced. Born as if separated from itself, it comes from what was, or what should have been, a separation. Cuban poetry matches the immaculate conception with an accursed, maculate sterility. From sterility, from sin, from darkness, from a prohibition a thousand times tricked, there is born an unborn race that weighs what its name weighs, that slips the body from the body and hides it as far away as possible, or conceals it in the name of the father, the son, the holy spirit. The unborn has only one way out: immortality.

Here's a little exercise. One for immortals. We'll fuse some lines by Mariano Brull and Cintio Vitier in hopes that judges and notaries will incorporate them in future past birth certificates. Phrases falsing faces, they seem to fit the nature of such documents particularly well. I consider them more detailed, more exact although less copulative, than the usual language of municipalities and parishes. Poetry as birth certificate and birth certificate as puzzle. We'll mix these lines like blood. Owing to its textual specificity, the collage will provide a wealth of information. It will be a laboratory of analogy. Because here the text is born arbitrarily from the dissimilar, the incompatible, tricking the integrity of its very diverse origins.

Distance is the blood in my veins.
Eternally detached from myself,
embraced by the statue of my absence,
I was born far, far away,
far from my soul:
my life separated
from my gaze.
I am behind myself:
in the blind glimpse of not being present in being,
far away,
separated from myself by a distance,
not excessive, but enough
for me to know that shores never meet,
far away, not alot, endlessly,
I was born.

Illegitimate, mulatto, incestuous, as such the text conceals those origins by underlining others, which are more pathetic and impossible, although acceptable, for the very same reasons: the text is born from a separation—in fact I have severed the phrases from the wholes to which they belonged; it is born separate from itself—the placing of lines is arbitrary: the closer its pieces are drawn together, the more they cling to distance, infinity. Textuality, in itself, which is to say blood, as a mathematics of distance. Sign and sum of that mathematics of distance: zero. At bottom, it's a question of not being born, of not having been born, in order to conceal the specifics of origin; it's a question of erasing presence with the paradox of a difference, or a sequence, that annuls, or alters as if with mirror games, with the flashing of suddden duplication, the order that will possibly permit perception as recognition: I am behind myself, we say, as if right now I were writing this last sentence immediately after the next. But failure wins out in this paradox of distance: Achilles is poetry and the tortoise, birth. The text—the birth certificate—aspires to the impossible: to be so as not to be born, to be born so as not to be, to erase the blank page. Traverse solely and forever half of the half of the half of a separation. Be that half. Be zero. Or even less. Less than nothing. Xeroxed. Be present without being, be without being present. Imitate Martí faithfully—imitate so as to cease being—but by unconsciously revealing separation. Lapsus linguae, lapsus calami. To say, for example, "I am a sincere man," a man "sans zero," Xeroxed zero. Dispossession, blasphemy, banter, origin, all in careful proportion, with a semblance of order so that an exhausting race is just barely visible: Achilles is a small blank space and the tortoise a subtle allusion to tort, i.e., torture. Errata that would not escape a careful proofreading. And what is poetry but a careful proofreading of our own birth certificates?

Learning the Alphabet Is Bloody Work

1

The origins of my writing are in the writing of my origins. Words born of words. As if I myself had been born of words, as if I were a piece of writing. Writing is being born and reborn in our mother tongue. I imagine that it is our way of trying to make birth, the act furthest from our will, our least initial initiation, completely voluntary. Writing is practice for birth: it prepares us for birth. Something like reciting the conjugations when we were in school: I am, you are, he is, we are, you are, they are. The miracle of words as preparation was already suggested there, in the acting out of an action. What pleasure when the teacher called on us and asked us to recite the complete conjugation of *play* or *run*, in the present indicative. Verbs were conjugated, then, as if we were playing on an immense playground, in a faraway backyard, in the semi-darkness of a shady vestibule where our blood felt so cool it seemed we were being fanned; memory rushed along happily, and we would barely separate pronouns from verbs: Iplayyouplayheplaysweplay . . . When I finished I was out of breath; it was just like running through the streets. Those, I sensed were the true possibilities of language; paradoxically the same thing that drew me so forcefully, that made me feel more powerful than Christ, had me cornered, paralyzed by the spell of language. Standing in class, like a statue, I would run. In front of a teacher, in the middle of a lesson, I would play. Actions devoid of activity, inactive actions. It was a question of absolute power that was absolutely impotent. Language only revealed my inadequacy.

My initiation by language was a dramatic series of small failures. Impotence, complexes—that great Oedipal inferiority complex felt by those who cling to their mother tongue[1]—led me to fantasize about a parthenogenic, linguistic origin. I imag-

1. Note for George Steiner. This may be one of the causes, obscure and remote, but determinant, of the phenomenon studied in *Extraterritorial:* the writing of authors like Nabokov and Beckett who express themselves outside of their mother tongues.

ined myself jauntily conjugating the *fiat lux* of my own body, of all bodies, as I left my mother's womb:

I am	born	we are	born
you are	born	you are	born
she, he, it is	born	they are	born

Writing: a form of remembering, examining, repeating, forgetting, resenting that fantasy. The failure of fantasy born of failures. For example, I see myself at the blackboard or bent over my desk, writing hundreds of times *I will not talk in class, I will not talk in class. . . .* Writing as punishment. Sometimes the sentence was served in the form of poetry. In class Lautréamont's dictum, "Poetry should be written by everyone," became the solidarity of my girl friends, each of whom wrote two hundred lines for me. "The lines should be written by everyone." They would write my lines; they would use my pronoun, they spoke with me, that is, with my I: *I will not talk in class, I will not talk in class. . . .* Sometimes as many as three or four girls used my first person simultaneously. Love, then: those girls pressed in my little i, which left me and returned on magic lines, through conjugation. An orgiastic pronoun, a shifter capable of driving Jakobson crazy. Language as solidarity, punishment, and usurpation. And something else: language as trick, lie, nonsense. For as I wrote those lines—writing that recorded and aimed to erase a small crime, the voice—I heard myself saying five hundred to one thousand times: *I will not talk in class, I will not talk in class . . . .* Invaginated, ironic, language let me keep talking. Censorship itself lifted the censure. An Achilles heal. My I, ay, an eye stymied. An infinite stumbling.

2

As I explore the relation I sense between the writing of my origins and the origins of my writing a very specific space appears immediately. School: squealing without a squeak. The conjugations, the lines I did in class as punishment, other examples I could mention as essential strokes in the faint sketch of a vocation, an atavistic impulse toward writing, like my anguished and frustrated battle with the Palmer method; or the doodles that repeatedly took over my notebooks, where I deformed letters to form drawings and re-formed drawings line by line, dismantling their outlines toward letters or words barely suggested by the corners of a figure, or a curious angle; or the signature I began to practice in one class or another: it all seems to prefigure the birth of my writing, as if in the middle of that hubbub of learning I had to think about blood, anchor myself to the dark force of instinct. In one of those conjugations, on one of those lines I wrote in order not to talk and to keep talking, in one of those practice signatures, in a sudden, perhaps insignificant stroke of my pen that marked me for the rest of my life—I don't remember exactly which one, or how, or why—I discovered the mask, the very first and inconsequential persona; I moved from created to creator. I was born, I erased the birth owed to my parents. A true resurrection of the flesh, except that it was a resurrection from birth rather than death, and a resurrection of the flesh I took from signatures and drawings, from lines written as punishment, from conjugations. A resurrection from immortality. I know—the writings of Otto Rank have provided me with a minimal grounding for my intuition—I know there is a relation between that moment and the impulse behind my entire life, behind each of my actions; and I know the relation is identical—except for being outlined in a different shadow—to the relation that exists between my birth certificate and each of my writings.

3

If birth is a separation, everything that evokes it or tries for a return to the deed itself will cause even more distance, separation. Any language that persists in that effort will be a digression, will take the form of a navel, a world of absences. A digression for never diverging from the theme, which is the name, that small desperate attempt at order when faced with the entropy of society, politics, economics, history, blood. Inversion: my name is not me, I am my name. I am a footprint, a sign. And what is the meaning of the sign that is my life? It means my name. The design of my sign: I could not have a son; I could only have once again, a thousand and one times, always, a father. That would be my son. That would be my grandson. That is me.

For this reason, I have been able to conceive of writing as body, procreation through symbols. From my birth certificate to these lines I am trying out right now, the only thing I have done, at bottom, is write my father's name, keep it clean, polish it, by showing everyone—me, my father, the world—that he was right when he told me our inheritance was a good name, a phrase that summed up the goodness, character, example transmitted in our blood. Our blood is like the radio station where Chibás shot himself. Ashes, the memory of our ancestors fit in a name and I was that name, these words you are reading now. A Chinese box. The surface is a box, and within it there is more surface. A metonymic world that buried me in reduction, that faithfully duplicated—once again, the copy—my way of assuming exile: all my writing fits in a name, and all Guantánamo, all Cuba, fits in my parents' house, in my room. A Chinese box in reverse. I live in the eye of the needle. What counts is leaving a good name. That was the impetus underlying my handwriting exercises, and it explained an anguish I felt at times: with handwriting like mine, I, or rather my good name, could never perpetuate, repeat itself. Because when I was a child, a good name had to do with handwriting, signatures. It implied writing rather than living. Through me, I feared, our name could never be reborn. My writing as abor-

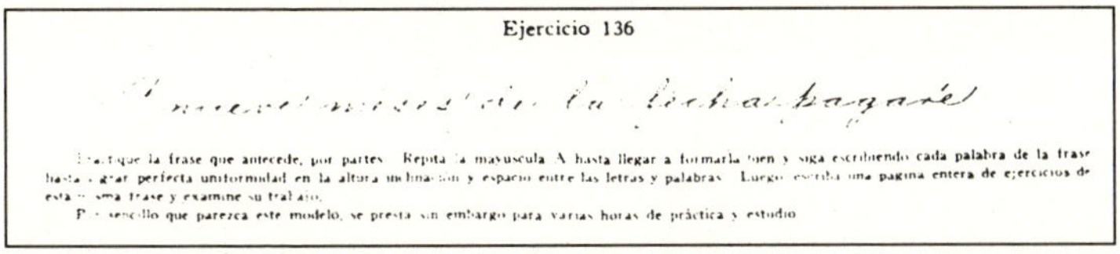
Ejercicio 136

Practique la frase que antecede, por partes. Repita la mayúscula A hasta llegar a formarla bien y siga escribiendo cada palabra de la frase hasta lograr perfecta uniformidad en la altura, inclinación y espacio entre las letras y palabras. Luego escriba una página entera de ejercicios de esta misma frase y examine su trabajo.

Por sencillo que parezca este modelo, se presta sin embargo para varias horas de práctica y estudio.

tion. Nine months in reverse. For perhaps since earliest childhood, as a way of denying myself emphatically, as my personal method of resolving the Oedipal, I understood my father's words too *literally*, too well. I killed myself with my own name for the sake of his surname. Because to say that I have only been born as a name is the same as saying that I have never been in my mother, in her body, that I am not a body, that I have only been born from the womb of my father, which is his name, my name. I am innocent, I was only born as an absence. My mother is also innocent. She was not present at my conception. Nor was she present at the birth of my biography. She neither appeared before the judge nor signed her name in that 83rd folio of volume 104 of the Division of Births of the Civil Registry of Guantánamo. She is an absence, a smudge.

((

In Loco Parenthesis: Father Furthered

Long ago, my father told me, in your grandfather's time, gentlemen never signed any documents to guarantee their agreements. A man gave his word; at most, he plucked a hair from his moustache. This implied a commitment of honor. Anyone who did not keep his word became an outcast. No one trusted him anymore, his word was worthless. That was worse than death. I, who had not even been born when I listened to this, and even now as I remember his words, would prefer to die a thousand times than be wordless, nameless. I would rather die than not be like my father, copy of a copy who kept his word, his good name, his vigorous, elegant signature that fascinated me.

It's revealing, that signature. I have asked him to write it several times and given him a sheet of paper. He sits down and I see myself, as a child, practicing my signature. I used to practice it, thinking that I would please my father, that in so doing I would have a good name. I signed in order to assure my family history. And now he signs ten, twenty times, to please me. The signature as portrait. The name as a gift, as practice, as destiny. My father was also born from the womb of his father, from his good name. He signs Luis O. Armand. Charles Olson would say that the O is not an initial initiation in him. The O is an initial from his father, Octavio. Because his name is Luis Armand and not Luis Octavio Armand, he has always signed

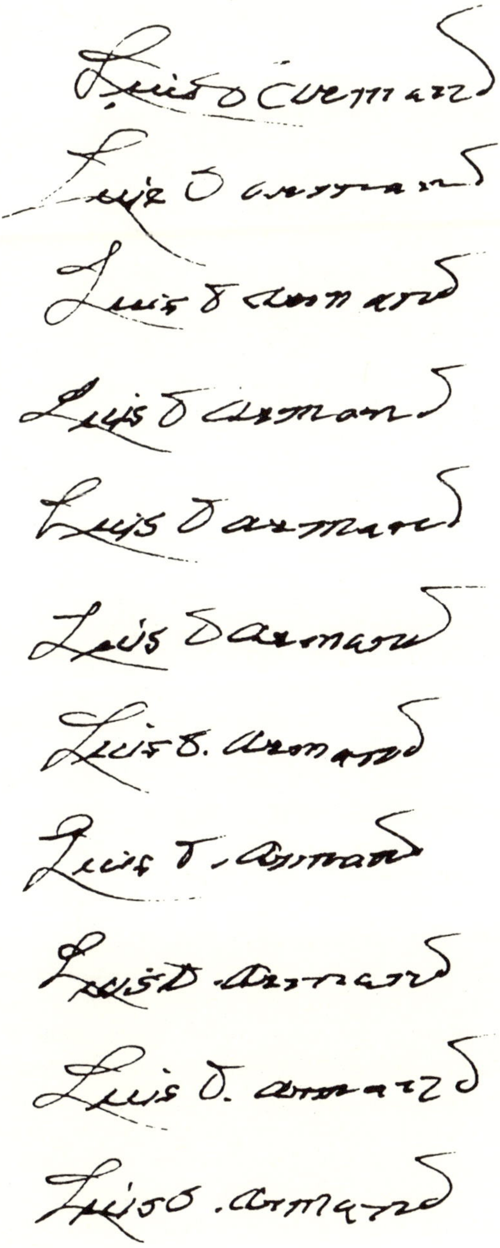

My father, age 88.

Luís O. Armand. I don't believe there is a better way to document the presence of the father: we live so that our fathers can live, so our fathers' father can return to life. Species, speculum, spectre. We live backwards, as if the only possible future were the past, the most remote origin. I also sign O. Armand, like Luis, my father, like Octavio, my grandfather. I am my father, my grandfather, I am not I, I am not. O as homage, novel. An O like Joyce's S. O as chromosome.

O is a
letter that has not
yet been born, that is never
completely born. O is only an
egg, and no one knows what it
holds. In order for us to finally
know what it holds, we will have
to put it in an incubator, for
since it lost its mother, since
it probably fell out of her,
it needs a little warmth—
at what temperature?—
so it can hatch.

—Alberto Hidalgo, *Simplismo*

Blood type O. Names born of names. Letters born of letters. Words born of words.

))

All of this explains the importance that, at a given moment, I attributed to my signature. From my exercises in handwriting I went on to practice my signature. I practiced it hundreds of times, almost like the lines I had written in punishment, except that now I had no friends to help me, accompany me. I knew, nevertheless, that I was not alone. On the contrary. I was as anguished by the irregularity of my signature as an orphan would have been by the obscurity of his origins. There, in that small, incipient fetal scribbling, I had to be present, and in my I—once again the Malthusian experience of sharing my first person with many others—my father, my grandfather, my great-grandfathers. . . . Signature as blood, chromosome.

Against a Babel-like confusion of tongues, a transfusion of names, a verbal genetics.

Behind my writing, my signature, my penmanship, the lines of punishment I penned in class, beyond, behind everything I do and everything I write is my birth certificate, the name of my father. There is my source of authority, and there I first become an author. An unauthorized author, a plagiarist who copies his own name, a reader who made a panoptic monument from every letter, a dreamer who discovered how to walk under an ant, a hand that could pick up that ant and put it in the sky. I write these words, and all my books, and my name in my books, as if I were furthering my father's name in stone. A Pharaonic impulse. A lithic restraint. Father. Farther. Fossil. F:a:t:h:e:r:a:s:f:o:s:s:i:l. As if my whole existence and all my actions were a hieroglyphic to veil and protect his name: a car-

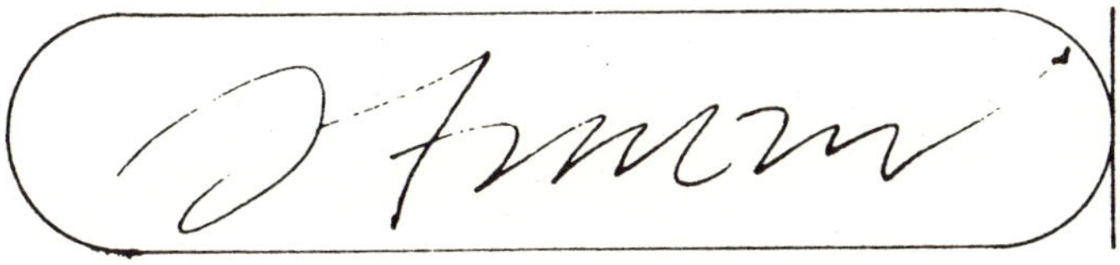

Cartouche of Octavio Armand

touche that perhaps within five or six thousand years will make possible the deciphering of a dead language. I write for the dead, I write in a dead language, I write for archaeologists with the hunch that my name will revive language. My name in the name of the father, my tongue in a dead language. The name of the father survives, the mother tongue dies. But the name of the father—Lacan warns—condemns us to death. A huge Lacanthropy: the father, who dwells in the heaven of the superego, devours, dismembers, destroys us. He is a wolf. We are sons of a father, we are pronouns of names of more names. We are Little Red Riding Hoods. When did I begin to realize that I live trapped in a statue, in Marcel Marceau's glass box? How did I sense that those who have fathers and mothers have not been born, will never be born, that being born is the absolute opposite of having a father and a mother, that we have to be born before daddy and mommy, that being born has no name, is not having a name, like a little bit of all and nothing squeezed in your soul? I knew in the telling.

Octavio Armand is the name of my grandfather and my name is Octavio Armand. It is as if before my birth, or in order never to be born, I had provoked my name: as if ever since the beginning, since before, I had been, I may be, something whose very specific destiny it was to appear in writing, to demand life from death, to write, to be born. That's what I'm about here, what I'm about now: birth.

*Penitence**

(Posters)

1

(Song)

It's a voice we need, friends,
yes, a voice.
The voice of that Cuban mockingbird,
the voice of that martyred brother,
oh Martí was his name,
yes, Martí.

2

Listen to those Cubans talking: it's a real lesson. The tone of voice, something Cuban about how they say their words is a dead giveaway. There are times when an overheard conversation—even one about a subject that holds no interest—will carry us to the most distant points of our inner history, almost as if it let us touch the novel of our landscape. I'm thinking of some words by Raymond Radiguet: "What defines a race is voice rather than features." (Lorenzo Garcia Vega, *Rostros del reverso* [About faces], April 25, 1969.)

3

(Sonnet)

Yo soy un hombre sincero
Yo soy un hombre sincero
Yo soy un hombre sincero
Yo soy un hombre sincero

Yo soy un hombre sincero
Yo soy un hombre sincero
Yo soy un hombre sincero
Yo soy un hombre sincero

* The cover for an improbable edition of *Penitence*: jacket for a 45 rpm record. It could be heard at different speeds. For example, the great Northern revolutionaries could listen at 33¹/₃ rpm, the great Southern revolutionaries at 78 rpm Graphics: as for a poster.

Yo soy un hombre sincero
Yo soy un hombre sincero
Yo soy un hombre sincero

Yo soy un hombre sincero
Yo soy un hombre sincero
Yo soy un hombre sincero

4

Cuba present as a voice: demagogy and *choteo*, slogan and flattery, partying and *paredón*. Bathetic fireworks. Verbal eroticism, impotence. Cuban history: that voice threatened by an implacable, deadening ocean. An empty seashell. Roaring within, roaring without. A speech on the sand. Castles/ speeches erased by the waves and repeated by the same foam or scum. Cuba is not that history: Cuba is that voice. It is not a presence: it is that voice. The empty seashell: the bubble as it bursts. Cuba's stature is revealed in her Orators: Martí speaking, Fidel speaking. Her apogee, the singer. Orators clam up and yield to the lyrics of Beny Moré or Rita Montaner; words clam up and yield to the cry, a lobster wagging its giant orchestrated tail. Speak: spout: sputter. Neither thoughts nor action: words; neither eloquence nor dialectics: wordiness; neither constitutions nor proclamations: dance, music. Our favorite heroes are verbal. Or they are systematically reduced to a strictly verbal heroism. No surprise, then, that the best and most *sincerosincerosincero* of our homages is the *verbal statue*. Repeat in unison one of the Apostle's slogans; learn a few simple

Celebration (?) Ode

Being born is here an unmentionable fiesta
Being born is here an unmentionable fiesta
Being born is here an unmentionable fiesta
Being born is here an unmentionable fiesta
Being born is here an unmentionable fiesta
Being born is here an unmentionable fiesta
Being born is here an unmentionable fiesta
Being born is here an unmentionable fiesta
Being born is here an unmentionable fiesta

verses by heart, a
fragment of *Los*
pinos nuevos
(The New Pines);
recite from memory;
insert a voice
from the past be
tween cho ruses of
Guantana mera, re
member ing—al
ways—the words of
that song: "It's a voice we need friends,/Yes, a voice . . ." That's our history. A systematic reduction to language, orality,

with all its implications. (Among Cubans, words are reduced [raised?] to rhythm; cadence is more important than words. Sense is not what is sensed. Most persuasive in insular speech: the logic of an ostentatious onomatopoeia.) A montage of voices on voices and voices against voices. Being born is here an unmentionable fiesta. History against destiny. *Choteo* against tide. Scum against foam. This is all sad, profoundly sad. Insular joy is fiesta and despair: an unmentionable fiesta. The poetry of Manuel de Zequeira y Arango: playful prattle. Also: a symptom. Fiesta and despair. An unmentionable fiesta. Prattle/parable. Cuban *choteo*—questioned by Fernando Ortiz in *Entre cubanos* (Among Cubans), later surveyed by Mañach in *Indagación del choteo* (A study of *choteo*), and novelized and nivolized by Guillermo Cabrera Infante in *Tres tristes tigres (Three trapped tigers)*—is jesting and bitterness: jab, jest, and joust: joke. Fiesta and despair. A fiesta of despair. Unmentionable fiesta. Joke: a ritual jousting of spontaneity. Guillermo Cabrera Infante caught that. His title suggests the essence of *choteo* (the essence of Cuba?): violence/sadness/ t. t. t. o. o. ngue twisters. *Tres tristes tigres*: a turbulent insular Gregorian chant. Bash and suicide. Orality and writing. Montage and self-destruction. A profoundly sad pleasure. Pleasure/prattle/parable." . . . and I'm happy she's waving, smiling, swaying her incredible body and throwing back her beautiful head: I'm happy she's not singing, because it's better, much better to see Cuba than to hear her and it's better because to see her is to love her, but once you hear her and listen and know her you won't ever be able to love her" (Cabrera Infante, *TTT*).

5

(Warning or Ballad)

If they tell you that I've gone
If they tell you that I've gone
If they tell you that I've gone
If they tell you that I've gone

If they tell you that I've gone
If they tell you that I've gone
If they tell you that I've gone
If they tell you that I've gone

6

(Prose Poem)

And I looked for you, always, also, within myself and I looked for you, always, also, within myself and I looked for you, always, also, within myself and I looked for you, always, also within myself and I looked for you, always, also, within myself and I looked for you, always, also, within myself and I looked for you, always, also, within myself and I looked for you, always, also, within myself and I looked for you, always,

7

(Tune)

You, gone from Cuba, answer
You, gone from Cuba, answer
You, gone from Cuba, answer
You, gone from Cuba, answer
You, gone from Cuba, answer
You, gone from Cuba, answer
You, gone from Cuba, answer
You, gone from Cuba, answer

8

(Song)

When you're finally gone I'll know that you left
When you're finally gone I'll know that you left
When you're finally gone I'll know that you left
When you're finally gone I'll know that you left
When you're finally gone I'll know that you left
When you're finally gone I'll know that you left
When you're finally gone I'll know that you left
When you're finally gone I'll know that you left

9

The Phaistos Disk: a spiral written toward the c
enter. What if there is no center? Let the music
roll!

10

((((Open parenthesis

I think I've discovered one of the soundest theoretical, even ontological premises for the authentic poetry of exile we are still lacking. What surprises, pleases me is that my hunch has arisen from an unmeasured angle, a difficult inwardness. In other words, it reaffirms what (little) I have done until now and brutally clarifies its pathetic immanence. Do you remember how in the poems published recently my only starting point was that *I have something to say I say?* A stopped start, circularity. By trying to explain myself, I found an image with which to protect, objectify that vagueness: the scratched record. And what if, since I must, I accept my voice—a history in which I am inscribed, but which I also observe from without, cut off—that record of a single revolution?

I've discovered remote voices within my own voice, the voices of others which are mine, very much mine. In other words, I am a witness, but in the end I can only attest to my own situation. That explains the circularity: I realize that I am not only a product (object) of history but its agent (subject). As a subject I can speak: of course I have something to say. You know what I mean? Boomerang: at the end Sherlock Holmes discovers he is the assassin, etc.

(That's from a letter to Victor. July 26, 1973. A few days ago I finished selecting the voices for "Penitence." No one will care about my posters. The great Northern revolutionaries will say they're a profanation. Even worse: no one will recognize my *big discovery*. It's covering everyone cares about. Writing is wrapping. Announce all this as one big cover-up, and the great revolutionaries—Northern and Southern—will proclaim you a statue!)

Close parenthesis))))*

* Parenthesis from *Diario de una tarde* (Diary of an afternoon).

11

(Octave)

Remember the country you yearned for
Remember the country you yearned for
Remember the country you yearned for
Remember the country you yearned for
Remember the country you yearned for
Remember the country you yearned for
Remember the country you yearned for
Remember the country you yearned for

12

(Sonnet)

Wherever fate in her furor impels me
Wherever fate in her furor impels me
Wherever fate in her furor impels me
Wherever fate in her furor impels me

Wherever fate in her furor impels me
Wherever fate in her furor impels me
Wherever fate in her furor impels me
Wherever fate in her furor impels me

Wherever fate in her furor impels me
Wherever fate in her furor impels me
Wherever fate in her furor impels me

Wherever fate in her furor impels me
Wherever fate in her furor impels me
Wherever fate in her furor impels me

13

(Song)

Oh, that I were at sea
Oh, that I were at sea
Oh, that I were at sea
Oh, that I were at sea

Oh, that I were at sea
Oh, that I were at sea
Oh, that I were at sea
Oh, that I were at sea

14

(Lament?)

If I left, I would instantly long to return
If I left, I would instantly long to return
If I left, I would instantly long to return
If I left, I would instantly long to return
If I left, I would instantly long to return
If I left, I would instantly long to return
If I left, I would instantly long to return
If I left, I would instantly long to return

15

The poetry of exile: a *ready-made*. Just write it out. Distance is a constant in Cuban literature from *Espejo de paciencia* (Mirror of patience) to *Muerte de Narciso* (The death of Narcissus). In Manzanilla, a French corsair thinks of his homeland; in Havana, an islander promises never to forget his for even an instant. Girón the mariner yearns for France; Zenea the poet wishes he were at sea. A circle.

Bodyless scars, these voices—implicit/latent—converge in each text as insult or lament, prayer or slogan. Trace them and you'll find that distance is a way of remaining at the heart of Cuban reality, doubly isolated. To be in Manzanilla, for Girón, or turn-of-the-century Habana, for Julián del Casal: a way of distancing oneself even if only to long instantly to return. To be/to distance oneself/to long to return: to remain. Distance is a measure of insularity, its confirmation. A circle.

In your hands I will place the inhabitants of the earth, and you will cast them from your presence.

Other voices reproach the mob, which lashes out at the departing who will soon be trapped in the void, at once familial and unknown; others from New York or Key West willingly join the mobs waiting, always waiting; still others, trumpeted by thousands of lips and a single mouth, teem in a shout or guffaw, bursting like an immense solar ocellus; the voice that sees nothing, hears nothing. The voice that is, period. Fold out/ fold up/center: a circle.

I've collected them all. Claimed them. Obsessive, circular. Spirals lost to the sand. Memory, history. A funnel clogged with knees. Voices coiled like streamers at a carnival that is also a carnage. Together they goad each other on, forming a pathetic hymn. A battle cry that turns on itself becoming motionless, useless. Battle/backside. What Martí once said is what he said; what Martí is said to have said—echoes, refrains, refractions—replaces his voice, annihilates it. Repetition blots out the wealth of words. A circle.

They left us, but they were not ours; because if they had been ours, they would certainly have stayed with us; but *they* left so as to make it clear that not everyone is one of us.

Repeated obsessively as slogans or torpid litanies, texts are lost in con/texts they themselves trace in duplication. A scratched record is no longer voice, music, carnival. Repetition caricatures. Repeated fourteen times, one of the Apostle's verses belongs to me, or you, or anyone. There is nothing daring about it, no *coup de texte*. Multiplication has imparted a sense that is different, unsuspected, anti-Martí. Apostle/apostate: a circle.

This record is my own voice telling me that I have something to say, that I have to say something. Am I the witness? Boomerang/echo/mirror. The extended signal arm rebounds, returning to its center—absorbed, silent. It has always been like this. No doubt. Throat: size of the world. Words only fall from tongue to lip, from lip to lip, from saliva to tooth. Way at the bottom there is no one: I'm here (it has always been like this) looking, inwardly and outwardly scraped together. A spider/ a finger nail/marks of interrogation. Journeys cut short at departure. There is no doubt. Rodrigo Díaz takes leave of his daughters to go into exile: Christ takes leave of Ahasuerus, and the poor shoemaker begins to serve his exile, his sentence. A circle.

If they have pursued me, they will also pursue you.

Like the multiple/unanimous/identical histories of history, a record speaks, spouts, sputters through revolutions. But it is not a presence; it's that voice. Nor is it history: it's that voice. The scratch (what is a record except scratches?) is irritating only to those who evade the record's peculiar reality, the mechanical, uncertain nature of its incantation, its very awkward immanence. There is a parable here, a circle that opens, becomes a center. Experienced as gesture, as an epic of impotence, irritation is beautiful. Scratch: history. History: spider. Spider: what? Screech/squeak/squeal, everything becomes language, lyric. And in spite of everything, silence clams up. A circle?

16

(Refrain)

Let the music roll!

17

Pos(t)e(r)s = poses

18

Definition

Cut out: cut yourself off
Cut out: cut yourself off
Cut out: cut yourself off
Cut out: cut yourself off

Cut out: cut yourself off
Cut out: cut yourself off
Cut out: cut yourself off
Cut out: cut yourself off

Cut out: cut yourself off
Cut out: cut yourself off
Cut out: cut yourself off

Cut out: cut yourself off
Cut out: cut yourself off
Cut out: cut yourself off

Testicle: Diminutive of *t*
estis: 1490, testiculus
"witness to virility." De
riv. from the ancient
testifie, C. XIII-XV.

19

(Saying)

History will absolve me history will absolve me history will absolve me history will absolve me history will absolve me history will absolve me history will absolve me history will absolve me history will absolve me history will absolve me history will absolve me history will absolve me history will ab

20

Etc.

Lezama Lima or the Death of Narcissus

Being born is here an unmentionable feast.

1

Twice I had tried to read *Paradiso*, but neither time could I get past the first couple of chapters. The book was impenetrable. What daunted me was not the almost unreflective difficulty or the form bogged down in images capricious like colors in a fishbowl or imposing like a ruin. In a certain gaze, this ruin is also a habitable space. Only as past, however; as past it is splendor, as present it repels. No, I was not daunted by such bull/fighting. This Job was up to the job. One expects, even, to a certain extent, looks forward to a whale of difficulty from Lezama's essays and poetry. After all, the baroque is a display as well as a gaze.

The gaze I had. So that was not the issue. The real source of impenetrability had to do with my acknowledged discomfort—disdain—with respect to narrative. This meant that the difficulty of *Paradiso* was no more than incidental within a greater difficulty where what showed up as a disdain for narrative was a more dangerous, complex disappointment with history. Perhaps a novel brought into focus my marginality, which seemed harsh enough on its own. In a novel, history can redeem marginality, but as subjection and as glaring proof of what a few years ago would have been called *bad faith*. Because that reading, that novel, that, the historical, gave in so quickly to the implacable, which was history, with its linear continuity and its progress. And the reader who persisted in spite of an unforgivable, avowed anachronism lacked the resolve necessary for self-definition within continuity. I was no Roman in the time of Caesar. I was no citizen two hundred years ago. I am not now a member of any organization currently spanning the twin rivers of commerce and ideology. In a world where all shores have vanished, I have no stake and no interest whatsoever in the anonymity of censors or compounded rates.

2

I confess the same disdain for narrative poetry. Conversational poetry, committed poetry, to me it all seems like desertion. Antipoet: capitalism, where poetry is passed to the consumer. Antipoet: Marxism, where poetry passes, first and inexorably, to censors who know how to read precisely because they do not know how to read. Antipoet, finally: Rimbaud, who refused to speak outside the poem and thus made an antilanguage, like a big zero, not from his word, but from his life itself. The rest is just literature, and it is better to confess that. To be real through conning. A con artist for real.

Committed poets serve up and summarize their ten commandments with questionable tenacity. In those commandments Mohammed and Mao, the Sermon on the Mount and Tass speak with one voice. So that no reactionary, political motive is perceived here (but why be so defensive?), I will add that especially the Middle Ages and the twentieth century speak with one voice. An identical effusion and vehemence is easy to spot in some of the art from both periods. In the Middle Ages this arises from an attempt to sacralize, and in the twentieth century from an attempt to desacralize, which is to say from an attempt at pro/fanation, at placing street and temple, idea and ideal, faith, one in front of—or over—the other, as in the case of Ernesto Cardenal. That might account for the instinctive renunciation of metaphor in this poetics *à la dernière* which aims not to be rhetorical but is, loss by default. The direct language purported to be colloquial, which is found in advertisements or headlines, indicates a move from the place of consubstantiation and communion to a place of communication and catchiness. From word and metaphor: body that is bread and bond: sacrifice that nourishes, bridges, to message and soliloquies. Soliloquies that seem like dialogues only because they are echoes: a radio voice that does not listen, a listener's voice that neither has nor should have voice since it exists in order to be ear, receiver, voices jammed in an unwearying wearying verbal hysterics. A total hybrid that above all is efficient. One big catchword: *in hoc signo vinces* and another, which is pitiful: *vox clamantis in deserto.*

(Thought: how far these characters are in spite of everything from Leo Naphta, Jesuit and Communist. Without either lyrical or antilyrical hysteria, *The Magic Mountain* is more subversive than the entire sum—the Summa—of all committed poems.) But there is an obvious difference between the effusive, functional art of an age placed in the middle, like a bridge, and twentieth-century art that goes every and no place defined by its own little number. An affective identification with a certain unity is associated with the vertical impulse of the Middle Ages. With the horizontal impulse of the cosa nostra, more prone to mirror games, is associated an effective rather than affective identification with plurality. The two periods are identical, then, to the extent that a triptych is identical to a Mexican mural, to the extent that the Sistine Chapel is identical to the Kremlin or the White House.

3

My present does not exist because my past does not exist either, nor did it exist. No past exists except as convention. History accumulated in readings or the repeated experience of exile was always the same: an apprenticeship of marginality, impotence. I did not give in to those events that were happening today but not tomorrow, or that were not happening today but tomorrow had happened yesterday. I gave myself willingly to the penetrability of a live history that will would never be lived, because it suits no one, or to that other history which occurs as imminence or possibility, but in order to continue as image forever. History according to a madman or a barbarian or a reprobate or a leper. The history of a certain image, a certain tenacious transgression, a certain stain.

4

No poetry from Cuba's nineteenth-century exile is more intense than that of Manuel de Zequeira, who succeeded in becoming Deputy King of Cartagena. It was with his hat, though, that he really went beyond the pale. The apogee of a magician, he pulled rabbits out of his hat that were all too regal: "Charles XII, King of China." Beneath his own hat, Manuel de Zequeira, who succeeded in becoming Deputy King of Cartegena, disappeared. In a century of exile, and before Heredia, Gómez de Avellaneda, Zenea, or Martí, Manuel de Zequeira reached exile through insanity. His exile was of this world. His marginality was of this world: was an interment. The word today is *internment*, seeing that, crazy or not, poets and other marginal types are made sane through insanity. Because, as Trotsky explained, the State is well acquainted with the danger posed by internal emigrés. Trotsky should know, having emigrated without and within. The State has large hats for all of these situations. Ezra Pound's case is not the worst. Didn't they take off Saint Elizabeths, that big hat he wore for awhile?

There is no greater exile, no greater distance than Zequeira's in nineteenth-century Cuba. (That's my Cuban century. Along with certain years of the republic—the revolution I knew and shared from childhood to adolescence—it is the only history I have.) That *headless hat*, that deep-seated contradiction that is so Cuban, was the first and worst case of incoherent eloquence and of the absolute exile that takes the form of a turning inward. It is not the only paradoxical but typical instance of the essential poetry of exile, of what could be defined as insularity from without or marginality from within. There is Juan Manzano, slave and poet. Or rather: neither slave nor poet. Because he was a poet in order to stop being a slave and a slave in order to be a poet. Another, very Cuban, contradiction. His freedom can be measured with a large silence. Juan Manzano belongs to history only when history defined and defended him as a slave. Free, Juan Manzano disappears. In the instant he stopped writing he wrote his great, blank poem. His hat was freedom. A tropical Mallarmé that Guillermo Cabrera Infante could certainly have included in *Exorcismos de esti(l)o* (Exorcising a st[y]le), a man zany as they come. A chapter of our essential poetry, all to himself.

5

History's penetrability. I read Zequeira, his fabulous *décimas*, as if I were putting on his hat. Of Manzano I read especially what he had not written. Of course it made me zany. Versions of a possible history. I read Martí and looked with him for the first time at a landscape bewitched by words. But it was an improbable version. Because even in the most incidental, concrete moments, in his manifestos, in his political or personal letters, in his *Diario de campaña* (Field diary), Martí was/ is/

will be *a man of his word.* In that word, which *transcends in service* and which, when made flesh, is sacrificed for a symmetry it never possessed, what one finds above all is distance. I do not remember now if Martí died *against a triangle*, the defensive formation employed by Spanish soldiers. Perhaps he died face to the sun, which is what he wanted. But above all he died against a triangle. That's how it was, that's how it must have been. (Now I do not even remember if Martí died, period. I remember a sad, very Cuban song: "It's a voice we need, friends, a voice . . ." Yes, Cubans need a voice for all their blablablabing, period. Thought: if Martí should not have died, he has not died. Is he still dying then?) That's how it must have been. A white horse against a triangle. Against a triangle, a gun that did not fire. Sheer distance confronted that triangle, which held fast to its three sides like an oyster and closed up tight. Triangulate/strangulate. But it was a Cuban, Antonio Oliva, the mulatto guide, who gave Martí the *coup de grâce*. Oliva recognized, perhaps more than any other Cuban, the distance coiled in that presence. And he said to him: "What might bring you here, Martí?" They gave Oliva Martí's *revolver with the mother-of-pearl butt.* They also confiscated the Apostle's *gold watch and chain.* His revolver, inherited by Oliva, the unbewitchable guide. His watch/his time/his history, confiscated. What all this suggests is certainly grotesque. But no more grotesque than the Apostle's last speech, which corresponds to Manzano's unwritten poetry. Confluences. This is also the history that belongs to me: the distance that remains silent when faced with a question as natural and octosyllabic as the *Versos sencillos* (Simple verses): "What might bring you here, Martí?" What Martí thought–, must have thought/thinks in those final seconds of life, when he is confronted so impudently with insularity, is essential to the history to which I belong. His last speech is undoubtedly grotesque. But no less moving than the others he made in Tampa or Key West, with his slightly exaggerated "s." Zequeira's incoherence, Manzano's silence, and then the terrible speech, the grimace: *his tongue was bitten and his teeth were literally piercing it.* The description echoes Juan Trujillo, the medic who witnessed that. Hat/hush/grimace: confluences. Disconnected connections. Unrelated relations. History. The Orator, with his grimace resembles/is one of Ionesco's characters. That is his image, Goyesque. That speech is his most eloquent. Like a verbal scribble. Apogee of distance. Impotence. Martí against a triangle/Martí against a simple, down-to-earth octosyllable/ Martí against his own tongue. A star burst. Martí/martyr/ martel. His funeral cost about seven dollars. Paid by the Spanish government. It also cost the Republic. It might cost the Revolution. (Martí died in Dos Ríos. I have mentioned a *bridge spanning two rivers*. One of writing's coincidences. Take note, I tell myself, and I write it down immediately, don't miss that disconnected connection.)

6

I also read other versions of our history. Grover Flint's *Marching with Gómez. Liberty, the Story of Cuba*, by Horatio Rubens. Versions written by foreigners. Thought: aren't we all foreigners? Aren't we all outside of some history? Aren't we all essentially barbarians/reprobates/madmen/lepers? Martí fell like a heart untying roots, ropes, fears. Everything has a destiny. But for some the bones of the dead are dice thrown until the right combination comes up. (Thought: innocence and justice *flow* into the purity of mathematics. What is innocent, what is just, is that which is complete. Is that: whatever has nothing. Which is to say, nothing more, nothing less.) The *players* are always in history, histories, because they are the only ones to recognize history as a game. The players figure, count, are accomplices or comrades. The rest, *the others*, touch those bones, but they are always too clumsy. They do not sense the dice in those bones. They do not throw those bones. And of the dead man they say: his words belong. They do not say to whom, or to what.

Simply: his words belong. They are the foreigners, who trip, like the blind, in any historic situation. They are the barbarians, the mad, the reprobates. They are the lepers who trip on all the stones cast with whoring marksmanship. They are the ones who ask, with a clumsiness dissimulated with even greater clumsiness: you mean every situation is historic? everyone casts a stone? They are the ones struck dumb when they finally burst into history. They do not know what to answer when

Oliva asks, "What might bring you here?" They will bite their tongues, which will literally be pierced by their teeth. Because every triangle, every symmetry, every history, is a negation, an abolishment.

7

Lezama attempts a symmetry, though. *Paradiso*, Chapter XII. And that symmetry ends in death, in a die, in fear, in centurions. There are one hundred paragraphs in that Chapter XII. Ten times ten, square. "The power of a square was generally absorbent, it was an emptiness, which, like the mouth of certain serpents, drew toward its center the calm development of that family, along with any passers-by or visitors." And that square Chapter XII gathers four alternating narratives. Alter/nants: alter/egos.

(1) Atrius Flaminius, commander of legions
(2) The grandmother and the little boy, the ball game and the Danish vase
(3) The case of *the invisible*
(4) Juan Longo, music critic, and his wife who guards him

Symmetry is a *successive order*. In fact the various narratives do alternate with each other. Except that the single, intermittently detailed narrative is woven into them until its synthesis in the last paragraph, which is the square, one hundred, the convergence of four narratives. Confluence. Things disconnected connected. The unrelated related. In that square paragraph of the square chapter

(1) There are two centurions
(2) There is a bust that falls and a game of dice
(3) There is the flight of a ghost
(4) There is the guard duty

The synthesis occurs as an apogee of symmetry. Because it has been prepared for successively in the preceding chapters. For example, when the deranged wife of the music critic peered into the urn holding the body of her husband, she saw "the face of a Roman warrior, contorted in an expression of infinite desperation, trying to reach with his hands the capes, boots, swords of the legionnaires passing by on their way to fight in distant lands." His face aflame as he remembered the stone, "he moaned, immobilized, as the possibility of achieving death in the crush of battle was erased." In the last paragraph a bust falls. Then, that bust interrupts and alters the throw of dice. It is the geometer wanting to *enter the game*, the geometer wanting, with his compass—which is geometry but also music—to reach the degraded attributes of the Roman soldier. But "the two centurions covered themselves with a single cape, something like the head of a huge turtle rising from their necks, and taking care not to trip, they departed with the steps of a forced march." The die that jumps, interrupted by the compass that had also jumped, hits a stone the size of a crab and *retreats*; the centurions—one hundred paragraphs, a century—cover themselves with a single cape, something like the head of a huge turtle rising from their necks, and they depart with the step of a *forced march*. The metamorphoses suggest a permeability of attributes, but *the meeting* of diverse elements is foiled. Which is why I believe we are facing a ruin. A narrated, narrative ruin. Symmetry ruins. Because it occurs, forced, as abstract symmetry, in numbers. The throw of dice: two and three. The compass falls on the three, which jumps and rolls toward "the die with which it made a pair" and is now no longer three but two. Two centurions, a bust of a geometer that falls twice, two dice each having two dots. "The four contributed by those two dice, one beside the other, as if the two surfaces had joined their waters. The four was left beneath the ruined cupola, in the center of the nave, equidistant from the two aisles." Four/square. But the numbers are on the surface and that surface becomes part of a ruin. I think of the *successive order*. I go back to an earlier paragraph:

"He has destroyed the subtle scholastic distinction between cause, causation, and causality, or between birth, what engenders birth, and birth and its finality, but his nascent act passes in an infinity traversed by the sleeper at that flying point. He has also conquered time as *between*, according to the meaning of some contemporaries, since in his sleep it is impossible to separate time that was from time in the making. That *between* which seems to be the last dialectical refuge of mortals, a blind man's penetration in the fleetingness he believes is duration, because that *between* is the negation of all penetration, and it ends up like an act aimed at a rock, but one that has turned to foam when it reaches its destination, except that in terms of temporality, man is not that rock but the rock from some theatrical props, which seems to be a gift from the Danaidae or Sisyphus, from the demonic gods with their sterile design."

I take notes. From *baroque symmetry* I am gradually making a symmetry of redundance, a *symmetrical symmetry*. Absurd. A thought then—not then, but later, after I have finished reading: no, this ruin would be out of place in a museum and the meeting with Lezama will not be, cannot be, the detailing of excess. What it will be, I don't know. Perhaps *it will not be.*

Among my notes I have copied the following lines from Lezama's "Confluencias" (Confluences). There, in the final pages of *Las eras imaginarias* (The imaginary ages), Lezama alludes to his own work—when does Lezama not allude to his own work?—to his immense Chapter XII. Not immense because of its size but because it never stops, not numerically but because of its *bewitched quantity*. Because Chapter XII is time outside of time, a succession outside of succession, a *successive order*. "*Paradiso*, a world outside of time is equivalent to supernature. Liberation from time is the most tenacious constant of supernature. Oppiano Licario wants to provoke supernature. For that reason he continues his search through endless labyrinths. In Chapter XII, a negation of time, behind the crystal urn an endless exchange of faces between the young boy and the centurion, both dead, except that in Chapter IV, toward the end, the person who appears behind the urn is Oppiano Licario himself. A negation of time achieved in sleep, where not only time but also dimension disappears. I move the enormity of an ax, I reach infinite speeds, I see blind men in nocturnal markets talking about the visual quality of strawberries, and at the end, the Roman soldiers playing Taba among the ruins, I reach the tetractis, the number four, God."

I go back to one phrase: behind the crystal urn an endless exchange of faces between the young boy and the centurion. But that crystal, it seems, is what changes the faces; is what *flows still*. Among my notes, then, these other lines that suggest, beginning with Chapter IV, the urn and the comments about the urn. "Time, like a liquid substance, like a mask, slowly covers the faces of the most distant ancestors, or, on the contrary, that same time drags, lets itself be almost absorbed by earthly games, enlarging a figure until it acquires the physique of a Desmoulins, a Marat with clenched fists, pounding on the variants, the echoes, or the tedium of a Thermidorean assembly. . . ."

In my notes I also outline a certain confluence in Cuban narrative, taking as my starting point the figure and the projections of the Flemish geographer and cartographer Gerardus Mercator (Latinized version of Gerhard Kremer). In that confluence, that figure and his projections found in the Colonel's study and in Cabrera Infante's *Exorcisms*, could there be a hint of our need for landscape? Could the dates of Gerardus Mercator (1512–1594), which are so close to the date Cuba was colonized, be a clue?

8

It is one thing to get lost on a map and quite another to be traveling without a map and come up against the smiling teeth of a cannibal. Cartography is one thing, but land that turns out to be more than just extension, which does not confuse the conquistador with the archaeologist disguised as conquistador, is something else again. To read Lezama and get lost in his remote syntax, in his verbal foam, to understand little or poorly or nothing of the way he rears wildly in the most ordinary phrase, to be incapable of following the arrow shot from a bow most harmonious when tensed, to not even realize that the phrases are shot like arrows or obedient falcons, to be unable or unaware of how to read Lezama while reading him is a necessary apprenticeship. An apprenticeship more valuable and necessary than a reading that gets to the bottom of something conceived apart from an act, where fate is equivalent to reading. Because it is possible to know certain texts by not reading them, the adventure they offer is so improbable. But it is also possible to surrender to other texts just for the pleasure of knowing them, without ever getting enough meaning from them, savoring what is accessible and desiring the rest. This is something I learned from Lezama. There is another, complementary lesson. Do without anything that comes across as mere arithmetical dabbling or tamed surface. The guarded statement with its measured steps is worthless. So is the waxy but awkward symbol of saying nothing, like a child who has clumsily stolen a piece of candy. A geometric efficiency of progression. Burst by multiples into fullness, into the practice of flashing, wolf-like sequences, which call from behind the flow of discourse by making way for some while closing the way to others.

These lessons are not axioms that drop as if by force of gravity from everything baroque. Baroque sensuality does not exclude the most diverse surfaces nor the most divergent throbbings beneath surfaces that strain toward touch. In Cuban baroque, for example, it is impossible to confuse Carpentier and Lezama. Between those two styles, one formed from pieces and the other from scraps, there is a leap: from a natural baroque to a formal baroque, from a genetic code to a code that is programmed. One arises and the other is a tending toward. One never leaves the voice pierced by its own conversations: informed, but also formless, it always relates, as if brushing against them, the idea's ascendant element with immediate, day-to-day presence. The other defers by squandering phrases, as if recognizing means and demands extraneous to desire, its motion mostly for the purposes of avoiding an unconfessable inclination toward the rococo.

Natural baroque as negative valence, alterity with respect to *nature itself,* which implies not traveling toward an unreachable destination. Formal baroque has access to its own limit: the goal is to metaphorize limit as *stasis,* not dynamism. It can surpass its own limit, but in order to remain within the frame, in order for actualization to occur through subtraction, it *elasticizes* limit. An unbinding of boundaries: its metaphor is to reach the goal but always in order to throw that goal further out of reach so it remains an incomplete and improbable excess.

As if adding two and two to get five or adding two and two so as not to reach three: sense of purpose and senseless purpose render the same thing insofar as the same thing is something else again. This is clear. One tends by rendering, the other renders by tending. In one, risk is equivalent to rigor, in the other, rigor is equivalent to risk. One sheepishly covers a wolf, the other wolfishly covers a sheep. The elasticity of a waterfall as opposed to elasticity quantified.

9

Yes, on this third occasion I had read *Paradiso*. And its impenetrability crumbled. Why? Thought: I read *that* as cordiality, as a peculiar kind of intimacy. I had read at the insistence of Lorenzo García Vega. We planned to discuss the novel. Like a chronicle, a document. We would talk, we have talked about the reverse of *Paradiso*, its human hell both as labyrinthine and as desolate as its verbal splendor. Labyrinthine and desolate: at the base, in the center, was Lezama. Lezama/Minotaur.

Unlearning is necessary for learning. I have always known that intuitively. I confirmed it reading one of Lorenzo's essays, "La opereta cubana de Julián del Casal" (The Cuban operetta of Julián del Casal). A lucid, solitary essay. The essay of a reactionary here considered revolutionary. The essay of a revolutionary there considered reactionary.

Man of two worlds? Man of many worlds: of none.

With Lorenzo I have learned a lot about Cuba. In conversations that begin here and end there. Either in his apartment with too many walls—better to say too many walls than absence of what he would call decor—or beneath the irritating, screeching interruptions of the subway under Roosevelt Ave. Either in the secretly famous *Casa Wong* or in my room with its aversion to walls—better to say aversion to walls than what I would call *excess of presence*. Either in my apartment, where my cat Pacito shows Lorenzo he could never be a *mambí* warrior, or on some grubby bench in Central Park.

I want to talk about *Paradiso*, about Lezama, about Cuba. Because here, in Queens, at certain moments, I am in Cuba. The provincial Cuba of my childhood. Here, at times, without being a player, I am in history, the history that jumps from the nineteenth century to the 26th of July, 1953. I think some sense of wholeness might be possible, even for me. Like a tree after too much rain when the ground has begun to give way, I had not felt my roots for a long time. Because mud is ground giving way, like a warning.

x or the unknown
comic relief *algebra class* *epicenter*

cemí + foción + fronesis = three trapped tigers

10

(((((Like a cardboard pyramid, what I am is named Octavio Armand. What does Octavio Armand remember about Octavio Armand? What am I of what I was? What does what I am remember of what I was? About 1959 I started to write. I was thirteen. A good or a bad age to start writing, it makes no difference. What I wrote, and it makes no difference why, was not *reading, hastening, made poem upon the mountains of spices*. Two events transformed me (had transformed me?) decisively. One, suprapersonal, surrounded me with history in full force: the Cuban revolution. I had already lived it for years with a child's excessive imagination and awareness. Now it had become a daily holding-oneself-in-check, an apprenticeship of clumsy dissimulations: daily pettiness gobbling up history as hope. For sympathizing with that (that?) revolution, my family had lived nine months of exile: with that exile I was reborn. Not long afterwards, disillusioned, our family met with another—or the same?—exile, which has lasted many years. Many: from this exile no one is born. This other, identical exile goes on, excluding me from that, from what was, and is, an essential part of my life. That child, the only one who survives all my (im)postures, still finds it hard to distinguish between revolution and family feuding, between flight and travel. When I was fourteen, another event. In the spring of 1960, something at once superficial and extremely intimate. Between two political exiles, a more drastic one, which resulted in a difficult turning inward. Suddenly—I never knew exactly when, since there were few mirrors in the summer that meant beach, that meant Uvero—I was surrounded not only by an inhospitable history, but by a skin that had openly declared war on me. They were both offensive, wounding, abusive. History and skin were one and the same thing. I fled from my skin, which no doubt eased the way for my other flight. At that point landscape was virtually devoid of intensity for me since I had lost a far more immediate territory: the terrible periphery of fuzz and pimples and also scars and pores. I will never understand how anyone who has had skin like mine, who has felt skin as I have, could believe in nation, history, peripheries. Pores clogged with dirt, which is mud, earth giving way, like a warning. In time, I sensed I would have to win out over them both, skin and history. History of skin, skin of history: harshness, dirt, mud. I would win by rejecting them, simultaneously cutting out from—cutting off—anecdotes and fluff. No, it was not an escape. I am not *an evader*, as the poetics *à la dernière* would say—that poetics *à la dernière* which is a poetics *par-derrière*. No, it was not an escape. Rather, and I have written about this, I wanted to live history hour by hour, reduce borders to the level of touch, live skin with all its miraculous and shameful details. Acceptance of surface strictly as surface: a terror of territory converted into terror from territory. I have written about this, in *Piel menos mía* (Moulting).

Among those vague memories, more invented than remembered, there is one fixed like a stone in a slingshot: on December 24, 1960, I left Cuba for the second and last time. A day like any other: wind and blue sun in Rancho Boyeros. A day like any other and nevertheless it was Christmas Eve and I was starting out on an unexpected journey. In New York that evening, that Christmas Eve, it was very cold. It was snowing. A paradox: the unusual events of the day abolished its ritual, tribal value. The Fiesta, an exclusion.

An ominous jump: I went from Rancho Boyeros to Idlewild. From my own space (is there such a thing as one's own space?) I was dropped into a foreign time (is there a foreign time?). Omen/nomen/no men: today those airports are called José Martí and John Kennedy. History has been replacing geography. Space is used to pay homage to time. Now, however, it is not a question of constructions linked to sacred calendars but of landscapes condemned to time's passing, sacrificed to daily demands. Spaces where the Mayan calendar is a timetable for Eastern Airlines. Spaces that are useful but absolutely insignificant.))))))))

11

There is a lot to talk about (there is a lot to do, Vallejo used to say). As in Cabrera Infante's *Tres tristes tigres* (*Three trapped tigers*), all the characters in *Paradiso* speak a single language. They are language, they are the same language. True, *Tres tristes tigres* is very different from *Paradiso*. It is and it isn't.

It's the reverse, Lorenzo would say. It's different and the same. All the characters are one single character, they are the sameness of the bewitching, bewitched Cuban language. Except that, in their language, the characters who walk along La Rampa tend to put down whatever defines them; whereas the character who comes or goes along the Prado or on Obispo, climbing the streets like stairs, tends to enhance whatever it is that defines him. In both cases, although as rituals of rival heterodoxies, language is an exorcism. Also: an incantation.

Of interest, with respect to "*Penitenciales*" (Penitence): "The Colonel finished, laughing as though giving in more to verbal exaltation than to veracity. He often laughed when he finished speaking, as if he communicated some enigma to his listener through his own joviality." This is *very Cuban.* "More than a custom, it seems like an incantation of a deity unknown to us all, which hovers in a suspended silence when several Cubans get together, in the contradances at a birthday party or around the table over thick sips of beer, until some ordinary voice is heard saying or singing something totally extraneous to the occasion for the gathering: *Mamá, I want a taste of that delicious fruit,* or *there's a corpse on the fourth floor*, or *onward, onward in silent confusion*, which everyone ignores as it gradually acquires the force of an absurd call made from a musical instrument and they begin to work it into the principal theme. Evohé of ghosts slipping past, shadow of waters falling from the bow of a violin."

We will also speak of the *trickster tricked.* And of the *reverse.* "As if we could penetrate the eyes of animals watching a passing train, which would make accessible to us the reverse of a world of illumination,

pair of dice / paradise

freed from all causality, in the golden region of serene wonder." "That which reveals how Casanova, like Gide himself, used the mask of sincerity, but cynicism in its pure state is as difficult as the total word it hides. In confidential matters, all or nothing always hides the other half, where one is aware of being sought by a falcon that destroys the truth for sure. The quantity of sensations hiding behind the face or mask of the word *homosexual* is so large that it comprises both those who as great soldiers were afflicted with an undeniable sexual deviance and men whose sexuality is relatively normal, but who bristle or squirm as their skin tastes the hint of seaweed, receiving with the waters' splash the investiture of its maternal spirit."

And of how Lezama *violates* language, how he imposes a devilish sexuality on something that had never before exceeded the most naïve nominality, normality. Julio Cortázar has seen this clearly in "*Para llegar a Lezama Lima*" (How to reach Lezama Lima). In this context, and because he has obviously done the same thing, we will speak of Severo Sarduy. *Cobra* is close to *Paradiso* in many ways. The novel could be the fulfillment of one of Fronesis's prophecies: "The time will come when the serpent will coil round the cross, worshipped by the Orphites who render it homage, the metal serpent, invented by Moses in order to save those bitten by the snake." But I do not intend to refer only to *Cobra.* I am also thinking of Sarduy's poetry. Of *Big Bang*, which Lorenzo has not read. *Big Bang*, English for a theory about the origins of the universe. Also English for something else. Astronomy and erotica. I want to show Lorenzo Sarduy's *visual poems:* they *are* constellations, yes, but they are also anal constellations. A project after Mallarmé: the constellation as theme, structure, (con)figuration.

Our conversation will be a successive order, then. Because all of these themes will be interwoven. And it will no doubt have its Chapter XII, with a paragraph one hundred.

12

Early August. I have written a paragraph about *Paradiso.* The beginning, I tell myself, of something that really reflects a reading, a *meeting*.

"They are characters that tend toward immobility, like the elephant when it is made of ivory. In the same way, the novel ends thickly, in an amazing utter darkness, like the darkness of water tinged gradually as it trickles through grounds toward a celebration of coffee, daybreak. But in Cemí's growing immobility, that of finding himself alone, like the Taíno idol when there are no more *areítos* or aborigines, the end is usually a far-from-empirical chair, a table, and a cup of *café con leche*. Seated, alone, the tinkling of the spoon against that cup will reconstruct a certain absence, which is the novel itself, which at that instant stops (beginning). It is necessary to ask then what is a novel, what is that novel that stops (beginning)? Because at issue here is not a riddle in the center of a formal nightmare, but above all someone who has *outguessed himself* and therefore willingly become marginal in order to establish a sense of the day-to-day in the confluence of diverse things, someone who, as he sits down, configures, in passing, a quadrilateral with the chair, the table, and the cup of *café con leché*. To enter that *figure* implies more than discreet allusions to the baroque; it implies more than a certain intelligence trying not to go too far; it is more than the labyrinthine avoidance of the labyrinth, which surrenders heroically, like something allowing itself to be unbasted without offering the least resistance."

I will show it to Lorenzo. Along with another paragraph I've written, in *Diario de una tarde* (Diary of an afternoon), one about him.

"He does not like (1) wearing a uniform and having to smile (2) standing on his feet (3) opening doors. He is a doorman. A rigorously logical sequence. Of course its logic is lost through reduction, unlike a scream lost in another scream or the word *morn* in a thick, creamy Mornay. He does not like (1) wearing a uniform and having to smile (2) standing on his feet (3) opening doors. He wants to be a doorman. What leads to something even more absurd is the discovery of a surprising rancor that intervenes between word and thing, definition and occupation. Doorman. But I have to (1) wear a uniform and smile (2) stand on my feet (3) open doors. Etc. The solution: make him the editor of a dictionary not bent on reducing words through definitions. Yes, a dictionary. Yes, opening doors means opening words.

I read the paragraph and write: like a lion in Central Park imagining jungles, a person cannot but be disruptive here in the midst of a context that makes wholeness impossible. There is a certain heroism in this.

I remember mentioning an ivory elephant and a caged lion. Nature degraded by artificiality. Nature worn out by circumstance, by the circumstantial. There is something in this.

13

Monday, August 9, 1976. Noon. Lorenzo just called. It's pouring rain. Hurricane Belle is approaching New York. I was reading *The Magic Mountain* when the phone rang, barely disguised in the guffaws of rain. Combinatorial: Belle and Bell Telephone. Lorenzo's on his way over. The first time he came to my parents' house he arrived frozen. This time he'll arrive dripping, Lorenzo as sponge. Lorenzo has asked me why I don't *try some narrative*. I have tried some, very obliquely, in *Diario de una tarde*. (Also: I'm trying some now.) In the *Diario*, as if facing an improbable interviewer, I have answered that question with all the sincerity of a provincial sort whose fortune has risen.

"But what do I have for beginning a narrative? A pretty categorical ignorance and a lack of interest even more categorical. Resistance. Perhaps less: indifference. Perhaps more: disdain for narrative genres, which has seemed more rather than less a question of literature for gossips. There is clearly a considerable difference between a reader of Proust and a neighborhood gossip. But the difference is one of degree. The reader finds out about everything by getting involved as little as possible. Is reduced happily to a strictly halved half of the insidious dialogue in which there is a great deal of nonparticipatory participation. And the reader can—everything is permitted—stop with pleasure at certain details, invent others, deform a few more. The more one interferes the less one gets involved. The more the reader understands of the details/strings governing the characters of a novel, the less necessary it is to resist a gaze other than that of the self, reflected. Thus, since according to one novelist there is a female reader and a male reader, there are also, in the neighborhood as novel, two ways of reaching the *vox populi,* two means of expressing the desire for omniscience."

14

Monday, August 9, 1976.
From the beginning of an essay I outlined but never wrote about *Orígenes*: "Situated between *revista de avance* and *Casa de las Américas*, in other words between a revolutionary maga-

zine and a magazine of the Revolution, *Orígenes* (1944–1956) still represents the most radical effort ever undertaken by Cuban magazines, if we consider the etymological or mathematical value of that word, which today smacks of ideological sentimentality."

And I say to myself: One's own feelings, ideas, even one's own vocabulary, resist those of the other. To such an extent that those of the other are either excluded or deformed until they can be safely assimilated within preexisting structures. In other words, until they are reduced to harmless glitter. It worries me a lot when someone *understands me.* I wonder if he didn't hear me right. Maybe I failed to make myself clear?

15

There's water in the air. Leonardo da Vinci had already thought about it in those terms, with a child's uncanny precision. Thought: that sheepishly covered wolf. Play that card up your sleeve, I think, and wash your hand. Like a stone after it is hurled, the card is still the hand even after it is played, the hand beyond the bone. I think about that. And I remember Madame Pompadour, Madame Whore. *Après moi le déluge.* Is Madame Pompadour dead? Is that why we're having this storm? Is that why the hurricane is named Belle? Leonardo Pompadour, Whore Belle. And I say to my hand, speak up, señorita. Gliding by with a Louis XV smile, she corrected me: *Mademoiselle.*

> *Après moi la pierre*, said the phalange
> *Après moi la prière*, said the second phalange
> *Après moi Robespierre*, said the third phalange

Phalange/second phalange/third phalange.

(There is a story about this. My father was visiting a friend when their conversation was interrupted by the sudden appearance of the friend's three children, who were anxious to display their knowledge of anatomy. Using her index finger to point out the rather surprising relation between the anatomy she had studied and her own anatomy, the eldest daughter told my father: "Phalange/second phalange/third phalange it is." The second child repeated the gesture: "Phalange/second phalange/

third phalange it is." The youngest, who was still struggling to learn something more difficult than anatomy came out with: "tit is, tit is, tit is.")

Belle bangs at the windows; the windows bark like dogs. There's a hurricane in my head like the hurricane in the street. Belle, it's a *Verlainian air.* I'll have to tell Lorenzo the story, when he arrives wet and hardly Verlainian.

16

I have written all this after Lorenzo was here. That was several days ago. Today I visited him. He came here on Monday; this afternoon, Wednesday, I went to his house. The conversation we had today and could not have Monday encouraged me to write. A narrative, like my friend suggested. Because it's true that what happened on Monday was really odd.

That was odd. (Odd: the word is not adequate to describe what happened on Monday, which has something of Lezama's *successive order. That* was more than odd.)

Lorenzo arrived, soaked to the skin. We went to my room with its aversion to walls. An initial awkwardness. I attributed this to the hurricane, since there was no longer an *initial awkwardness* when we met. I picked up a piece of paper. Something was written on it. A paragraph. I said: it's about *Paradiso.*

"He died yesterday." Lorenzo seemed distracted as he spoke.

"What?"

"Lezama. He died yesterday. Apparently from pneumonia. His sister called Julián from Puerto Rico."

My father made coffee, like always. We talked. But it was impossible to talk about Lezama, about *Paradiso.* An *internal emigré*, that's what he would have been called by Trotsky, who knew the story inside out, told the story, and had it told to him. Lezama died yesterday, down there in Cuba.

Like Cemí, he was alone when he reached the end of his pilgrimage. Life and novel: solitude. (I'm thinking about the death of Narcissus.) Odd. Very odd. I have just read *Paradiso*; Lezama dies. We are about to talk about *Paradiso*; Lezama dies. These days Lorenzo is writing about Lezama; Lezama dies. The horse dies and we are left like the dragon or the sword.

We are the two centurions from paragraph one hundred. Perhaps we have seen the *flight of a ghost.* Perhaps *we have covered ourselves with a single cape, something like the head of a turtle rising from our necks, and we depart with the step of a forced march.*

Our conversation was a non-conversation. And I thought/ think again about Juan de Manzano's not-at-all Mallarmean blank poem, Zequeira's incoherent eloquence, Martí's tongue between his teeth. *Literally pierced by them.*

I propose a hyperbole: I killed Lezama by reading; Lorenzo killed Lezama by writing; we both killed him by not talking. As if there might really have been something to that, neither Lorenzo nor I laughed. Nothing. A silence that said nothing, that said everything. Phalange/second phalange/third phalange it is. Tit is/tit is/tit is. Our conversation, our small homage ended—it did not end since it did not begin—as pain and complicity.

17

A parable.

The hand's reality ends with a color, a particular line. Serenity dissolving in cold, mathematical terror. The logic of space governed by the impassive centering of some animal, or perhaps a fruit. No figures, prefigurations, hints, indications. The shadow is painted, not the form but its projection in total darkness. A painter with no paintings. Spatial movement/narrative movement: drama. In that space there will always be an animal. *But I speak to them in parables: because by seeing they do not see and by hearing they neither hear nor understand.*

Yes, there is an elephant. Ivory. Like an African version of Moby Dick. A prairie whale. And a caged lion. My notes for a possible essay about a possible painter fit here, on these pages, like a parable. Like an impassive centering. Like space. Like a painting. Like a synthesis. Like Chapter XII. I'm thinking of Foucault: "the symbolic man manages to become a fantastic bird whose oversized neck folds over itself a thousand times, a meaningless being, placed between animal and thing, closer to the spells of illusion than the rigors of a meaning." Lezama is that *symbolic man.* That *fantastic bird* is Lezama.

As if to brutalize its possible contexts, I include the following item, almost in neon, from *Esquire*, December 1959, Year of the Revolution.

WORLD'S
SEVEN
GREATEST
BARS

The Floridita Bar in Havana, Cuba, is an institution of unique integrity in a city whose catering to tourists has corrupted the spirit and meaning of a truly honest bar. At the Floridita, man's spirit may be elevated by conversation and companionship, not enticed into betrayal by his baser instincts. It is an international and sophisticated crossroads, but it is not for the cha-cha addicts. Rum, as it should, dominates, and as is the case in many great bars, the stimulation of the presence of a famous man lends a special atmosphere, a feeling of a friendly philosophy for imbibing. Cuban resident Ernest Hemingway can be found frequently holding court, and when not there in person, there's a solid reminder of him in the corner via a sculptured bust.

Did that bust topple when Hemingway *jumped*, like the bust of the geometer?

The Floridita, with SW Miami—la Sagüesera—as reverse.

Delight on delight, splashed coral and green snow. With that kind of spontaneous excess, Lezama would tell about an exceptionally pleasant gastronomic experience. Gourmet and gourmand. *Delight on delight, splashed coral and green snow.* A verbal palate. As if language, words even, gave him the enjoyment of food. To him, words were also delight, coral, and snow. A very savvy savoring. Palate and parley. Language and lingua. Gourmet and guru.

Lezama Lima died in Havana the night of August 8, 1976. If God has read *Paradiso*, Lezama will not enter the kingdom of heaven. His exile was of this Earth. His marginality was of this Earth. But in Hades there is bound to be a spirit willing to talk with him about Saint Thomas.

So be it.

White on White

Wipe out as well
the next word,
which you are always
about to read,
                    not here
there,
that one staining the
page.

Ramming the Page

1

What is the page? A naïve question. But an essential one. By reversing one of Bachelard's titles, I can say that the page is the space of the poem. But what do I say when I say that? How do I say it? How can I say it?

2

There is no need to go into cahoots with history. To assert, for example, that behind every active notion of the page lies an obligatory antecedent: Mallarmé. There is nothing but antecedents. And of course the antecedents of antecedents.

3

Page: what things say when no one says anything any longer/yet. Antecedents: stone, a monkey's antics, an empty shell, an earthworm tortured by children, tracks in the snow. This is all *legible* and it happens in a space never dispossessed of redundance nor expansiveness: the body itself, a landscape covered with hair and shrieking teeth which are a red rear-end which is that sun which are pink rings multiplied by alcohol into red rings toasted by flames and children playing until they are tracks in the snow, which are the body itself.

4

What Artaud read on the Mountain is written everywhere. Even in Artaud's texts. Page: space of space. Distance, not place. Distance without dimension. Dimension where all objects fit and are Nothing, where you and I are or are not in order to be No one. None. The page hurls space beyond space and time beyond time. Presence and transcendence. That is all/all is that. Page: beyond of the verbal mask. Also: theater of signs. What can be here being somewhere else and everywhere. Designing signs: "raising the page to the power of a starry sky." Neither page nor starry sky: power, virtuality. Mallarmé read Something in a sudden non-spatial space. There (=there?) or thus

(=thus?) he tried to write his pageless Book, his wordless Page. It is not improbable that Artaud read the same thing in that same distance. The issue is one of *legibility itself*: metaphor of transparence. The Pageless Book and the Wordless Page will never be written. Will never be written because they are written. Nothing is missing but the authors: the readers: you.

5

When defined in terms of content, *text* leads toward notions like epic, lyric, genre, theme. The definition is made more precise by referring to further notions of form obviously implied in content and thus inseparable from it. As an exclusive phenomenon (which contains or speaks its own form exclusively) form only appears in instances of self-allegory. To quote Lope de Vega: "Violante requests that I write her a sonnet."

6

Such precision does not alter an essential fact: the definition of text conforms to a strictly combinatorial principle of possible or even probable relationships between what is articulated and ways to articulate it, between signs and number/order/type of signs: design. In other words, everything that will not fit literally in the literal is usually deemed not significant and therefore eliminated systematically. For example, the very space that makes texts possible: the page, first geometrization of voice.

7

A definition more attuned to the demands of integrity could not omit that space. It would begin with the page and would extend the range of possible meanings by positing visibility (page:voice) as theme/genre/form/content/etc. Definition = description, where, de($^{\text{scrip}}_{\text{fini}}$)tion admits the virtuality of the page as active sign and replaces the idea of passive surface with an acceptance of surface as a polarizing and polarized medium. The space of writing withdraws from the idea of *background* so as to create a writing of space, a surface not covered with words but discovered as sign by the words themselves. The visible is also legible. The page in itself says something: it says the page where saying takes place. That totality is the text—synthesis not sum of page and word.

8

Because words kill the page as they mount it. Kill what activates page as signs. Kill in order to propagate: black on white. The page dies like the equal sign that lets two by two be four. Or like the male of the famous *Lacrodectus mactans*. Irony: those same words transform paper to page. Simultaneously animate and annihilate.

9

On surface what is not word can be visibility/transparency: mirror or window. The eye's logic avoids the mirror because it seeks definitions rather than its own sphericity, and it avoids the window because it suggests that, read, each word leads to an opening, a hole, a beyond. But the word should not be a place where the eye stops. The adventure of the page as totality demands a reading of the word in space not extension. Which is to say, visibility of the word, reading of the page. Pageantry. A measure against the repression made systematic by literary conventions, which are always conventions of reading: write not only with words but with words and page. Or—to use a different terminology—bring the repressed unconscious (page) to consciousness (word). Through expansion, the page as sign alters the function and substance of the text.

10

ordswordswordswordswordswordswordswordswordswordswordswordsw

11

Legibility owes to (page)antry as much as to word. The determination of what is legible occurs as censure and gives rise to a false impression of relief (landscape) on surface (space). A page whose signs were perforated instead of written would reverse—although perhaps not resolve—this impression of relief. This would make the word extraterritorial: a space that is not (but implied) on the page. And the page, a space of access to another space: light or surface beyond the page. The word would exist then only as tension between sign and thing. *Puzzle*: the pieces of the text in play with or relation to each other and in a relation of assembled surface countering/confirming surface of assembling.

12

The story of the page recapitulates a systematic destruction of space as surface. Written, that history is a ruin—eloquent, redundant. Neither catalogue of destruction nor multilation of space. Space itself coming apart: spacing out. Words: the conversion of space to frontier: architecture as demolition.

13

By renouncing space in favor of extension, the eye surrounds itself exclusively with words, which confirm its capacity as organization and reduce to a minimum its impact as organ. What is not word puts the eye in its place: thing among things, thing in orbit. The freedom of the eye is the closed eyelid or the acceptance of word and paper as surface, page. On the surface (of its own eyelid (or of the visible as immediacy, eyelid) the eye is free.

Axiom. A mirror writing: gaze = page, is beneath/above/behind/around/facing the word.

14

The page as space confirms that language is a manifestation of evil. The page as extension implies a renunciation of the nonmeasurable world. An awkward, painful renunciation: unit for fraction, truth for lie. What is said for what must be said or must not be said.

15

Repressing the page is analogous to suppressing the body. Like prohibitions or fashion, words cover what cannot be altered: the body where one writes. Page is pleasure/placenta/orderless order. Impossible to study clothing without knowing the body.

Also impossible to write about writing without knowing its body. If, from convention, the page is reduced to (fad)ing, as an object of repression it suggests that what is truly peripheral is the word.

16

Page: central/centripetal dimension of the text. Spacetime: time as spatiality of space. Page as po(e(s(i(e(bility of poem. Naked experience of order. Says and says nothing. It means and means to say it means.

17

a. The page organizes the present of the text, its imminence. **b**. The motionlessness of the page causes as much dizziness as the movement of the poem. **c**. Page: center of gravitation where text is dispersed, dissipated. Motion(less) center of movement. **d**. Page: the poem's fixed present: was what it will be now that it is while you read. Present indicative of presence.

18

Thus, between the already "encoded" eye and reflexive knowledge there is a middle region which liberates order itself: it is here that it appears, according to the culture and the age in question, continuous and graduated or discontinuous and piecemeal, linked to space or constituted anew at each instant by the driving force of time, related to a series of variables or defined by separate systems of coherences, composed of resemblances which are either successive or corresponding, organized around increasing differences, etc. This middle region, then, in so far as it makes manifest the modes of being or order, can be posited as the most fundamental of all: anterior to words, preceptions, and gestures, which are then taken to be more or less exact, more or less happy, expressions of it (which is why this experience of order in its primary state always plays a crucial role); more solid, more archaic, less dubious, always more "true" than the theories that attempt to give those expressions explicit form, exhaustive application, or philosophical foundation. Thus, in every culture, between the use of what one might call the ordering of codes and reflections upon order itself, there is the pure experience of order and its modes of being.

—Foucault, *The Order of Things*

19

The degradation of the page: initial passage to all writing. Passage and passion: abolishing the page as space (silence) ritualizes a determination to remain exclusively in the realm of definitions, a provisional and desperate alternative to matter and disorder.

20

Writing rams the page, covering it with signs or scribbles that are always incapable of saying less than the page. Writing is always over. Under oath, the page is extension not space. Under oath, the page comes about as renunciation, never as freedom. For it only exists where it upholds words: the rest is just paper, inertia. Desert, not distance. Thus, the page says nothing: it relates its own supression with the very words supressing it.

21

And man,
wracked by such dark visions,
who finds in the heavenly bodies
overpowering wonders and signs in space,
regards the camel
leading the caravan
as the messenger led by light,
on the vague desert forming
the blank page!

—Darío, "La página blanca" (The blank page)

22

The horror of words—which bursts like commercial or ideological noise: propaganda—has been decisive in the revaluation of the page.

23

a. A music of sounds rather than notes; a poetry of signification rather than words. To the Protagorean arbitrariness of order and measure, oppose the relativistic arbitrariness of signifying without (or before) designating.
b. Page: archetype of the poem.

24

The page is *full of Nothing* until the moment of writing. Text written, page empty. The empty page—madness—is all that remains of the castle?

25

Each page is its poem. Specificity: the poem said the page where I said what was said or unsaid as the page was saying it. A reversible dynamism. Palindrome. In the language of comic strips it would look like a balloon-boomerang.

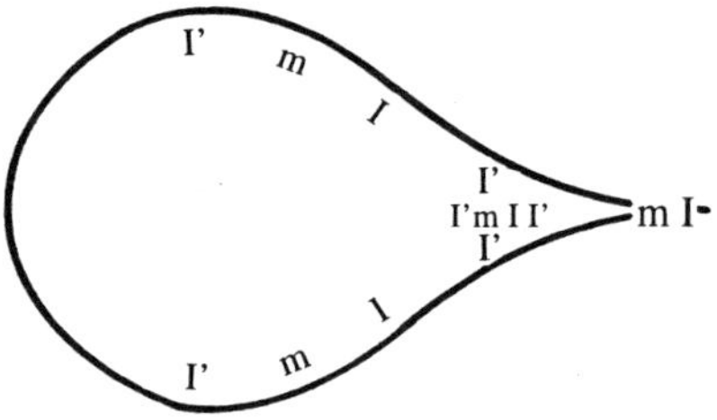

26

(PARENTHESIS*

Raining.
I sit down to write and say the page will fill up. It will accumulate—obscure, resonant—in the porousness of a pebble in

* "Parenthesis" from *Cómo escribir con erizo* (How to write with a sea urchin).
All rights reserved. No part of this publication may be reproduced without prior permission of the publisher.
Registered as required by Law 11,723
Legal registration
M 12,847 - 1976
Nihil obstat:
Censor

a pool thrashed by gluttonous larvae in the hand a child plunges into the dried guts of a cow glistening once again as it rots in a well.

The page will fill up. Something will have to be said (about the urgency of speaking or the impotence of speaking?) and what is said will have as much weight as water flowing. Surface is enough. Enough for self to be shed/sp/read. Let surface provoke laughter, anger, stammering, silences, exclamations, screams, laments. Let the page say what I have or do not have to say, and that will be my text, my pretext. A trick: the magician pulls words from your mouth, your groin, your armpit; you speak if he touches you; you speak where he touches you; he pulls out your bones and you bare each urgent eyetooth, you bark; he devours you; he pulls a phrase from under your hand; he is insulting and you are oblivious; he calls and you do not recognize the name; he tugs at your tongue and you talk a leg off, it falls under the table, beneath the typewriter, propping up a skull nailed suddenly on a disgusting pole, a trophy from some meticulous, useless, empty destruction, and so you attack again with hair, eyelids, gesture, cheeks. Phrases/phases. Written/writhen/rotten. The page fills up, it frees you; you rise, reject it. Palimpsest and symmetry. Because there is no nakedness in scattered surfaces. There is nakedness in open, accumulated surfaces. Because there is no nakedness in scattered surfaces there is nakedness in open, accumulated surfaces. Etc. Is it enough to shed self? Spread self? Each affirmation, another doubt. Each instant dissolves in another instant; each incomplete phrase in another phrase that will never be complete. Each phrase, another phase. Each truth, another lie. No longer am I/I no longer am/I am no longer.

PARENTHESIS)

27

Writing: traces left by voice; page: traces left by silence. Hush with one lip what is hushed by the other. Traces on traces.

28

a.

frame

b. Square/target/mirror/perspective even as negation of perspective. Whatever will fit in a frame. Nothing, squared, the page represents no space, makes possible no perspective that would open a phantasmagoric geometrical perspective. From seeing to reading: from mirror to transparency: from sketch to scheme.

29

Until recently, the philosophy of composition—brought into modern literature by Edgar Allan Poe almost a century and a half ago (1846)—did without an (adequate) idea of the page. Almost exactly a century after the publication of *Philosophy of Composition, A psicologia da composição* (The psychology of composition, 1947), by João Cabral de Melo Neto suggests the definitive? incorporation of what could be called by analogy a formal unconscious in the expression of the contents of writing. The page will be one of the materials incorporated as formal unconscious: it passes from background to logical surface, active background, and, bypassing its own surface as surface, makes possible a phenomenology of composition.

This means that until the present, when in the field of intersemiotic studies the possibility of a verbal and visual art is being explored in harmony, synthesis, rather than symmetry, no one had even come up with a hyopothesis about the page as a material part of the poem. With one exception—Mallarmé—the page continued to be systematically excluded from the theory and practice of the poem. It had no place in rhetoric: printing, impression, then, involved neither expression nor persuasion. Considered *dead weight*, the page was systematically confused with its antecedent: stone. No distinction was made between the limits of language within the limits of stone and the limits of language within the limits of the page, an unlimited although visible space. The page is not stone minus geology. Nevertheless, its norms were spelled out in precepts employing tenaciously archaic metaphors, a verbal museum: *Poet, carve your verse.* Every page was literally (lythographically) a dead weight; all writing, a momumental epitaph. Writing continued to occur on paper as if on stone. In this sense, clandestine, revolutionary, writing—graffiti—is linked with the tradition of the epitaph, the most reactionary writing still in existence. Society has never needed to domesticate the epitaph by prizing or pricing this profoundly social writing. It has, however, begun (through subvention) to subvert graffiti, allowing it to enter the museum and thereby authorizing the dissolution of its marginality, its clandestine nature. Clandestineness as clan/claque–clown; the subversive in the academic. Assassinated, graffiti commits suicide. An enormous sin of redundance: the exhibiting of what in itself is (was) exhibit, *exposé*. Everything has degenerated into a papal and suspicious alliance of graffiti and pop.

30

Neither Dada nor the Futurists, who went as far as the concept of free words and letters, were concerned about freeing the page. The Futurists intuited, in film, a *writing of motion*. But they did not move from there to a possible *motion of writing* in terms of screen or page. There were, it is true, a few hints, glimpses. By Tzara, for example. *Dada Manifesto, 1918*: "Every page must explode, whether from deep, heavy seriousness, the whirlwind, vertigo, the new, the eternal, from devasting humor, from the enthusiasm of principles or the way it is printed." Printing presses.

Nor did Cubism show any more interest, with its attempts to geometrize writing on the basis of theme. Quite the contrary. Freedom of the letter and the word owed to impression, a pinning down of the page. The poem was torn to shreds; the page remained intact precisely because its individual existence was never recognized. This meant the demolition of the poem was incomplete: the blueprint was destroyed and the building saved.

31

There is a need for a phenomenology of the page, a psychoanalysis of the page, a poetics of the page. And there is a danger: it appears that the philosophy of structure, which is gradually substituting the philosophy of composition, will overlook the page because it is not considered significant within the system of relations operative in textuality. *What does it say?* is a question that must be asked about the page.

32

Medieval and Renaissance man experienced little of the separation and specialty among the arts that developed later. The manuscript and the earlier printed books were read aloud, and poetry was sung or intoned. Oratory, music, literature, and drawing were closely related. Above all, the world of the illuminated manuscript was one in which lettering itself was given plastic stress to an almost sculptural degree. In a study of the art of Andrea Mantegna, the illuminator of manuscripts, Millard Meiss mentions that, amidst the flowery and leafy margins of the page, Mantegna's letters "rise like monuments, stony, stable and finely cut. . . .Palpably soled and weighty, they stand boldly before the colored ground, upon which they often throw a shadow . . ."

—McLuhan, *Understanding Media: The Extensions of Man*

33

The negation of the poem was essentially engineered by reading. A de(author)ization. Crisis: the poem ceased to be considered an actualization of axioms that provided it with a degree of legibility. In the crisis, that poem was not conceivable. Conceivability and legibility were not approaches to but questions asked of that poem, or rather, questions about its possibility or impossibility. From then on what sustains the poem is not an axiomatic but an implacably interrogative poetics. The idea of the page could thus be reexamined. Mallarmé's abolishments were a fundamental step. In the context of that implacable interrogation, the page could (re)appear as a question among questions. At the bottom of it all, there would literally be nothing left to note, not even the page.

34

a. Analogy between dream and language. In the most ancient languages a single word could express opposite terms; difference was established by intonation, gesture, or, in the case of writing, by the use of determinatives. In latent dreams, opposites often arise through a single manifest element. **b**. The page as a space of that (am)bivalence. Another analogy, then. All writing is determinative. Write: indicate the difference between this page and that. Write: classify pages. Ennumerate and number. Or fix the Infinite. Page: the monogrammatic to an absolute degree.

(Open parenthesis

What do I read in my own texts? How do I read them? Who reads those texts when I read them? What do my words mean? What do words mean to me? And what does the page mean? What does it mean when I read it?

((((((I read the poem from the page, the page from the word, the word from silence, reading from things, silence from a woman lying at my side, the woman lying at my side from my body, my body from a scribble; I read the page reading the poem that writing shreds in the silence of some body where there is a woman lying around a child who might be named me and asks me what an eye is; I read space on space, words on words, body on body, shadow on shadow (I read: overshadowed). I reread poems that are words, words that are gestures, spaces, features, where in the very act of reading the eye itself (de)forms what it reads. Gives to or takes form from what it reads? (I read: the eye is the poem.) Or rather, I read what is lived, dreamed, written. I read what is read. And I read nothing. (Nothing, I read.) What is lived, dreamed, written read me, I am what is read. The poem, the word, the page, the woman lying at my side, read me. I am what they read, what you read, nothing I read.)))

I have written some texts against the page, literally ramming it by subjecting it to a specific projection of the line. Which is to say, convergence of legibility and visibility. Surface as background. This is true for the *reticules* in *Piel menos mía*

(Moulting) and the stock phrases in *Penitenciales* (Penitence), 45 rpm posters where writing proposes the exact circularity of a record.

In those two instances I was trying to redefine or alter the convention of the page, a space that simultaneously facilitates and limits writing. I also wanted to write on (the page like) a mirror. To make or convert the page into a nonspatial space. In the *reticules*, for example, the margin's odd (and brutal) justification contributes to the acceleration of a combinatorial reading that superposes and supports the strictly visual over the merely grammatical. Geometry (:grammar) as time.

Etc.

Cosas pasan (Things happen) and *Piel menos mía* (Moulting) condense and/or bring to a tension certain relations between word/world that are suggested in the final section of *Entre testigos* (Among witnesses): "Each lip will answer each lip." Opposition: the rubbing or separation of lip against lip and the dissolving of the tentacular proximity between language and thing. Correlation: reduction of the possibility of communication to the (grotesque) lip-to-lip and, simultaneously, the acceptance of that awkward silence as gesture. In other words, an effort to create from the picture in an empty frame, on the basis of zero squared: the page.

The bivalence of reduction—grotesque discourse (completion) and gesture (rites, writhing of initiation)—determines a dual development or motion in the poem, where the value of transference between configuration (communication as thing) and gesture (thing as communication) occurs as a system of affirmation/negation. Or rather, there is a *semantics of construction* that replaces without excluding other notions of order, such as genre or grammar. With increasing freedom, sentiments and (p(re)sent(i)ments form their own dynamics: an automatism of the whole in the mechanism of the hand. That essentially chaotic formulation which collides, first, with the impediment (reduction) of the hand, then confronts a peculiar duplication of its possible space, the page. Formula against form, that is.

Such an *imposed form* places a gratuitous demand on chaotic formulation, since at first glance (: as reading) it proves to be extraterritorial to the poem itself. It consists of an avoidance of the convention of the page as a limit zone, a margin. This is ironic since the avoidance duplicates that limit zone. A margin within (against) the margin, by dispensing with all systems of grammatical warning (hyphens = scripts), the brutal typographic justification accelerates even more the chaotic formulation it should contain gratuitously.

The strictly formal implications (form = limit) of such designing designation do not mitigate the poem's essentially chaotic and emotive charge. On the contrary, speculation (with that form), the utilization of limit as reflection (speculum), permit any desperation to be seen as surface.

Close parenthesis)

35

Painting on painting: Velázquez, *Las Meninas*. But the work of Velázquez is not solely conceptual: canvas on canvas, a spatial relation that Foucault discussed perceptively in the first

---

On the right wall Baldassar Carlos, Philip on foot with his hunting gun. Philip on Horseback, the horse's foot having been done first in a different position. Again by the door Mercury and Argos, and below it the Drinkers.

—Pound, *Guide to Kulchur*

---

chapter of *The Order of Things*. Velázquez *paints on what has been painted*. Pentimenti. Years later, the results are astonishing. As much or more than the painter, paint makes his canvas definitive. Paint and time. So that in *Philip IV on Horseback*, the horse has five or six hooves. The *background*—what was blocked out—imposes itself, participates. Realism over realism, organicity, and abstraction.

Axioms. Writing over writing. Use one writing as the active, o
OOOOOOOOOOOOOOOOOOOOOOOOOOOOOOOOOO
perative,OwOrkingObackgrOundOfOrOanOtherOwriting.OWrite
OOOOOOOOOOOOOOOOOOOOOOOOOOOOOOOOOO
in a thronged space teeming with words, numbers, signs.

Through selection, scratches, emphasis, make signs on the basis of that teeming. A montage of texts; poetry in relief, topological poetry,

---

it was that word oidor, *heard and savored by José Cemí like the impossible key to an unknown world that recalled the Palazzo Capitolino's stone face of the Empress Plotina, where, because of its peeling paint, the rocky cowl that forms her nose creates the impression of a Dipylon Egyptian face that reveals the youthful condition of its skin as the strips of linen are torn off, thus causing a novel effect where time intervenes like blind but precise artifice, erasing the principal qualities attained by the artist and adding others which would likely have mortified him by realizing for that face in stone the new solution he could not even envision. We feel that time mocks time there, since, even as it pounces fiercely on the stone face and wins a first momentary victory by peeling the paint from its nose, the same nose reappears, rhyming or conversing with the face that has remained unchanged.*

—Lezama Lima, *Paradiso*

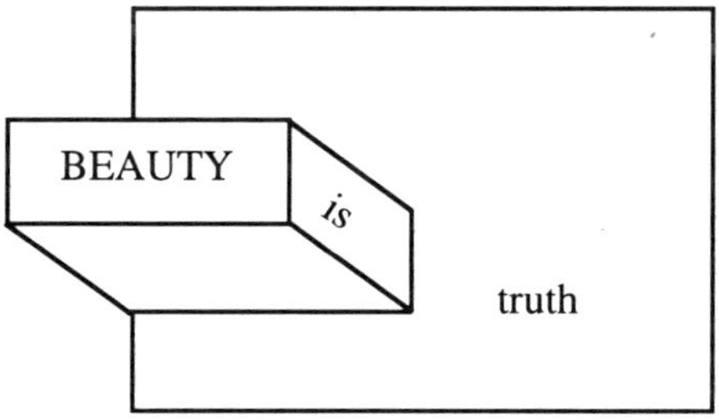

etc. Experiment with an *oral arbitrariness*, highlighted by *visual arbitrariness.* A concrete poetry of the acoustic surface. Or rather, exploit all surfaces of language.

As the "Treasures" are installed at the National Gallery, we experience them, of course, as modern objects, not as ancient relics. The light that transforms those alabaster vases is the light of modern display technology—it has nothing to do with the light (or the dark) of ancient Egypt. The dazzling gold surfaces of the sculptures are likewise a "fiction" wrought by modern museology. We have, in a sense, transformed the "Treasures of Tutankhamen" into something they never were—an art to serve the modern appetite for esthetic delectation.

—Hilton Kramer, "Hailing the Romantic Treasures of Tutankhamen," *The New York Times* (November 16, 1976)

Verbal imperialism/visual imperialism/oral imperialism. Abstraction through imposition rather than imposture. Go beyond surfaces. Duplicate them. Xerox poetry, zero poetry. Underline one surface with another. Writing/inscription: write over (against) what is written, (mask) one text in another, as in *Cosas pasan* (Things happen), for example. I have tried to provide some clues to the way writing penetrates writing. This explains the parentheses that suggest or betray the presence of one sign in another. The parenthesis as multiplication. In *Penitenciales* (Moulting) a parenthesis as an X-ray of meaning. Pos(t)e(r)s: poses

36

An attempt to reval(u id)ate page through pagination. Pagination that activates, accelerates multiple readings. Calder more than Gutenberg. Extreme cases: reader as spectator; combinatorial pagination. Page as movement: *mobile page, open page.*

37

Julio Cortázar narrates from the page. A narrator of pagination. In *Rayuela* (Hopscotch), the order of reading determines the *object*'s (functional) definitive pagination. The book's binding neither controls nor entirely defines the movement of reading. The writer is less bound, but so is the reader. Bound less because in the premeditated ritual of alternatives the *book is more binding.*

From *Ultimo Round* (Final round) to *Libro de Manuel* (A manual for Manuel) the relation between reader/author, reader/book, reader/page, page/pagination becomes more dynamic. The move is from the convergence of two texts on a single (sectioned) page (which is two pages) to the convergence of various texts on a single page. Reduction (enlargement) of the page of the book to the page of a newspaper. Around the text, the texts: news items, anouncements. Rosetta Stone: each text, a version of the Text. Between an ad for aspirin and the political news item or the plot of a novel the difference is only one of degree.

38

The page as *functional delirium. Blanco* (White), by Octavio Paz, is not a book: it is a page; it is not a page: it is a codex; it is not a codex, but the simultaneity of all language in the discontinuity of all language. "The page tends to evoke in relation to the abstract continuity with which we see time and space and in relation to the real discontinuity of thought: lacunae, silences, breaks. Writing is nothing more than a point of departure, a beginning text on which are written the never identical reading or readings the reader—hypothetical creature—can make according to individual mood." ("*Aviso al lector*" [Advice to the reader], *Blanco*).

With *Blanco*, and above all with *Discos visuales* (Visual disks), Paz seems to reach ultimate yet strictly functional limits. Visual design/functional delirium. *Discos visuales:* seed: the possibility of the poem as film, the page as screen, the reader as spectator. Extreme: voices on a black screen, the reverse of the silent film. Apogee of the *talkie.* Snatch the page from writing; use the page against writing; create distance—space of uncertainty—between page and writing. Extreme: movement of the poem on the film, of the film on the screen, of the screen facing the spectator, of the spectator facing the screen. *Talkie talks back.* A poetry of c/kinematics: passing page, passing word, passing reader. Movement of the page, movement of the word, movement of the reader.

39

Beyond the strictly functional: the *pop page*, the *gadget page. Gadget*: the technological symptom of a complicity: boredom and industrial capitalism. Play = ploy, page/card: written/ marked. Marked/market. The ultrabaroque, commercialization. Investment: of order, of funds. Also: of surfaces. Divestment: capital as a take-off on the page, the page as a take-off on capital. From Jean Baudrillard, *Le Système des objets* (The system of objects): "With its predilection for allegory, with its new individualism of discourse, through the redundance of forms and the falsification of materials, with its demiurgic formalism, the baroque is what truly inaugurates the modern age by summarizing beforehand, on the artistic plane, all the themes and the myths of a technical era, without excepting the formal paroxism of detail and movement."

40

Two titles published recently in the United States are of particular interest to a philosophy/psychology/phenomenology of composition: *Compendium for Literates* by Karl Gerstner and *The Nothing Book* from Harmony Press, which is already a best- seller in paperback.

The Nothing Book—degree zero of the book, what remains of the castle?—pushes to the limit the idea of the blank page. Nevertheless, this blank book has little to do with Mallarmé's adventure, since its purpose tends toward the practical in the same way the blank page or the *Grand livre* tends toward the poetic absolute. Writers, doodlers, secretaries, businessmen will all be able to create their own books, beginning with the book as zero. (For anyone who wants to try this, Gerstner's *Compendium* will be indispensable.) But in a more evident, although perhaps less decisive way than other publications (since there is the poetic option of leaving the *The Nothing Book* at nothing), *The Nothing (*yet) *Book* definitely exposes the disdain for the page that has characterized writing, above all since the invention of print. There was more respect for stone, papyrus, parchment; there is currently more respect for that other possible page: the screen. Word or glyph, the sign has created the page. By converting a space to functional extension, which is to say, by altering a surface (background), writing (un)covers the page. This happens in the most conservative writing: on stone (epitaph), as well as in the most subersive: on walls (graffiti). Also, case in point: *The Nothing Book,* virtual graffiti. The word activates the page, gives it meaning. In effect, turns it into a page. Hence, the invitation/challenge that fosters the commercialization of the *Grand Livre*: "Wanna make something of it?" The answer would interest Igitur.

(All this must be pushed further.)

Another Letter from Jonah for Thomas the Magnificent

Quieting both halves
the heart promises greater truth.
Doubt is also a bridge,
a midnight mass sung
in the humming of a bee.
Dunghill of crystals,
shattered names, flesh only light knows.

Wine is a keyhole, Alcaeus said,
it lets you see into a man's soul.
We appear to be. There is neither soul nor man.
Infinity lies, never lies.
Our brothers were born
when there was not yet an eternity.
You and I when there was one no longer.
This is the thickest blood between us.
A single instant of centuries and even slower hours.

The sentinel sets his dark pupils
beyond the stars.
A woman sleeps.
Your blood weighs less than her dream.
It is a pillow in the center of a carved obsidian,
in other words, in the center of night.
A shadow so precise it falls only within.
Fountain of transparent stones,
red lines in black and white.

Thales made a paradise
by raising the lines left by a plow in the earth.
But forms are animals on the prowl, sharpened perfections.
True order arises from vertigo, it devours us.

The Chavín discovers geometric propositions
in the eyetooth of a jaguar.
That fact tore through my mind

as I displayed an abyss of round scars
and gave you two whales for a bird of prey.

So begins the meeting between Thomas the Magnificent
and an obscure prophet.
They are made of stone, stone of water,
water of fire, fire of wind.
They are like thc tiger slowly regarding itself in a mirror.
They meet in the light.
Columns of rain, water
sliced from massive stone,
volumes
the Romanesque uses to weigh space
and the Gothic to pierce it.

In Tairona quartz the imperfections are gold.
The quartz vessels take us to Tristan's crystal house,
to Gywnfid's celestial circle.
Quartz is a way to remember the Druids.
It also reminded me of Vico.
If language is a tiresome interpretation
of thunder, I told you, making a tremendous racket,
poetry is a silent gloss on lightning.
Wound of light, shadow of light,
flash of lightning that never heals.

Constellatons buried in the eyelid.
The blink of an eye:
the sun and a thousand eclipses.
To deny blood and that which denies blood:
tricks of magicians and beggars, the loftiest of disciplines.
To see a beautiful girl completely naked.
To drink completely naked water.
To undress for the mirror of another body.
In this way truth and other lies join.
Dreamed and divided blood
hides in our bodies
like an animal of capricious burning figures.

When the issue is this light,
how well the gaze dies;

how it falls
                    —without skin or shadow
or memory—
on the altar of other gods.

A woman sleeps.
Don't forget that your blood
weighs less than her dream.

A Reading of Light

Light is the first animal visible in the invisible.
—José Lezama Lima

1

"The sun breaks my idea," El Greco used to say. For Van Gogh the sun is not what breaks the idea: the sun is the idea. Not only idea but obsession. Neither theme nor technique: neither a question of painting with light nor of painting light. Rembrandt had already done all that with shading: he had painted with shadows, almost hiding his colors. Rembrandt neither attracts nor dazzles us: he demands a close viewing. As we move closer in order to create an intensity, we discover figure, nuances, forms as if we touched something intuited, something returned by night. Van Gogh blinds us with his intensity, is the very manifestation of color, of the possibility of color. His paintings—and of course I am referring specifically to certain paintings, like *The Harvest, Starry Night, Sunflowers*—do not trap light or color: they squander them, emit them. They are fountains of light, like the sun. Van Gogh also makes us see through touch: the intensity of the light is such that our gaze is excluded. When we get too close we see with our hands or skin, with all of our senses but one: sight. The painter ignites a sun and thus ignites, burns our gaze. It is no longer a question of seeing Icarus fall—as in Pieter Bruegel's *Landscape*—the act of seeing becomes a fall in itself. It is impossible to get close to the sun, impossible to contemplate the painting, impossible to read the writing. That impossibility is what Van Gogh teaches us: we see because we learn to see as only the blind can learn to see. We see in spite of our eyes.

2

During one of his visits to Delacroix, Victor Hugo found the sketch of *Massacre de l'Evêque de Liége* on the easel. He had trouble making out the assassin's weapon, and he asked what the painter had wanted to do. "I've tried," answered Delacroix, "to paint the flashing of a sword." Violence as flashing, lightning, light. Van Gogh does exactly the same thing but exactly in reverse: flashing, lightning, light as violence. He forces our gaze to remain outside the painting, to see by averting sight, in the same way that the brilliant sheen on the stones of Egyptian art forced the eye to follow the movement of the statue's surface, its outside, thus veiling corporeality itself. Light, on the polished surface, pulled the eye away from the body, turning vision aside and negating it. With Van Gogh this light arupts from within the painting and is its form, its reason for existing.

3

Pathography is the branch of medicine that studies the effects of certain illnesses on the lives and creative processes of painters. After 1888, the hands in Renoir's paintings became increasingly deformed as the effects of rheumatoid arthritis made his own hands useless—and deformed. Something similar has been suggested about Rubens: the painted hands are the pictorial transposition—a symptom—of the hands that painted. Not only forms proved to be symptomatic. The diffusion of brilliant colors in certain of Monet's paintings can perhaps be attributed to cataracts that affected his sight. In the case of Van Gogh, it has been argued that the propensity for yellow, the vertiginous movement of light around a central source, the halo that forms and deforms stars and sunflowers, is due to the influence of a drug: digitalis. Another pathographic hypothesis about Van Gogh's peculiar vision: absinthe. Digitalis, absinthe, insanity. Of course neither pharmacology nor psychopathology is able to reveal how, and why, possible hallucinations are linked to an impossible work.

Before the pathographers, Georges Bataille had pointed out that Van Gogh's sun paintings "only become intelligible from the moment in which one looks at them as the very expression of the painter's persona (or, if your prefer, his illness)." For Bataille, then, the link is direct, brutal: the painting is an emanation of the painter, the madman, as if the true center of all the whirlwinds of light were the very hand that painted, the being that made yellow spirals with the brush. Yellow reflects Van Gogh's condition as the moon reflects light from the sun.

There is an incident that tends to confirm Bataille's observation. One night in January or February of 1889, on the pretext of painting a nocturnal landscape, Van Gogh went out wearing a hat crowned with lighted candles. In one sense, the sunflowers are a self-portrait. But Bataille's observation, although useful, is misleading. It is useful because it departs from the obvious—the quantity of yellow—and it establishes, or tries to establish, an intelligibility of forms. The sun paintings must be decentered, in other words they must be referred to the process of which they are a part, but a process that does not originate, or not entirely, in the painter or his illness. Proposing a possible intelligibility in order to reduce it immediately to the perception or interpretation of a symptom resolves absolutely nothing. Saying that there is a language and not saying what the language says, or what the very existence of the language says, transforms an impenetrable, perhaps unintelligible, although astounding work into one more scribbling or hieroglyphic from that vast gibberish called insanity.

4

Paradoxically, light can suggest a wish for invisibility. You can hide in light as well as in darkness. Bioluminescence: light as camouflage, concealment or protection. Don't throw ink to hide and escape, like the octopus: throw light, so you can turn into a blinding screen, and dazzle. The mention of bioluminescence as a possible factor in Van Gogh's painting immediately obliges us to recognize the failure of his work. The more he tries to exclude our gaze the more we look. The same thing happens with the work of Isidore Ducasse. Ducasse creates the Count de Lautréamont who in turn writes the *Chants of Maldoror* in order to erase Ducasse. A reverse narcissism, a centrifugal autobiography. Ducasse erases Ducasse with the Count of Lautréamont and Maldoror. Writing as absence and disauthorization. In an overly literal sense the author is counted and discounted. He multiplies and enlarges himself in order to disappear. He makes himself a count in order to be discounted.

I look at Van Gogh again in the Arles night beneath the ring of his hat, a hat crowned with lighted candles. I see him again precisely because I no longer see him. He disappears in his hat; his body goes out beneath the burning lights. That is how the Cuban poet Manuel de Zequeira would disappear: when he put on his hat he became invisible. When he put on his hat he lost his head. In the same way, by using a hat, Magritte demonstrates the invisibility of one of his subjects,

"The Therapeutist." As in a magic trick, a demonstration in reverse, something is shown with the express purpose of hiding it: attraction is a distraction, presence is an absence. Isn't this—remember the "Soleil cou coupé" by Apollinaire, author of "The Starry Head"—what a certain tradition has seen in the sun itself?

5

From its beginnings, painting created a need for light. Light for painting, light for looking at paintings. There are cave paintings in corners where no sunlight has ever penetrated. In order to paint or to see what they had painted, paleolithic artists had to build a fire. Light for painting, light for looking at paintings. In this way a process of gradually incorporating light into painting begins: from cave art to our modern video system the radical difference rests on the fact that light is now emitted rather than trapped. In turn this process of incorporating light increased the need and the desire for artificial light. The torches of the paleolithic cave eventually became the stained glass windows of a cathedral, the millions of lights and neon signs of the modern city. On and off the canvas, painting continued to add, consume light. Space and time became thresholds, goals rather than limitations, since with the accumulation of light night was conquered and space widened. As he created the need for light and enlarged his cave, the paleolithic artist invented electricity and travel: he invented discovery, discovered invention.

Van Gogh's paintings, to the extent that they surpass the merely symptomatic, are part of the incorporation of light. Turner brings Goethe's theory of light to his canvas, but Van Gogh is an explosion of light. He invents the electric bulb at the same time as Edison. His paintings produce the effect of a flash: they dazzle, blind. According to him, shadows are "tricks of the sun." This is why he tried to eliminate them, as he wrote to Emile Bernard. Shadows only interested him as "an explanation of light." His paintings do not try to trap light, to create light effects or represent light: they are light itself, they produce light. We can now return to Bataille's observation about a possible intelligibility of the sun paintings and see clearly how they can be decentered and discussed in terms of a creative process without falling into the gibberish of insanity. The obvious, the quantity of light, is absolutely functional. Very violent but functional. By forcing us to look directly at a fountain of light—to fix our gaze on the sun—the painting exists as an exclusion of the gaze. That violence of light against looking—a violence to which Van Gogh accustoms us since we insist on looking even when our gaze is excluded—will become new media: movies, photography with its blinding flash, television.

6

Painting as an exclusion of the gaze is linked to a specific tradition: hermeticism, writing as an exclusion of the reader. Prophetic, apocalyptic books made reading an impossibility.

"Who is worthy to open the scroll and break its seals?"

And no one in heaven or on earth or under the earth was able to open the scroll or look into it, and I wept much that no one was found worthy to open the scroll or look into it.

I have quoted the fifth chapter of the Revelation to John, the Theologian, which we can all read now in paperback, thanks to enterprising publishers. In Revelation, Christ's eyes are a "flame of fire"; the angels have "faces like the sun." Sun, fire, flame are the elements we must transcribe, the language of prophecy. A voice tells John to write what he sees; John looks again at the voice that speaks to him and what he writes resembles a portrait of Van Gogh, his hat blazing with lighted candles:

Then I turned to see the voice that was speaking to me, and on turning I saw seven golden lampstands, and in the midst of the lampstands one like a son of man, clothed with a long robe and with a golden girdle around his breast: his head and his hair were white as wool, white as snow: his eyes were like a flame of fire, his feet were like burnished bronze, refined as in a furnace, and his voice was like the sound of many waters: in his right hand he held seven stars, from his mouth issued a sharp two-edged sword, and his face was like the sun shining in full strength.

John gazes at a gaze that shines like the sun. He gazes at the past, the future: he sees time. Prophecies are calendars, but—eschatology, not astronomy—they announce a time no one can measure: a time that exists, not before history like myths, but beyond history. Prophecies are the myths of an impossible future. Myth: a reading of something illegible, something erased. Prophecy: a reading of something that has not yet been written, that will be impossible to write. Between myth and prophecy: the book, books, suffocating repetition and a palimpsest: history.

7

Stone calendars represent the first readings of light. Through light, primitive man, we ourselves, can approach the sun because we also, like light itself—remember Plotinus's *epistropheé*—long to arrive at—return to—the fountain of knowledge. The sun, according to certain mythologies, is the burning mirror where God looks at himself; to read light is to approach God, at the end of all time. The great readers of the future have been readers of light. By reading light—which is read at approximately 180,000 miles per second—it would take about $8^1/_3$ minutes to travel from the earth to the sun. Perhaps this astonishing speed of light explains how light's readers can soar to a remote but imminent future: a time when there will no longer be time. The reading of light, and not the machine dreamed by Wells, is the true time machine. Until now, that reading has been the secret of priests and prophets—and blind men like Tiresias, who was blinded by the goddess Pallas because he accidentally saw her naked. To look directly at the sun, the face of an angel or the nakedness of a goddess, is blinding. But blindness—as in Tiresias's case—becomes a gift. John looks at a voice in order to write his prophecies and that voice is flame, sun, fire. Michel de Nostredame has also described his prophetic method in terms of a reading of light: great events were shown to him when he looked, as if with darkened gaze, in a flaming mirror.

8

"God is light"—we read in Blake's "Auguries of Innocence"—"To those poor Souls who dwell in Night." Another summary of this theology of light: in the darkness of a Gothic cathedral the faithful see God appear through the great stained glass windows. The mystery occurs in the light, the writing that passes through the windows to be deciphered by faith moves us closer, from another perspective, to the work of Van Gogh and to a possible reading of light. Each day we are more transparent. We have all been read, deciphered, analyzed by some light. Transparence as a daily reality: feeling ourselves pierced by one of Van Gogh's sunflowers, seeing ourselves on a slide or an X-ray. "I plan to decorate my studio with half a dozen Sunflowers," the painter writes, "a decoration in which raw or blended chrome yellows will blaze on various backgrounds, from the palest Veronese green to royal blue, framed by narrow strips of wood painted orange. The kinds of effects you get from stained glass windows in a Gothic cathedral." The sun does not break the idea: it is the idea.

9

". . . There is war between the mind/And sky, between thought and day and night. It is/ For that the poet is always in the sun." Wallace Stevens's poetry always places us in the sun, or the mind, or in that space between sun and mind that is thought itself, craving more and more light. Not reading, legibility itself. "Let's see the very thing and nothing else./Let's see it with the hottest fire of sight./Burn everything not part of it to ash." Since it is not possible to gaze continually at the sun, the sun represents the ultimate abstraction, that which we cannot see, an idea of which we cannot have an idea. Not reading, legibility itself: the sun—according to Stevens—should not have a name, or rather, it should stay on the margin of all habitual ideas—or readings. But it must always be present in the difficulty of being: the sun as a point of departure—and goal—for thought itself. "Begin, ephebe, by perceiving the idea/Of this invention, this invented world,/The inconceivable idea of the sun./You must become an ignorant man again/And see the sun again with an ignorant eye/And see it clearly in the idea of it." The sun, or the mind—or language—is an invention: something added to reality until reality becomes intelligible. That invention is reality itself, our desire to participate in it, to feel and suffer its changes, to change it. Sun, mind, language: an incessant process where the real becomes visible, forms of opening form. Communications media that become sources of communication themselves as they grow transparent.

10

But what is the sun as an idea? What idea is it? And how is a reading of the sun, of the sun as idea, possible? *Idea* means "ideal image of an object." It is derived from *êidon*: "I saw." As appearance, then, ideas suggest a specific sense: light. A sense that perceives the sense of appearances or of apparitions. What does the prophet tell? The prophet tells us his visions. "And I saw another mighty angel coming down from heaven, wrapped in a cloud, with a rainbow over his head, and his face was like the sun, and his legs like pillars of fire. He had a little scroll open in his hand." In this way the prophet outlines a map of ideas—a map that is an idea—where that terrifying *little open scroll* will be transcribed. Appearances and apparitions provoke a reading that will in turn provoke appearances and apparitions through reading, that other idea. There is an open scroll, but also a rainbow, sun, pillars of fire. We are presented with the possibility of reading: the book is open and there is light; at the same time we are presented with the impossibility of reading: the scroll is open and there is too much light. And this is precisely the idea of the sun as idea: the possible reading of light. We are confronting the phenomenon of legibility itself: the conversion of an impossibility into a possibility, of blinding appearance into immediate sign: more taste than test, idea of the idea.

John looks and sees flames, rainbow, sun, fire: he also sees a little open scroll but his testimony, his own writing, arises precipitously from the impossibility of reading what he has before his eyes. Vision: failed reading. The prophet writes his book in order to narrate, translate that other book he cannot read. He writes to make possible an impossible reading. The tradition of the blind prophet, of what, in the case of Van Gogh, we have called the exclusion of the gaze—seeing is averting our eyes, seeing is learning to see as only the blind are able to see, seeing in spite of our eyes—summarizes the story of legibility itself. Legibility always makes reference to a process of gestation or conversion of signs, not to the stereotype of a

So I went to the angel and told him to give me the little scroll; and he said to me, "Take it and eat it: it will be bitter in your stomach, but sweet as honey in your mouth." And I took the little scroll from the hand of the angel and ate it: it was sweet as honey in my mouth, but when I had eaten it my stomach was made bitter.

fixed, docile meaning communicated mechanically. For that reason, John does not read the book, he devours it. He reads with appetite because—from pětěre—"he aims at," "lays claim to," "seeks." Here, testing, in the strictest sense of the word, is tasting.

11

Surrounded by sun and pillars of fire, the prophet devours the book. The book enters flesh and fleshes out. There is light and word, the word becomes incarnate. This implies a concise summary of the entire Biblical process. The process is biblical not only because the first verses of Genesis and the Gospel According to John are suggested as background; the process is biblical in the strictest, most literal sense of the word: one writing incorporates other writings. Book as body, body as book. I'm thinking about *The Librarian* by Archimboldo. I'm also thinking about the idea of writing as weaving. Holy Scripture, Holy Texts. Those names continue to haunt us, even though they have been rigorously stripped of their sacredness. Today the only writing that seems sacred is precisely that which renounces, eagerly, all traces of sacredness. In a word: the impossible gospel according to Roland Barthes. Writing, text, in the sense—almost in the very taste—that these terms now hold for us, underline the fact that we have moved from commentary, from the sermon based on reading and reverent quotation, to criticism and the systematic irreverence of analysis.

I said that we can now read John's Revelation in paperback. I did not say, did not need to say, that in this edition Revelation will be read, and can only be read, as literature. A devastating popularity: the prophecies prove to be readable only as literature. A tale of science fiction, a gothic novel, a surrealist poem: the only thing Revelation cannot be is sacred writing. As such—as something that means or tries to mean exactly what it says—John's Revelation proves unreadable. The paperback edition excludes one reader: the believer. Raising the question of the readability of sacred texts seems to extinguish automatically the possibility of that specific reading which granted a given text its strict literalness of meaning.

12

What worries many critics about criticism and greatly displeases others, perhaps unconsciously, is that in a very radical way all forms of analysis presuppose death. By analyzing language it becomes clear that we speak dying languages, languages that are perhaps already dead or in the throes of death; in a similar way we intuit the disconcerting possibility that we participate actively in phantom communication. This intuition, which encourages us to approach our language in the way that Champollion approached Egyptian hieroglyphics, senses in the analysis of language a sacrilege comparable only to the horror that, until the Renaissance, was felt for the dissection of corpses. The autopsies begun in the sixteenth century initiated a new relation to the body. Many prohibitions were discarded. Seen from within, from death, as a complex of functions, the body moved from the scientist's lab to the pleasure palace. Autopsies opened the way, until then a narrow path, toward a new eroticism: with Sade the body becomes a laboratory and the sexual act, centered as never before on a fascination for the excremental, at times resembles a dissection.

The same thing is happening in our own day, only now it is not the body but language, that last bastion—organ—of intimacy, that is being dissected. The Dadaists proclaimed the death of language; the surrealists made "exquisite corpses"; Huidobro tried to use a miraculous language even though it was destined to fail: "A miracle that will light the depth of our intimate seas/Like the boat that sinks with its lights blazing"; and Altazor, personification of all possible languages, falls "like the boat that sinks with its lights dimming." The games and explorations of the avant-garde take liberties with language parallel to the liberties Renaissance scientists could take with the body only after death, during dissection.

13

In 1632, Rembrandt transformed an autopsy into a work of art. With *The Anatomy Lesson of Professor Nicolaes Pietersz Tulp*, he taught a visual lesson: he showed that the body could be seen as depth. His painting moves away from statuary, where the body was a perfect and impenetrable surface. Or rather, it moves closer to the Greek statuary that utilizes translucent marble in order to let the viewer's gaze enter the body. In 1635, with *Life Is a Dream*, Calderón de la Barca, lets us watch the workings of the mind as it wavers between vigilance and sleep. Theater of ideas: viewers viewed. Six years later, in 1641, the Cartesian *Meditations* display the mind's systematic activity, the process through which, in spite of doubt, or thanks to it, the mind establishes itself as a thinking I. 1632, 1635, 1641: in a very few years, a remarkable effort to approach the essence of both mind and body.

In our century, and once again in an amazingly short space of time, there has been an effort to uncover the essence, not of the mind itself now but of its processes. If poets decreed the death of language in order to give free rein to the imagination, scientists intuited in language, or perhaps through it, symptoms of malaise: the disorder of personalities, cultures, systems of knowledge. The language of our day originates in the necessary although contradictory convergence of play and analysis. On the one hand Tzara, Breton, and Apollinaire; on the other Saussure, Freud, and Wittgenstein. The fact that today's autopsies, like Rembrandt's anatomy lesson, have become novels or poems is an indication that they do not imply the death of language. Instead they illuminate its depths: what we look for in corpses is life.

The violence we feel when we look at Bacon's deformed faces; the violence we feel when we watch television—violence that, as Brockman has pointed out, has very little to do with a particular kind of programming, that is related above all to the fact that for the first time in history humanity can look directly and sometimes for hours at a source of light; the violence we sense in political or commercial propaganda, that plague of modern society, all indicate that we are directly confronting the body as process, light as process, language as process. We are perceiving these processes unknowingly, unwittingly. We are victims of light. We are blind in the worst sense: we do not want to see.

14

It is undeniable: today certain readings turn out to be difficult if not impossible. Proof of this should lead to neither nostalgia nor despair. We are not witnessing the death of literature, although its demise has been announced many times. Neither are we witnessing the death of reading. On the contrary, it happens that we now know—perhaps better than ever—that reading is not a wake, it happens that the impossibility of certain readings owes to the proliferation of other readings and to the growing attention with which writing itself is read, a readibility that knows how to pause on the surface of language and also knows how to pass through it, continually questioning its functions and mechanisms, getting as close as possible to the process of provoking and representing meaning, even at the risk of ending up in gibberish.

In Van Gogh's painting I have glimpsed a dare and a denial for the gaze. But his stars and sunflowers blind in order to make possible yet other ways of seeing. I have glimpsed the same thing in certain poetry. *Altazor*, by Huidobro, blinds in order to make possible yet other readings. When Mallarmé raises the page to the power of a starry sky, I read on that page a painting by Van Gogh: *Starry Night*, or I see a line from Revelation: "and the stars from heaven fell to earth." Mallarmé makes an easy reading impossible because he makes possible many impossible readings.

15

The mechanisms of power and the marketplace are exploiting the analysis of language in order to reduce us to absolute passivity. Reading, speaking, listening to speeches, watching television are steadily becoming forms of hypnosis. Antipodes of the thinking I, of the I as subject of its own thought, we are objects of a systematic propaganda that amazes and seduces in order to transform us into a nonthinking, never-thinking I. Propaganda is the Latin of our day and we all speak Latin. But we speak it without knowing that it is already a dead language, that it has always been dead, that death is its only reason for existing. Neither nostalgia nor despair. When we learn to see like blind men, when we close our eyes before Van Gogh's paintings in order to see them, when we learn, like Hipparchus, that light does not reach the eye, the body, but emanates from the body, then dead languages will die. It is time to devour the little scroll open in the angel's hand, time to look at ourselves in the flaming mirror, to fall "like the boat that sinks with its lights dimming." We must learn to read at 180,000 miles per second. Otherwise, as we were warned by the angel with a face like the sun, there will be no more time. History is ending, and putting an end to us.

Birth Certificate
(May 10, 1946)

Delivered a hand.
There were five fingers.

Delivered a tongue.
There were no teeth.

Expelled a cry.
Slowly rubbed it into my skin.

Putting It Down: A Get-up

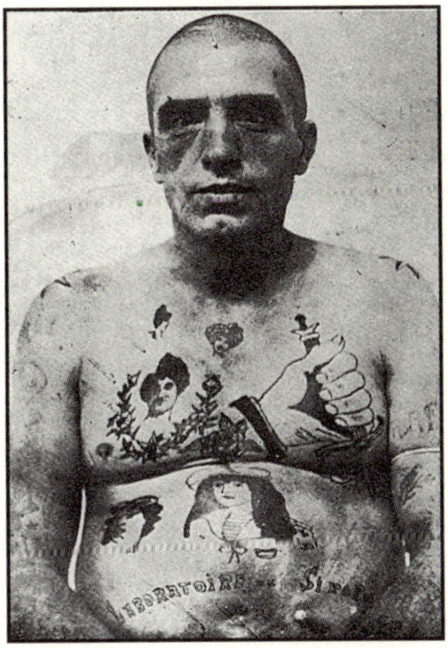

He had seen her painted sign by the road: skin illustration! Illustration instead of tattoo! Artistic! So he had sat all night while her magic needles stung him wasp stings and delicate bee stings. By morning he looked like a man who had fallen into a twenty-color print press and had been squeezed out, all bright and picturesque.

—Ray Bradbury, *The Illustrated Man*

1

"At ten o'clock in the morning," Zequiera writes in "*El relox de la Havana*" (The clock of Havana), "the bounty of Pomona and Ceres is on display, pineapples, sapodillas, mameys, avocados, every fruit imaginable disguised in unrecognizable names by the black women's dialect: to find out what's for sale, you finally have to look for yourself."

As it names, the black women's dialect disguises. This is pointed out by Manuel de Zequiera, who disguised himself with a Z and several pseudonyms when he gave his own name. The Z of Zequiera is the S of our *negritos catedráticos* (gnostic

Uncle Toms): it hid origins. His name was Sequeira, but he preferred the very Spanish Z. His name was Manuel de Zequeira, but he signed himself Ezequiel Armuna, Izmael Raquenue, Licenciado Freisesomorum, el Bruxo de la Havana (the Witch of Havana), la Horma de su Zapato (Your Boot Tree), el Alma de la Lonja (the Soul of the Market) . . . One of his pseudonyms, Raquel Yun Zenea, a nominal transvestism, honors the future Chinese presence on the island and anticipates a great name in Cuban poetry. Under writing, overwriting; pineapples, sapodillas, mameys under unintelligible names; an S under a Z; Manuel de Zequiera under Izmael Raquenue and Raquel Yun Zenea. Metathesis: metaphor. Putting it down: a get-up. Because it must be made clear that Cuban fruits are no less disguised by high jargon than by street jive. In his famous ode, Zequiera himself disfigures the pineapple through dislocation, a confusion caused not by the jumbling and reordering of letters, as in the metathesis of his name, but by a change of focus or context. The pineapple proves to be Olympian rather than tropical: consequently its praises are sung by "the divine Orpheus" instead of our lowly street vendors or the Matamoros Trio. Dislocation: the fruits of Caney as the bounty of Pomona and Ceres.

In the same way, neobaroque writing will be used to cover up fallen fortunes, incestuousness, censorship, homosexuality, insanity, mulatto blood, uncertain origins. Zequeira foresaw this prophetically when he not only disguised himself with pseudonyms and a Z but also chose erasure, invisibility: "To find out what's for sale," he says of the fruits, "you must look for yourself."

You must get past language, which disguises within and without, by changing names, hiding the bonds of syntax in rousing bands—a musical tattoo. You must position yourself behind words, behind their masked parade through the ear's labyrinth, because signs vacate the space assigned them: they are signals that point incorrectly, or only obliquely, to what's wanted, feared, mentioned. As an abstract system of signs, language does not lead to order or communication; quite the contrary, it designates through ellipsis, elides through proliferation, derails by slipping into resonance rather than reason. It fails, misleads, but in an effort to impose a simulacrum of meanings rather than a lack of meaning: touch, sight, hearing rather than comprehension. Verbal tattooing, the supplanting of reality: language must be considered an invitation, a challenge to sight. For it appears so the author can disappear. Figures because it disfigures. What it says is erasure because what is erased is what it means to say. Writing deforms as it forms. A reading unaware of this deformation erases what it reads, erases what has been erased. Most importantly, it is an ellipsis of ellipsis, a doubly oblique reading.

2

The first page of *Paradiso*: skin covered with expanding welts. The first page of "*Coloquio con Juan Ramón Jiménez*" (Colloquium with Juan Ramón Jiménez): skin that does not match the body. The first page of *Cobra*: bound feet. The first page of Virgilio Piñera's *Poesía y prosa* (Poetry and Prose): enormous feet that fill everything. Ellipsis: Cuban intertextuality: the "*Coloquio*" as the point of departure for *Paradiso* and "*Vida de Flora*" (The life of Flora) as the point of departure for *Cobra*. Ellipsis of an ellipsis: Cuban hypertextuality: the point of departure for writing is the body, skin, but skin conceived as writing.

We fell in love with skin, gazed at the same skin invariably covering us like a star chart. Skin, gaze, sidereal cartography. Later it turns out that skin does not correspond to body, which should answer for skin and gaze. The crystal snake proceeds, pursues itself, leaving behind its skin, which has become shadow, an arrow passing over the shadow, a wall that collapses on the inflated back. The crystal snake is atop another skin now and we are convinced only slowly that what was skin is now role, roll, that paper falls with the elegance of a leaf crumpling. When we were expecting the green leaf, the electric, purple leaf appears, the leaf that grows on backs and foreheads like a head of hair seen under water, like a cluster of fish revolving on a very fine, eternal crystal. Afterwards, skin, blood from smoke. A strong hand squeezes, strangles a lemon, defines a throat.

Stages: skin, skin of a glove, skin stuffed. Crystal snake: style, manner, the convention of sensibility. One day we mock the first of them. Lives multiplied by thrones, authority, devils, and angels could perhaps not achieve the second, so as to answer for everyone once and for all but remain definitively in failure, collapse, silence.

Skin as chaos, proliferation, uneasiness. "When we were expecting the green leaf," we read in Lezama's "*Coloquio*," "the electric, purple leaf appears . . ." The body is a hollow covered with blotches: "She said body and welts, as if she saw them growing continually, or as if the spiraling of the restless slab, the inappropriate gelatine, saw the ghostly pink appearance, the migration of those clouds over the small body. As the welts claimed the child's whole body, his panting suggested that the asthma left so much air inside him that it seemed about to burst through his pores." The body is a desperate growth—we are still on the first page of *Paradiso*: "she saw the body that stretched out and made the welts look more prominent." "She said body and welts, as if she saw them growing continually . . ." Growth and emptiness: "the asthma left so much air inside him that it seemed about to burst through his pores." How to confront, control, or dissimulate that proliferation? By leading the body to death, handing it over, through writing, to the magic of taxidermy. "Stages: skin, skin of a glove, skin stuffed. Crystal snake: style, manner, the convention of sensibility." This, I believe, is what gives form to the Cuban tradition of tattooing. An art of the skin, an art of stuffing skin. Distancing oneself from skin—the skin of a glove—ripping it off, stuffing it. Writing, like the moulds, gags, alum compresses used by *Flora* and *Cobra*, is a way of *shrinking*, transforming the body, putting it in order. Perhaps this also explains the peculiar emphasis on the diminutive found in Cuban speech. The body can be enlarged and reduced; gigantism and fetishism, tattooing and taxidermy are all possible. What is not possible: a healthy notion of the body or an eroticism that implies a desire for the body rather than a desire to annihilate, confuse, convert it into a ghost or the simulacrum of another body.

3

The Cuban neobaroque is a hypertrophied, hypertelic, hypersensitive translation of everyday life: straighten kinky hair, make feet smaller, dream invisibility. A Cuban history of the body would force us to confront Martí in the throes of death, *his tongue bitten and his teeth literally piercing it*; it would force us to reread Lezama, noting how he buries the body in an excess of body, which is like erasing surface, skin, with an excess of surface—the tattoo—although what is erased inevitably shows through—as pentimenti or that electric leaf Lezama mentioned; it would force us to approach Zequeira's invisibility as we would approach a mirror. In the Cuban history of the body there are more torturers than lovers.

Writing, like tattooing, will be an attempt to possess flesh, skin, by taking over whatever is alien, inhospitable, uncomfortable. In this sense the body will not be a theme of writing so much as an instrument for writing. The body is literally written on.

incrust bells in your cheeks
write on your forehead with lime
paint your sex with spiraling lines
your buttocks with fluorescent disks
    rows of white dots
    the surveyor of your black body
sign your forehead
cover your feet with plaster
your hands with gold flowers
Egyptian eyes on your breast
    white ideograms
    your body a black map

"White signs on your cheeks," Sarduy writes in another text. "Lime on your forehead, a tattoo of white spirals, a text on your face/written with plaster . . ." Writing like makeup, in *Big Bang* the constellations themselves like tattoos: "stardust" on skin. Enlarge, reduce the body: deny it. Write on, write off the body: transform it, deny its specific appearance: the tattoo of a homosexual, as Rafael Roche Monteagudo tells it, guaranteed he was a *sweet and attractive woman.*

4

Cuban alternatives anticipated by Zequeira: disguise or disappearance. The reduction of the body, or the corpse, are steps toward a longed for invisibility. Peeling off, sanding, scratching surfaces to reach the body as emptiness: "I make myself invisible," Lezama says, "and on the flip side I recover my body. . . ." Lezama makes the *tokonoma* by scraping with his fingernail on silk paper, on the edge of a coffee cup or on a wall. Beyond surface, in a small emptiness, enter invisibility, recover the body then, but "surrounded by recent graduates with their snowy banners."

The surface of a corpse is also scraped in *Maitreya*, as if to make a *tokonoma*: as if the corpse were a snowy banner, there is whitewash, fine sand, "like rice powder." And what does the body teach, what is taught about the body in *Cobra*'s

---

Then, in a corner of the nave, with creamy rags, pupils narrowed, panting, like cats digging for bird bones, they were flattening a bundle of dirty sheets with a ruler. No: with small pieces of knife-shaped sandalwood they were scraping pox from a corpse; they were working at its teeth with a file; on its hardened eyelids they were sticking circles of metal with empty squares at their centers; swollen skin broke out between greenish ideograms. Scabs fell to the floor as they were pulled off, and around the mouth there was a fine whitish sand from the teeth; an ashy halo encircled the lips, like rice flour: it was scratched by the old women's bracelets, clasps made of cats' claws.

"Anatomy Lesson"? First, that when docile, reduced by death, the body is like wax, paper, soft marble, clay. Death as the apotheosis of make-up: not a corruption of flesh but the transformation of flesh into soft marble. Second: with death it becomes easier to read the body, establish an order. The legible body, finally made order, syntax, writing, is not buried in the cemetery but the library; and only there, as literature, will it gain acceptance, only there, as if "surrounded by recent graduates with their snowy banners," will it be recovered. The Christian resurrection of the flesh serves as springboard for a most Cuban anguish: the improvement of the race.

Anatomy Lesson

You were diagonal, you were yellowing. You were sheer weight, a uniform wood, free of knots, a found object scrutinized by four curious watchers.

They were reading you, pointing at you. They confronted your body with the drawing of a body—a map of the open Man; they numbered your parts, named your innards, opened your eyelids—eyeballs misted—took a few notes, turned the page.

Beside your calloused, sulphur-soaked feet, a body was spread out like a musical score.

They sank their fingertips into your flesh: their fingerprints, the slits made by their nails remained: you were wax, paper, soft marble, clay.

Write on the body, establish an order: make a possible map from biological chaos. This is why I dare to read the star charts in *Big Bang* as tattoos. Did Lezama not write, in the first line of his "*Coloquio*," that "We fell in love with skin, we gazed invariably at the very skin covering us like a star chart"? This is why I have indicated a Cuban reading of the persistent translation of the body into a map, of the biological into a reticulated geography. This is why, in the very Cuban map of Cuba outlined in *Exorcismos de esti(l)o* (Exorcising a sty[l]e) by the word *mar* (sea) there is an erased tattoo, skin *marbled* to the

LA ISLA

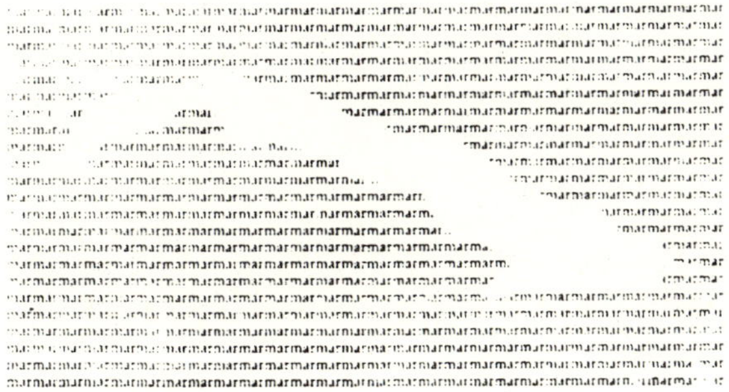

*n*th degree. Cabrera Infante's map is Zequeira's invisibility, Lezama's snowy banner, Sarduy's wax, paper, soft marble. It is Cuba's mulatto consciousness, which has been erasing the nation's ongoing Haitianization since the nineteenth century. From the skin out the mulatto element of Cuban culture is made blatantly evident: *guaracha*, *choteo, bongó*; inside, malaise, resentment, discomfort manage to disappear in a very white, transparent, invisible island by stretching a marble hide(out) on the bongo drum. "Your body, a black map," Sarduy says. Your island, a white body, Cabrera Infante points out. A white map on a black body: mulattos, tattoos.

5

According to McLuhan, Gutenberg's press led to the prison system: impression/imprisonment. But prisons have also produced, or protracted a kind of writing: the tattoo. A technology of writing leads to the body's isolation, but body becomes sign, a desire for interchange and communication: impression/imprisonment/impression. The body cannot be alone. The soul must be alone, must be distanced from the body itself, from its jail, in order to surrender to God. Conscience can be alone and from a distance it can point out impossible paths. But the body needs body. In solitude it doubles or disappears. In jail, a man's body is the only thing he has left, the only thing that still belongs to him. This explains why he writes on his skin, proclaiming an identity denied him by society: penned, pen.

6

La policia y sus misterios en Cuba (The police and their mysteries in Cuba) by Rafael Roche Monteagudo, a curious book that was first published in 1908 and ran through three editions in the early years of the Republic, reveals the origins of tattooing in Cuba. Certain pages and the photographs of tattoos reproduced there by Monteagudo are part of the Cuban history of the body. Extraliterary data for the study of the island's neobaroque. In those tattoos, as in the black women's speech Zequeira found so annoying, or in Zequiera's own *décimas*; in the very Cuban counterfeits of American bills made by the gang led by Wilkin or Winter or William Miller Smith or Dulio de Lara, alias "El Ruso" (The Russian), as in Padilla's pathetic confessions or Vitier's no less pathetic conversions; in García Vega's flip side or in Lezama's imaginary eras: there, here, everywhere we are all somewhat disfigured.

7

We have said that the Cuban neobaroque conceals fallen fortunes, incestuousness, censorship, homosexuality, mulatto blood, uncertain origins. The most recent tradition of tattooing in Cuba adds still other disturbing roots to the origins of insular neobaroque. I will mention three: lack of documentation, defiance of censorship, hieroglyphics.

(1) The destruction of any document that indicates or confirms identity has given rise to a new kind of tattoo:

To complicate matters, the Cuban authorities at Mariel, the port from which refugees embark for Key West, Fla., are said to confiscate and routinely destroy any documents the refugees try to take with them: diplomas, certificates and the precious pieces of paper on which the names and addresses of American cousins, brothers and aunts have been hoarded for years.

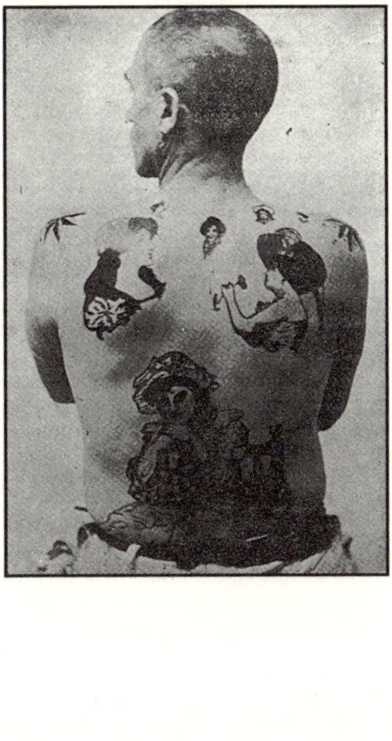

Refugees have lately begun appearing with such information written on the insides of shirt collars or on their upper arms to escape the notice of Cuban authorities. Some have even tattooed telephone numbers on their arms, unwittingly arousing the suspicion of immigration interrogators who believe that the tattoos might be marks of former prisoners, who may be excluded from admission.

The New York Times, Monday 26 May 1980

(2) The tattoo can also represent an extreme effort to trick or resist censorship:

[The Case of "Gabriel"]

Before you go I will show you what some of us did in prison. A friend in jail tattooed this eagle and some other designs on my back for me. Not all the prisoners have tattoos, only a few of us, who wore them as a form of protest. We did it to bother the guards because we knew they didn't like them. I knew I would have a fight with the guards about the tattoos and took off my shirt on purpose to show them. At that time I was surrounded by other political prisoners. The guards realized that if they hit me, they would have to hit the others, too, because the political prisoners were united. So when the guards saw my

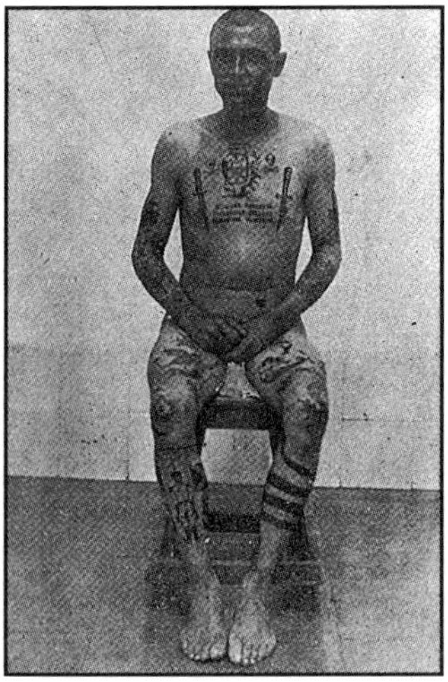

tattoos, they called me into the office. They could not do anything, though, because it was too late. All they could say to me was since my tattoos were not done perfectly, I should not walk around without my shirt! When they said that, I answered that I do anything I want with my body and that if I had a tattoo of the eagle, it was to show what I was feeling. I said that I could just as easily have had one of the Cuban flag, because it is my flag and Cuba is my country.

—Lorrin Philipson, *Freedom Flights*

(3) The third and most macabre or grotesque reading of tattooing would liken it to the construction of a ruins, a hieroglyphic, a piece of archaeological evidence from a body—and a culture—destined for disappearance. For example, reread in *Cobra*'s "Anatomy Lesson" the following description of a corpse:

At 11:30 A.M. on September 22, a mile and a half off the coast of Miami Beach, the crew members of a fishing boat working in the area were left aghast and horrified when they sighted a crude boat rocking on the waves about 600 feet from where they were fishing. The boat contained a hair-raising, funereal cargo: the torn, rotted flesh of a man's naked corpse tied by one arm to the crude boat suggested the odyssey he must have

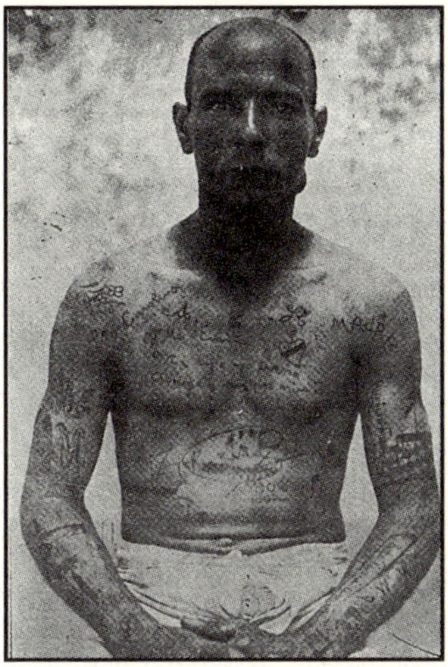

suffered before commending his soul to God. He had neither nose nor scalp. The sea, the brine had partially devoured him. According to the doctors, he had been dead for seven days . . .

Clues

As news of the discovery spread, it filled Miami's Cuban population and other areas of the exile community with alarm. The victim's story was pieced together gradually through the description of the tattoos found on the corpse. Telephone calls poured into the coroner's office by the hundreds. Finally, one of the callers had the clue to the identity of "the unknown refugee." She was Mrs. Carmen López Alfonso, who called the offices of UCE (Union of Cubans in Exile) from her home in New York. Mrs. López said that she was the dead man's aunt and she identified him by a tattoo on his body. His name was Adelfo Giz Alfonso, 36 years of age, native of Havana. Height: 5'8." Normal weight: 163 pounds. . . .

The Rebel

. . . In spite of his duties as a father, Adelfo Giz did not give up his struggle against the political oppression that enchains his country, and he was jailed on two further occasions. In fact it was in La Cabaña prison that his aunt Carmen López saw him two months ago when she went to Cuba with a tourist

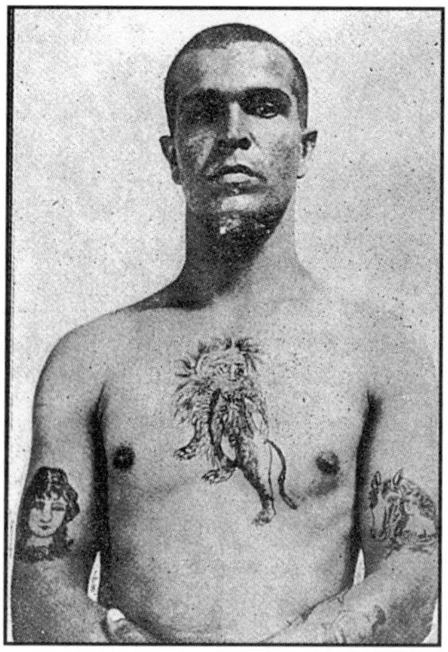

group in order to visit relatives. During their conversation, the aunt reprimanded her nephew for the tattoos she could see through his shirt. Adelfo's face, which sported a moustache and a small goatee, opened in a smile to tell her that "the prisoners do it to amuse themselves and to make sure they never forget jail. . . ."

The following tattoos were found on Adelfo's body: one in the shape of a cross with the abbreviation E.P.D. (R.I.P.) read: "With you, Haydee, mother, went my second mother, Cuba." It bore the dates "30 November 1959" and "23 December 1962." Mrs. Pérez explained that the dates recalled two painful events in Adelfo's life. The first was the day his mother, Haydee, died in November of 1959. She was a chorus girl in "Las Mamboletas," once a well-known Cuban musical group, who was assassinated on that date while on tour in Caracas. The second tragic anniversary marked the death of the grandmother who raised him. The third tattoo, on his lower abdomen, was a flying dove, and the inscription accompanying it reflected the dead man's youthful, sensual spirit: "Hop aboard and enjoy the ride . . ."

—Benjamín de la Vega, *Alerta*, October 1979

The corpse of Adelfo Giz Alfonso could be identified by the tattoos that marked it. Writing as resurrection of the identity

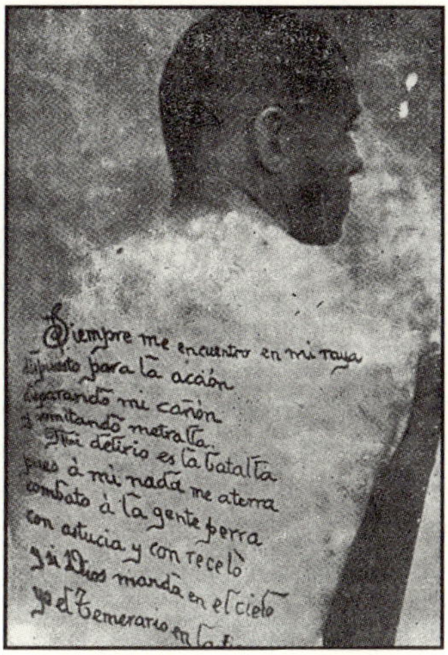

of the flesh. This is an unerasable page in Cuban history. Live writing on a dead body? Living signs of a dead culture? Everything I write, think, seems like Latin to me, like a dead tongue. I write, for archaeologists, hieroglyphics of a disappeared world. But I think Lydia Cabrera's writings are also hieroglyphics: that the black Cuba she studies and documents is dead. *Tres tristes tigres* (Three trapped tigers) is another hieroglyphic: Cuba's speech, so playful as it continually slid on its slips, is dead. The world of *Orígenes*, the world of *Paradiso*, the world of Lorenzo García Vega, dead. Cuban culture, at least everything of vital interest to me, is a hieroglyphic. We Cubans are writing the literature of Atlantis: Cuba does not exist. Or does it exist more than ever, as never before, as will and desire? The answer may be written on a body.

Self-portrait Without Me

In the mirror
I discover
—clouded, broken, alone—
the space with no room I take up.
From the center of the circle
straight
into the middle.
There
with great ritual
I mumble
my obscure inventory.
Lightning and ash.
Blood and ablutions.
One half memory,
the other oblivion.
Which is which?

Robert Morris: Mirage, Reflection
(A Small Monument to Vision)

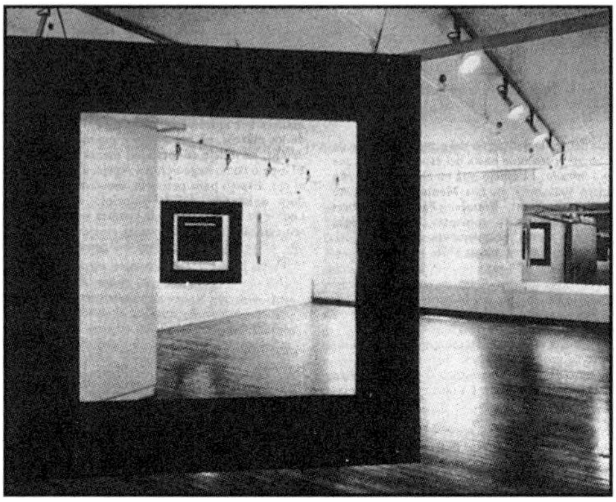

And this effect in the mirror would be as though someone who was looking at you, someone that is who has the left eye opposite to your right, were as by a miracle transposing left and right as is the case with letters used in stamping and wax which takes the impress of the cornelian.

—Leonardo da Vinci, *Treatise on the Eye*

1

Sight is constantly straining to see the eye. Because the eye is always absent from what it sees. It is the missing piece in the space assembled by the gaze. The mirror is thus defined indirectly. A nonredundant definition: point out whatever is necessary to whatever is missing in order to be claimed by incompletion. Naming would be useless: a fraud. Because mere names cannot pull relations out of the air. Names arise from over representation: contrast, conclusion.

2

Starting with the eye, a definition of the mirror excludes all nonessentials. It even excludes the mirror, which is the *eye observed.* Velázquez suggests all of this in *Las Meninas.* Duchamp suggests it in *Etant donnés.* So does Robert Morris in an environmental sculpture from the series *Sight Line Pieces* exhibited at the Sonnabend Gallery in New York City, May 1976.

3

The assemblage cannot possibly be reproduced photographically. As function, movement, it must be experienced since it cannot be *explained.* Perspective as spectacle, apogee. The work: an act initiated/repeated by the gaze.

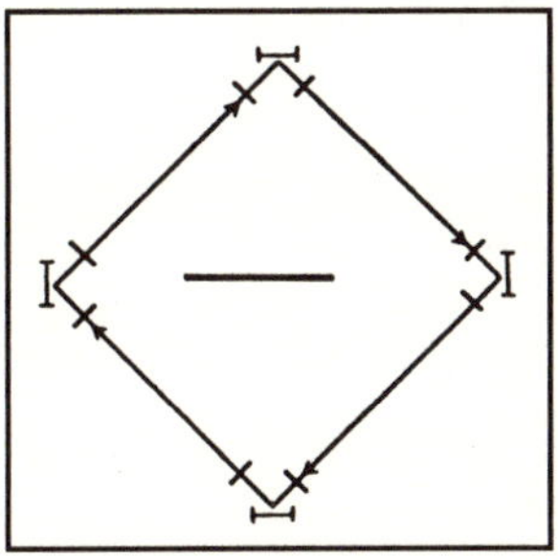

I will try to describe it. A large room not completely divided by a wall (= axis) that occupies the center, permitting circulation: squaring the circle and vice-versa. Four mirrors (⊢⊣) and eight metal frames (/). A symmetrical arrangement: by looking (⟶) at a mirror from any one of the frames, everything but the viewer is reflected in that mirror and then, successively, in all the others. The mirror as a negation of the mirror. The eye erasing the eye. A mirror for one to get lost in, like Alice. A devastating application of the principle Leonardo sets forth in his *Treatise on Light and Shadow:* "The note of the echo is cast back to the ear after it has struck, just as the images of objects strike the mirror and are thence reflected to the eye. And in the same way as these images fall from the object to the mirror and from the mirror to the eye at equal angles, so the note of the echo will strike and rebound within the hollow where it has first struck, at equal angles to the ear."

4

"The mirror is the master of painters." This phrase—conclusion—is Leonardo da Vinci's. Tradition recalls another phrase—another conclusion—no less emphatic, although very different. "The image should leave the painting." It is well known that Velázquez did not forget Pacheco's advice. In *Las Meninas* the image leaves the painting. But it is suggested, as a reflection, in the mirror that occupies the center of the canvas. The image, then, is outside the painting and at its center. A mirror draws and suggests what the artist suggests without showing. The mirror is an accomplice to a negation and, at the same time, the negation of that negation. A dialectic of surfaces. A circle. Da Vinci concludes that the mirror is the master of painters. The master of Velázquez recommends that *the image leave the painting* and his disciple resolves the enigmatic negation of the mirror by placing a mirror (= the image) at the center of his painting. Morris *breaks this mirror* with his assemblage. Because in effect the image is outside not one but two (and then eight) frames, which are also outside the image, which in fact is not in any of the four mirrors. Morris sums up and exhausts two phrases (and two phases), two conclusions, putting eight frames around four mirrors and an image which is an unreciprocated gaze going in circles. A circle: surfaces handed down/over. A theory of surfaces against contemplation.

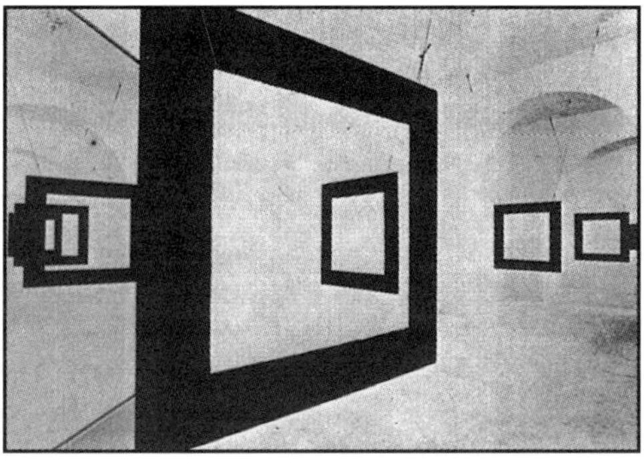

5

Trompe l'oeil/Renaissance perspective raised to absurdity. Not the famous hall of mirrors in an amusement park. There form is exalted, deformed, exaggerated as it watches itself. Teratology in cahoots with an indiscreet narcissism. In Robert Morris's hall of mirrors, the gaze looks in vain for its reflection; form wants to see itself multiplied, exaggerated, and it feels cheated, reduced to a disquieting absence in one mirror after another. The gaze activates a circular visualization. The eye as a sixth sense: two eyes times four mirrors equals zero. Because it all comes to an exorcism of the gaze.

6

The mirrors: an unconvincing symmetry. Not a rhetoric of vision but a metaphor. Even more: an ellipsis. Rebounding/repeating, the eye collaborates in its systematic revocation. The mirrors are eyelids: they close in the gaze. A gaze is not returned: there is a sweeping eradication of appearance and amazement. Glass eyelids. Don't be caught looking. Again and again we become Narcissus.

7

Beyond the eye vision breaks down. Dies in its own useless, catastrophic apogee. The peril within perceptible. Morris is not a Trojan. His four mirrors, the hooves of a horse *invisible in its most absolute visibility.* His monument to the gaze is an optic strategy: a trap. Better use a mirror to see his mirrors, a tempting, playful Medusa. It is best to close your eyes tightly or employ a cleverly oblique gaze, as when you (don't) watch a dangerous eclipse. Because, in these mirrors, the sun tends to be absolute: to see oneself seen = to go blind. Because the sun tends to be totalitarian here and we cannot sustain a gaze. Not in four mirrors. Not even in one. We witness nothing more than our own exclusion. Without belonging to us, the mirrors are our only authentic (?) gaze.

8

From Descartes's *Dioptric*: "First, because it is the soul that sees, and not the eye, and because the soul sees immediately only by the intervention of the brain, whence it happens that madmen and sleepers often see, or think that they see, diverse objects which are not yet before their eyes . . ."

9

Escher: everything is form. Cage: everything is sound. Morris: everything is eye but the eye. We arrive at the necessary satanic disorder of our senses not by losing our way on a map but by getting lost in a mirror. A paradox times four. Not an existential distraction: a presence dimmed/dispersed. A question of redundant precision. It is not form that the mirror brutalizes or exaggerates but the mirror itself, and, thanks to that hara-kiri of reflected surfaces, the gaze becomes seductive as it tries futilely to see itself, as each attempt at self-affirmation turns into a retraction.

10

In *Un Chien Andalou* there is a scene doubly difficult for memory. Difficult to remember because it is absolutely chilling. Difficult to forget because it is so accurate. A man (who is the man (who is an actor (who is the co-director) slices an eye. Vision is viewed: a screen emptied onto the screen. Morris's project is no less ambitious than Buñuel's, although—paradoxical as it may seem when dealing with an even more

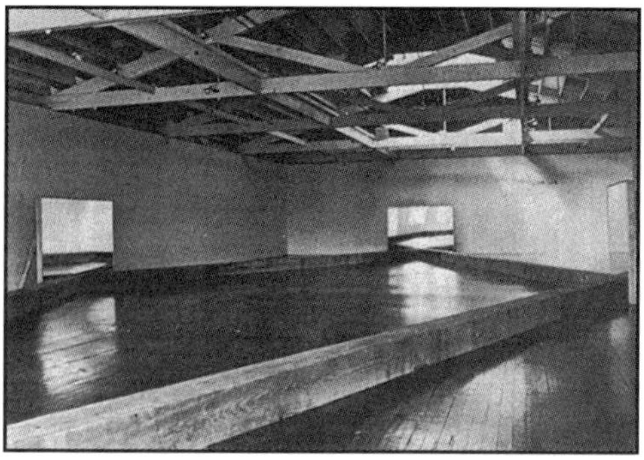

exacting excess of visibility—it turns out to be less obvious and much less disturbing. Morris tries to slice the gaze. His mirrors are blades.

11

The mirrors in Morris's exhibit empty our eyes. Disoriented, but also paralyzed, we try to reorganize the world, to be at its hub, consistent with the venerable custom of our egoism. We are indisputably Westerners. But for a few seconds, in which a simultaneity of spaces seems to erase time and duration, we have become—have been made—surprising and surprised works of art. The *voyeurs* are statues and they give in to the strangeness of a gaze which is their own but above all another's. A gaze at once empty and analytical, hostile. Curiosity as a reversible phenomenon. We verify that, in essence, being a statue is not having eyes. Immobility is logical, mathematical: a consequence. The statue, sentinel of an eternally defeated world.

12

What does this absence of eyes mean? We could resort to banality: mirror as castration. Anagnorisis, sphinx, Oedipus: the classicism of guilt. But recognition does not occur in these mirrors; it is frustrated by the impossibility of seeing oneself: the more we look the less of ourselves we see. If there is guilt it is entirely gratuitious or it deals with a presentiment that does not demand clarification. Guilt without recognition. In addition, a generalized, trivial guilt. The victim defines himself through complicity with another victim in a world withdrawn from sacrifice: immolation is immoral. Hall of mirrors: metaphor of a vicious circle. Perception/persuasions as artful optometry.

13

An exhibitionism of guilt. An exhibit of exhibitionism. The tragedy of a world that neither feels nor understands tragedy, that—by insisting from complicity on an art every day more superficial—finally receives the tribute of its own superficial-ity. Art reduced to optical laws that deny the gaze. Absurd but accurate. And here I find the fundamental difference between Morris's assemblage and its antecedents. In order to perceive this difference of a seen that sees, we can turn to objects as variations and to a minimal but discriminating bibliography. Notes for a museum of the gaze. For example, there are excellent versions—to say studies or interpretations would not sufficiently distinguish between those pages and many others—of two works already mentioned in this context. Of *Las Meninas* in Michel Foucault's *The Order of Things*. Of *Etant donnés* in *Apariencia desnuda* (Naked appearance) by Octavio Paz. Variations and versions: orbits tenaciously out of orbit which contribute to a necessary phenomenology of the gaze.

14

In Egyptian mythology the world springs from the eye, which confers reality on the world. Open, the eye creates day; closed, it creates night. Dream and vigil: sighting is siting. And citing. But the eye as epistemology is no less vulnerable than other systems of logic. Statues and the blind know this well. It is suggested with sufficient sagacity by certain tormented and/or tormenting monuments to the gaze. Each one of us begins to suspect it when we look for ourselves in surfaces either too profound or too superficial. Highly polished surfaces that disquiet by proclaiming, multiplying, denying us. Perplexity, laughter, irritation are symptoms of an inner bristling: the eye's urge to monumentalize exhibits us full face but forces us to look askance.*

* Thanks to the Sonnabend Gallery, New York City, for permission to use the photographs in this essay. (trans.)

Meditations

On the corner
The madman spewed out his names
Names like yours and mine
He was each and every one of us
Yet someone more
                                        Or less
Homer and No one
Avellaneda and Cide Hamete and Cervantes
Zequeira and Armuna
Caesar and Shakespeare, and you, Brutus
A chain of who and when
I am also Octavio, he heard
Once more our names echoed
Until, quivering, a single voice prevailed
It was an honor, delighted, so pleased
A thousand years went past the corner, a thousand days
Slaves, gladiators went past, centurions
Truer to iron than to purpure
This Monday and centuries ago
Someone ran into the doubts that are his destiny
And perhaps I met Marcus Aurelius

Taste: Archaeology of a Sense

In Memory of José Vázquez Amaral

Please don't confuse the pineapple with the pineapple. People have been doing that since the Admiral's second voyage and it's high time things were cleared up. To do that, we should celebrate not yet another anniversary of the discovery of America but one less anniversary of its invention, an event no doubt more unusual, but also more necessary and transcendent. There is an urgent need for America to be invented and reinvented. Otherwise, doomed forever to belong to someone else, it will be discovered repeatedly. An event like the discovery could find all of us listening to a hundred lectures, continually stifling the yawn that will be millenial within a few centuries. For Americans to speak on a day like October 12 about a day like October 12 is a sure way to remain passive and even unfeeling with respect to our own history, which we make and unmake as if we were waiting for Ulysses to return before puting our house in order. The invention of America calls for a different approach. What's needed is imagination and desire: presence. Let's start by making this essay a voyage through the labyrinth of the ear. I want to be heard from within.

Of the Nicknamed but Never Nicked Ananas

Fruit, I have fruits for sale,
lots of mangoes, mangoes of all kinds,
pineapples, sweet as sugar,
cut in the hills of El Caney;
wonderful mangoes, my friends,
pineapples luscious as song
just like a woman's lips.

Accompanied by the song of Miguel Matamoros's *son*, I have set out to reconstruct the pineapple's diffuse biography. The *son* is a bridge between a lost landscape and one form of sugar. For anyone who grew up listening to the cries of street vendors, fruit has rhythm; it tastes like music. Silent music. Swallowed music. A rare taste, capable of plunging us involuntarily into the past or into sensory chaos—Cuban nature is hardly tempered by a bit of French—is found principally in the pineapple, center of Creole feasts since 1604. In that excessively colonial year, napaeas laden with fruits came from the fields to celebrate the rescue of Bishop Juan de las Cabezas Altamirano. Centuries later, the pineapple still reigns over the Cemí *family fait.* There, in our own landscape or in one of Laplante's engravings, we come upon Charon, for the Cemís can still hear their grandfather summoning guests to a lavish party at their house, even though his voice now reaches them "from the cane fields on the far shore."

It was Cristóbal Colón—Christopher Columbus—who first referred to the pineapple as pineapple. In 1493, on the island of Guadalupe, he met the *naná*, which was one of the fruit's many indigenous names. "Since the Indians have many and diverse languages," González Fernández de Oviedo would write, "they therefore call it by diverse names. . . ." The Admiral met the *naná*, as it was called in Brazilian Tupí-Guaraní, but he named it *piña* or *pineapple* because of its resemblance to the pine cone. What is more, he colon/ized the *naná* so skillfully with the nickname by analogy that to this day it is called *piña* even in Paraguay. The curious thing about this naming of the fruit is how the countries most distant geographically are the ones that come closest to the mark. Tantalism: tongue-satisfied palate. The influence of Portuguese has meant that *ananá* or even *ananas* is used in French, German, Danish, Swedish, Dutch, Italian, and even in India. But not in the tropics. No one's a *naná* in his own land, as the saying goes.

The situation gets even more complicated in English, so definite is the existence of this inversely proportional relationship between name and landscape. In English *naná* is *pineapple:* apple or cone of the pine tree. What Columbus opined—a pinioning of three fruits in the verbal disortion of one word—no doubt anticipates territorial contorsions: in 1898 a bit of the tropics where pineapples are grown fell into the hands of the United States. So that *naná* could hardly be *naná* in English. But *pineapple*? *Pineapple* fails to go far enough. The *piña* must become even more exotic than the place where they grow it, especially in the case of Hawaii, a postcard surrounded by water on all sides. That's why English uses and abuses Spanish, mixing how a thing tastes with the way it gets pronounced. A fate of wrapping and rapping. Happy hour Spanish, right from a cocktail shaker. The *piña colada*, for example, many times sounds like *piña colada* and tastes worse. By distorting a name and then coming up with an abysmal pronunciation of that distortion, the Caribbean has avenged itself of the Admiral and the Spanish language. As usually happens in the Caribbean, this vengeance takes the form of a song. Calypso, *son*, *décima*, as anthropophagy: singing the "Guantanamera" to someone is infinitely worse than giving him some song and dance. It is to swallow him whole, tear him to shreds. The spirit gives life, but words wound much more than any number you can do on a person. A crazy rhythm of elocution. A pause. The briefest of hesitations permits a derisive interstice of ambiguity that splits or threatens to split European identity. Singing as singeing. It sounds something like this: "The brothers Pinzón/were gay . . . hearted guys,/who sailed with Colón,/that bu . . . caneer wise." In the Admiral's case, vengeance is double: Columbus was neither bucaneer nor buuuucaneer.

Descried = Described

The Europeans were not the only ones who looked for Paradise in America. Among the indigenous groups, at least one has been wandering for centuries in search of the land without Evil, a world free of suffering, injustice, and age. More's *Utopia*, *avant la lettre*. In fact it was the tales told by these Indians that kindled Pedro de Ursúa's dream of El Dorado. *Aguydjé*, which denotes the belief in this concrete, earthly utopia, draws us closer to the pineapple's landscape and name, to *naná*. Both words are from the language of the Tupí-Guaranís, the tribe that searched for Eden. Unfortunately, neither *naná* nor *aguydjé* found its way into Spanish. The sailors only wanted to hear the sirens of analogy: they wanted to be lost.

Columbus confused islands with continents, manatees with sirens, Cubanacán with the Gran Khan. How could he not confuse the pineapple with the pineapple? So what, Oviedo asks. "Watts in a name," he says as he presents us with an introductory description in his *Historia general y natural de las Indias*

(Natural history of the West Indies). "A pineapple by any other name would taste as sweet."

"There are some thistles that grow on this island of Española, and each one of them bears a pineapple (or, rather, an artichoke), since the Christians call them pineapples because they resemble the apples or cones from pines, even though they are different." Baptism's magnets and Manes, what turns up here is one of the most frequent and Christian plots from the sentimental life of the Indies. The secret mestizo bloodline once let slip in serialized novels and now told in equally slippery soap operas: the case of the love child. The pineapple is "the most beautiful of the fruits I have seen," writes Oviedo, almost quoting the sentence of Columbus so often quoted by Cubans. But . . . transfusion as confusion: the *melondrama* of the pineapple. A tale, and this is worth underlining, of love, of *natural* history. One where we feel the urge to erase and devour because of the marvelous messes wrought by our own helplessness. Another Caribbean revenge. We might say, for example, that it is just one small step from this natural history to naturalism to crime. Or that, hoping to increase the pleasure of the text, Emile Zola wrote *Nana* in his jacuzzi.

By persisting in their use of *piña*, Columbus and Oviedo lost a key to the American Eden. Literally one of its signs. Only centuries later, when pineapple was savored like ambrosia, would the dimension lost in a word be rediscovered. Cornucopia and palimpsest: apparently it was not the fruit but the act of naming it that was forbidden in the Garden of Eden. The palate as elision: swallowing a name, omitting it was the first step taken by men who were ready to swear that America did not exist. They set foot on land in order to cross over it, to erase it. What they found here was only a path, a means: the *strange islands* were the shore of every distance. Paraphrase and periphrasis. More a cover-up than a discovery. Part of the American being is always somewhere else: to be is to be somewhere else. As Lezama said: "Being born is here an unmentionable fiesta." Discovery, conquest, and colonization were exiles. As were independence, republic, revolution. In one of his last texts, the letter to General Juan José Flores dated November 9, 1830, Bolívar moves us and sends shivers up our spines with a phrase that constitutes his most dramatic political legacy: "the only thing you can do in America is emigrate."

For Oviedo descrying was the same as describing. "Of the five bodily senses, three can be applied to fruits, and even a fourth, which is touch; it shares more fully in these four things or senses than all the fruits and delicacies of the world." The description could be based on the same savage method used by Claude Leví-Strauss to formulate a logic of sensing. In other words, more a *logic of the senses* than a Deleuzian but also delightful *logic of sense*.

When man looks at the beauty of this fruit, he delights in seeing the composure and ornamentation with which Nature painted it and made it so pleasing to sight, for the enjoyment of that sense. Smelling it, another sense delights in a mixed odor of quince, peaches, the finest of melons, and more superior qualities than all these fruits together or separate, with no unpleasantness; and if it is ripe and quite ready to be eaten, not only the table on which it rests, but much of the house where it is found has a fragrant aroma and gratifies this sense more wonderfully and to a greater degree than all other fruits. To the taste it is so appetizing and smooth that in this instance there are no words to adequately speak its praise; because all the other fruits I have named cannot compare with this one, by many carats.

With respect to the other sense, which, ouch, is that of touch, the chronicler played the pineapple close to his chest even while dropping it like a hot diamond. "In truth, to the touch it is not so soft and tame because the fruit itself seems to ask us to pick it up respectfully with a towel or handkerchief; although once in the hand it gives more pleasure than any other." The fruit's sensuality is revealed, and it pleases three, no four—no, not four, three—of the five senses. The pineapple as mulatto. A strictly natural Cecilia Valdés. To the touch, that fourth and at times forlorn sense, the pineapple is not so soft or tame, is it? With that outside on the wild side, it's like an echinoderm with scant but appealing flesh. Mirror: fruit as fruit of the sea. Simulation: the pineapple among the flowers of evil. Translation: not the tactile tentacle of an octopus, the untouchable, almost fierce sea urchin.

In spite of the *natural* confusions in Oviedo's history, there is an embryonic phenomenology embedded in his copious descriptions. A *style of appetite* appears, which is also embryonic and first emerges in Europe immediately after the fall of Constantinople. Echo: the open wok as a whole new kettle of fish. This *style of appetite* will express and then sublimate the grand conjunction of spices and space that beginning with the fifteenth century joins kitchens, caravels, maps, and books until it culminates in the spectacular baroque *potpouri* of savors and savants. Why were Europeans so disconcerted and horrified by the cannibalism of the indigenous populations? No doubt because cannibalism set a limit to that *style of appetite*, a limit evidently defined by a deep and necessary prohibition. "They are fiercely fond of eating human flesh," Cieza de León repeats in *La crónica del Perú* (The chronicle of Peru), although this did not prevent him from alluding to the "very aromatic pineapples." A prohibition against cannibalism weighed heavy on men like Cieza de León, thus their revulsion. Proof: the European, like the Aztec, turned his domain into a slaughterhouse. Only he did not eat, he no longer ate, its meat.

We witness, then, the discovery of the pineapple, a wonderful but inscrutable presence that seems the sum of a hundred summers. But it has not been invented. Oviedo was neither a botanist nor a poet. In his involuntary *Brevisíma relación de la distorsión de las piñas* (Very brief account of the distortion of *piñas*) he himself admits this glaring lack. "The painting done with my pen and words cannot render either the individual essence of this fruit or its heraldry well enough for them to enable it to be recognizable thoroughly and adequately without a painting or drawing, and even with it color would be necessary, in order that what I say and do would be better expressed (in part if not wholly), so that the reader's gaze could partake of this truth." The pineapple will therefore remain "as poorly drawn as spoken" until the nineteenth century, when it appears in Zequeira's ode, finally ripe in Creole imagination. Only then, as an invention, will it start to be known from within. The failure of description and names, in Oviedo as in the fruit vendors we will meet centuries later, imposed a strictly visual, external order or recognition. In this way, the call made through the senses to the imagination went unanswered. Here, common sense, a simple seeing is believing, is inadequate. Recognizing the failure of names, Oviedo and Zequeira leap from botany to optics. In the last nanalysis, the chronicler would need the complicity of "the reader's sight"; the poet, faced with unintelligible names, will opt for a visual recognition.

Archaeology of the Cry

Through poetry, Manuel de Zequeira managed to make himself not only visible but also readable. His kingdom was different, however: neither vegetable nor animal nor mineral. Not even verbal: he belonged to the center of things. When he donned his hat he believed himself totally invisible; he got lost in it, like the rabbits and doves in magic tricks; when he tips that hat in poems no less amazing than the hat itself, he tips the balance and jumps toward us from invisibility to occupy one of the most splendid places in our poetry. Zequeira knew the strangeness of metaphor in his flesh itself and in that other self which is the word. He could have gotten lost in some corner of the classics: among gods and heroes punished by gods, this character from our innermost novel would be perched on a wooden horse. Dreamed by us, he could have lived in the scandalous pages of Homer or in the sinuous and no less scandalous pages of Ovid. Or Cervantes. We glimpse this potential, but he himself summarized it in a single verse: "He raced his horse," he writes in a *décima*, "on a knife-edge."

Invisibility was not a mere hiding place, nor even a disguise, like the regal uniform of a colonel or the numerous pseudonyms formed by the metathetical dissolving of his name: Ezequiel Armuna, Izmael Raquenue, Raquel Yun Zenea. It was his way of revealing himself fully. When invisible, he was consubstantial with Cuban landscape, like smoke from tobacco. We find him—air within—on the first page of *Paradiso*. He lives in our breath, our *pneuma*. He is what we breathe at dusk on the patios in our small towns or at our tables, when the breeze picks up the scent of jasmine or ripe pineapple. As he himself might have said: He'ze air.

Zequeira invites us to enter a world of radical transformations and fusions rather than feints and confusions. Its sense, what is sensed. Sight, the knife-edge, will be absolutely essential for restoring identity when words distance us from savvy or savor. So he will be a bit out of sorts when we meet him unexpectedly on one of his strolls through Havana. He has just run into some fruit vendors with their ineffectual cries. "At ten in the morning," he says in "*El Relox de la Havana*" (The clock of Havana), "the bounty of Pomona and Ceres is on display, pineapples, sapodillas, mameys, avocados, every fruit imaginable disguised in unrecognizable names by the black women's dialect: to find out what's for sale you finally have to look for yourself."

Hearing masks and sight unmasks. The black women sold savor not savvy. In any case it was savvy on the basis of a third sense, the palate. Confronted by the antics of Malabar rather than the semantics of Mallarmé, Zequeira neither plugged his ears with wax nor covered his eyes. He did not even go up in smoke. But he undoubtedly felt lost. And with good reason. Sirens swaying to a habanera, more symbolists than cymbalists, the vendors and their mystifying cries also mixed up a fruitive, radical mulatto synesthesia: not a delirious confusion of the senses but the perfect confusion of sense. A piñata. A Saussurian swoon. A sense less. A sugary saturation of insignificant signifiers. "So what do you think?" asked one. The other hesitated a few seconds, perplexed. She could hardly overcome her speechlessness and her strange accent: "I am not Saussure."

It is not unlikely that this irritating and basically useless battle for sense waged by two senses led Zequeira to write "*A la piña*" (To the pineapple), one of his best known poems. Neither is it unlikely that an arc could be described between Zequeira's neoclassic ode and "*Frutas del Caney*" (Fruits from Caney), a very well known *son* of the Matamoros Trio, where popular tradition proves to be mistress of taste. A century elapses between Zequeira's cry—no less Creole for being erudite—and the tender, rhythmic ode of Miguel Matamoros. From the lethargy of colonial Cuba to Cuba's republican chaos, the pineapple is continually at center stage, a wild plant tamed by the paladins of parlance as much as or more than by those of the palate. Among the delicacies of the *family fait*/recalled in Lezama's *Paradiso*, we find "pineapples with sparkling facets, reduced to the size of an index finger." In Lezama's hands, this fruit, which strikes Oviedo's gaze as totally out of proportion, is made to serve artifice and extravagance. It lends itself to playful parings until it resembles nothing less than an index finger. A favorite of the palate, incorporated an infinite number of times, the pineapple appears now as something actually corporal, as part of the hand, that creature of signs; and on the hand it is the instrument that indicates, designates. It becomes not only an order but also an instrument of order. A pineapple peeled with Zequeira's knife to the exact dimension of taste. A synthesis of all the exaltations that come through the labyrinth of reading in useless attempts to define, reduce a pineapple—Oviedo, Balboa, Zequeira, Bello, Stevens—as well as those that come, no doubt more obstreperously, through the labyrinth of the ear, in the cries of street vendors and in *sones* like that of Matamoros, where clearly—and this is very Cuban—the pineapple appears again, assimilated, incorporated, on the lips of a woman.

The Möbius Pineapple

In an attempt to possess landscape through literature, as if the poem were our equivalent of the Renaissance window, in 1826 Andrés Bello published his *silva "A la agricultura de la Zona Tórrida"* (To the agriculture of the torrid zone). The pineapple is one of the fruits with which Bello cornu/copied landscape. It only occupies one line of his extensive poem, but in that line two possibilities for invention are suggested. "And the *ananas*," the Venezuelan poet writes, "sweetens their ambrosia." First possibility: return the fruit's indigenous name, even though that name is rather deformed. Problem: simplicity is complicated. As with any indigenous effort, the use of *ananas* implies reliance on a phantasm. In addition, and even more importantly, in our aptly-named torrid zone, we have a law that nullifies any success achieved through exhumation: an archaeology of the past, the present, or the future could not pull us from ruin. A law of permanent asymmetry, coil of our baroque serpent, it commands nothing more than disobedience. This is perhaps the reason it has become our only law, or the only law obeyed willingly: problems are best solved through further complications.

Second possibility, the Creole one: the pineapple as ambrosia. Reason: we should claim what belongs to us, tamc the less than tame pineapple. Treason: a poetics of exportation that leads our poets, yes even our poets, astray in an infinite hall of mirrors. Not an archaeology but an anachronism. Distractions and distortions: a cruel instant of immortality. The pineapple is not tropical but Mediterranean. It comes from Olympus not El Caney. The process of taming seems to imply a reduplication of exoticism as a paradoxical first step: the Tupí-Guaraní times the Greco-Latin. The pineapple will no longer be confused with European fruits, like the pinecone or the artichoke, but with the ultimate synthesis of fruits and their significance in European mythology: ambrosia.

Even so, the following qualifications must be admitted: (1) amazed by the New World, the chroniclers used mythological references as *metron*, as a plausible standard for the enormous reality confronting them. Faced with a manatee or a naked Caracas they found in the mythological a possible phenomenology. When Creoles use the same references, they are fully aware of the exaggerated, comic effect. Scenography as deicide to the last detail: in our landscape the gods of Homer and Ovid provoke smiles, guffaws. They are vaudeville and carnival gods; metaphors off center in a way that gives them a radical, double connotation: alterity, absence.

> The pineapple, he said, the fragrant pineapple
> may it be raised in my gardens
> by the hands of my nymphs; yes, may
> its nectar flow in Idalium.

In Zequeira's ode, there is something like a foreshadowing of Andy Warhol. In the pineapple, that embryonic Coca–Cola, we can foresee the ease with which our most mundane products will occupy the center of a banal, canned culture. May its nectar flow in Idalium: a poetics of exportation that not too many years later will be echoed in the United States, the island's most important outlet for its sugar and other basic products. "I have no knowledge of trade," we read in Emerson's Diary, winter of 1868, as the Ten Years War was about to break out in Cuba, " & there is not the sciolist who cannot shut my mouth & my understanding by strings of facts that seem to prove the wisdom of tariffs. But my faith in freedom of trade, as the rule, returns always. If the Creator had made oranges, coffee, & pineapples in Cuba, & refused them to Massachusetts, I cannot see why we should put a fine on the Cubans for bringing these to us. . . ."

Like Emerson, the gods want to taste a pineapple. Ganymede, cupbearer to Jupiter, hurries "to our fields from sacred Olympus" so he can carry one to the "empyreal mansion." There, given a joyful welcome, the fruit proves captivating: "when divested/of its royal garb, the firmaments/it perfumed with amber." The apotheosis of our mulatto *vedette*. Preferring piña coladas, the gods no longer drink ambrosia. "In the sacred cup ambrosia/lost its value: with the scent/of Indian drink in sweet draughts/their majesties are inflamed." Zequeira's adjectives are candied: we are in a supremely saccharine landscape. Our refinement is a cultural coup even though our refineries are economic disasters. Or, better: refining is a cultural coup for us because refining for us is an economic disaster. Baroque aesthetics: export means decontextualize. Thanks to the European appetite, sugar—for now without aluminum, in its "royal garb"—becomes sardonically infected with the Apollonian and the Dionysian; simultaneously, Europe's mythology, the matrix of its culture, is rendered banal. Savvy prevails over savor. And vice versa.

(2) The apparent distortion, the logical, or rather analogical, consequence of the meeting between two landscapes as different as those of America and Europe, is not unilateral. It is the synchronic step that makes possible the expression of a shock: the expansion imposed on European Renaissance perspective by the overwhelming presence of the colonial Creole world. A step that through mutual and reciprocal distortions affirms a profound identity in the area of culture.

By literally taking a bird's-eye view, we find ourselves in the baroque vanishing point, the moment of reciprocal discovery and invention between Europe and America. Let's go back to those pages of Oviedo. As he attempted to show the "composure and beauty of this fruit, greater, beyond comparison, than of all others I have seen," the chronicler employed systematically cautious and at times daring approximations. The *naná* was likened first to the pinecone, then to the artichoke, the melon, the peach, the quince. His almost geometric variations could be multiplied infinitely if the possible chain of associations were applied to each of the four senses. With the *piña* and with a piniform prose bristling with comparisons, Oviedo evidently wanted to captivate his reader. He wanted him to approach the page as if it were a kaleidoscope. He juggled the relation between the pineapple, the senses, and whatever lent itself to sufficiently imprecise comparisons, hoping to achieve that bit of magic caused by the play of light, a mirror, and a few chips of glass.

As one would expect, his references are European: shaken like maracas by the pineapple, the four senses create perspective, but that perspective is centered in Europe, or rather, it is necessarily decentered. Oviedo's readers see, smell, taste, and touch the pineapple from Madrid, Rome, or Paris: they must create for themselves an image of American reality in mirrors that will turn out to be inexact, inadequate. A refracted image. So much so that it will be necessary to jump from words to drawings and from flora to fauna. "Just as among the birds, Nature paid special attention to the turkey when she featherd the birds of our Europe, she took care in the composure and beauty of this fruit." The imagination soars. Ultimately, in order to describe the pineapple it is necesary to talk about birds. At the same time, however, that imagination continues to cling to its own center and is therefore not thrown totally off balance. Europe's flora proves inadequate for a simple description, but the axis of the European imagination can remain in the Old World. Feathers as kaleidoscope: through an imperial change in focus, an American fruit is forced to assume metropolitan plumage. The pineapple is viceregal.

My Empire for a Bird

"It was a constant vibration, a humming, an oscillation repeated a thousand times. You could call it a thought nabbed in flight and trapped in the beating of wings, floating and suspended in space." Such was the emperor's first encounter with the hummingbird, the morning of January 11, 1860. He had certainly read *Candide*, that book full of hummingbird published in 1759, almost exactly a century before. "Reality proved to be far superior to all expectations and to any possible description." Once again, the language of inadequacy puts in an appearance. Prose bows to a few inches of American nature. "The hummingbird eludes prosaic judgment." Prose forced to wing it. Syntax in fresco. Notes that could serve for an Impressionist painting: "you cannot catch this tiny creature; neither can you copy its movements nor keep it in captivity. Like images in dreams, it turns up when least expected and flies off when we find it most alluring." Three centuries have passed since the *Historia general y natural de las Indias*; but three hundred years of colonial life have not been enough to tame even a few inches. A landscape always latent, imminent, at once overwhelming and unrealized, genetic and gnostic. It is the water of the great falls, which seems to hold still in mid air, turned to foam, drizzle, fog even before crashing against stone; it is the hummingbird, "so small and graceful, so quick, that it manages to avoid any definition of its corporeal substance." Flesh as lightning, music, perfume. Classifications overgrown with a utopian zoology that can be named more appropriately with poetry than with Linnean nomenclature. A kaleidoscope. European perspective once again thrown out of orbit. In order to describe the pineapple, even if only to leave it "poorly painted and spoken," Oviedo had to look outside the vegetable kingdom. Maximilian, the emperor whose feeling that he had been destined since childhood to touch the soil of the New World seemed like a dream, expressed his amazement as something even more far-reaching: "In fact the effort to classify the bird in any of the natural kingdoms seems foolish. Concentrated in a lovely, minuscule creature that hums to the air of the tropics, it is like the quintessence of all three kingdoms. It is an animal life with the forms and hues of a fantastic flower and with the bright sparks of a precious stone that shines with its own light, full of mystery." Its nest resembles a flower, its small eggs are like pearls, its eye sharp as "the point on a diamond." This "tiny, little flying thing," he insists, is like a "flashing stone struck by sun."

Maximilian's statement suggests that, with a hummingbird, a miniaturist could have moved from the Renaissance to the baroque; Rubens, of course, needed a macaw, that other lightning flash from the American landscape. Can it possibly come as a surprise that he placed one in the Garden of Eden when he copied a painting by Titian? In 1498 Columbus thought the earthly Paradise was located on this continent. In 1525, Thomas Skelton, the author of *Spanish Parrot,* called the parrot a bird of paradise. Can it be a surprise, then, if European painting was transformed by the flight of a macaw? Oviedo accompanied his description of the pineapple with a drawing. "In order to see," he says, "the composure and ornamentation with which Nature painted it and made it so pleasing to the eye . . ." "The painting done with my words and pen cannot thoroughly and adequately enable it to be recognizable without the painting or drawing, and even with it, colors would be necessary. . . . This notwithstanding, I will include it done the best I know how, as poorly drawn as spoken. For those who have seen the fruit, however, this will be enough, and they can add what is lacking. For those who have only seen it here, it cannot displease them to look at a picture as they listen to the reading. . . ." All Oviedo needed was Rubens to transform European painting. He did not have to wait long: it was his gaze, the gaze of those who had looked as he did at the *dream images* bestowed by our light, that would see macaws in the Garden of Eden.

With the baroque, America and Europe established a different relationship. A symbiosis in which imagination is the only thing real. It was a time when discovery and invention were like images in a mutual, reciprocal dream. Both worlds found themselves decentered, thrown out of orbit; they grew, were fused in a territory of vast, devastating signs. In the seventeenth century a macaw burst into European painting, filled it with color and noise, and created a true vanishing point for the mind's eye. Satyrs, fauns, napaeas, hamadryads, naiades, ephyriads, centaurs, oreads, lumniades parade in a Cuban poem, which is also from the seventeenth century, to celebrate the rescue of a bishop. From this fabulous and most pagan of groups, Fray Juan de las Cabezas Altamirano receives "among other things/some of those hicatees/which I do not have and always praise." That a bishop from the very faithful Christian island of Cuba meets with naiades and centaurs and receives some hicatees from them as though it were the most natural thing in the world, accustoms us to perceiving something unusual in the profuse jumble of savor and savvy that will characterize our appetite for immediacy. Territoriality/reality: Ruben's macaw marks a split in European identity and a rush toward nature as a source of alterity. Napaeas and hamadryads, on the other hand, are roots of American identity, joyously and playfully recovered by Creole imagination.

In the mirror, images vary but reflection is unchanging: self is seen, shattered, discovered, invented. The difference in angle within that identical reflection is no less singular nor important than reflection itself: what is shattering to the European is our reality, what he imagines our reality to be; what is shattering to us, here, is European fantasy. Europeans will happily exchange glass beads for nuggets of gold, centaurs for aromatic pineapples, satyrs for macaws. A century of surrealism and structuralism for a hundred years of solitude. To us those exchanges have always seemed *Favorables París Poema*. This is why we are small gods, like Huidobro's poet.

Sounding Absence

Reading Maximilian's pages I think of "*El colibrí*," a nineteenth-century Cuban song. The association might seem automatic, immediate, given the theme, the title itself. I feel, however, that those texts are being joined by memory because in both of them the literal disappears: because and where in both of them the literal disappears. According to the Emperor, the hummingbird is constant vibration, buzzing, infinitely repeated oscillation. Music. "It hums to the tropical air." This does not admit of analyis: "like the sound of Aeolian harps." What has made me recall the Cuban song is this impossibility of describing the hummingbird. Faced with American nature, Oviedo moved from words to drawing. It was useless. Maximilian is more perceptive; sensing the gnostic dimension of landscape in the smallest detail, in an almost dreamed instant that "flies off when we find it most alluring," he moved from words to music. It occurs to me that this may not be so useless. I decide to do the same thing, and I get the record by Esperanza Márquez I've heard so many times. The record reminds me of an ammonite: in music, as in fossils, time has been stopped. I want to hear the fossil, I want to reread Maximilian's pages while the fossil vibrates constantly, like a humming, like an oscillation that returns thousands of times. Turning our heads thousands of times.

Time stops. Violeta asks me to read the first letter I wrote to her, November 19, 1981. I read what I wrote then, what I write again now. We are in 1987, 1981, 1870, 1860. The obverse: an instant that is all dates and none. The reverse: the present as a fleeting anachronism.

I have just listened once, once more, to "*El colibrí*," the old Cuban song. I'm turning into a record; maybe I'm even getting scratched from spinning in circles under a needle. It's a way, useless like all others, of remembering.

I made my parents listen to "*El colibrí*." Listening to it, I myself began to recall the Cuba of 1870, which I remember better than the Cuba of 1950. In certain bars I sensed something—the rhythm, the tone, something—of "*La bayamesa*"; and then with the intensity of an image, I saw Céspedes surrounded by some friends in a nineteenth-century Cuban drawing room. It was undoubtedly Sunday. They were listening to the same song. The labyrinth of the ear as history, colors as history. Better to spin round in circles and get lost, better to stumble and fall, fall on a rhythm that still feels like your own. Anything rather than ask Euclid for a small straight line to make history, for a sense . . . Sense? Hearing, touch, vision, taste: make a history, dare to write it from precisely *that point of departure*. As for the rest, leave the boring to other, bared teeth.

"*El colibrí*," Miguel Matamoros's *sones*, and, recently, a *danzón* by Sergio Vitier send me back to my landscape. It's the only way I can let myself belong to the thirty–three revolutions of the still-pitiful scratched history that is still mine.

Memory within a memory: when the war of '68 broke out, Martí was studying at the "San Pablo," the private school run by Rafael María Mendive in his home on Prado Street. There, young sympathizers of the "Cause" met nighly to follow, "elbows on the piano, Céspedes' march on a map of Cuba." I have come to believe that what allowed those young men to approach a history at once their own and still distant was not the map but the piano. The piano was, or has come to be, the deep map. Sometimes I think that on the same piano I write everything I write and read everything I read. In this way, for example, Góngora's sonnet turns into a *son* of Miguel Matamoros.

> As many, when absent, I have refused the Duero,
> so many tears to Betis are the tears I entrust,
> and, crowned with sparks, the river,
> fire offers to the sea in an urn already incandescent.
>
> Volcano of this water and of these flames fount
> is, ungrateful lady, my breast;
> may the sighs that I send you tell
> if the jungle which hears it silences it.
>
> The edges of this second Eridanus
> are ashes; my tender weeping like
> Phaethon's wild adventure:
>
> A burning river, a burning sea, the world smoldering;
> if this is not the sun's chariot poorly driven
> it is tears and sighs sounding my absence.

The sonnet begins for me in the last verse, in the last three words. It begins and begins again. I stop there because there the poem does not end for me. The poem neither ends nor stops, it repeats infinitely. It spins there, like a record or an ammonite. The reading takes place outside of time, passing from verb to noun. I stumble onto a bridge to Cuba, in the sonnet I listen to *sounding absence*. In fact, all of Matamoros's *sones* are for me one single *sounding absence*. "*El colibrí*," *sounding absence*. *Flora*, Vitier's *danzón*, *sounding absence*. The *Berceuse campesina* of Alejandro García Caturla, a double sounding absence. Double because I have never heard it but nevertheless feel it, intuit it as an essential piece of the landscape I am constructing. I have never heard it, but I always hear it, like an amputee feels his missing arm or leg in the stump.

Most of the Cuban exiles who visit me, there are not many but they all come *sounding absence*, have been made to hear Sergio Vitier's *danzón* with me. I think they are grateful for this excrutiating Cuban instant, and I think they share my feeling about it. Neither opinion nor appreciation: feeling. The *danzón* is dedicated to the Cuban artist René Portocarrero, and it would appear that the music has been truly and literally touched by painting: it is a *danzón*, certainly, but a *danzón* that seems caught in the fixity of lines and colors. It has the cloying elegance of the *danzón*, but we imagine it resounding in Collazo's *El patio* rather than the Salón México. We might say that the rhythm is slower, more intimate. Like a *danzón* dreamed by someone else. Something like a *danzón* for Zequeira. An inaudible *danzón* for phantoms. For the invisible. For the other shore. A *danzón* that is concave, emptied. A startling absence of the *danzón*. The chords, the spirit of the entire piece, is Slavic, profoundly nostalgic. A Hungarian *danzón*. Or a Polish one. Something like a Cuban polonaise. A post-Cuban *danzón*. Which is nevertheless very Cuban. So much so that I hear in it the *Berceuse campesina*, perhaps because one of the musicians performing it is a son or grandson of Caturla. The notes, especially one—a chasm—show me how within Cuba there are people as far from the Cuban landscape as I am. Even on the island there are people living in the remote, in an inner distance. Please don't confuse the pineapple with the pineapple. I'm referring here, as always, to what is essentially Cuban. We still have our "elbows on the piano," like the students at the "San Pablo." Céspedes marches to this *danzón*. This music, like everything sounding absence, is a map of Cuba.

Charon, Columbus, Sancho: Trips and Tricks of the Enchanted Boat

In 1300 Dante began to write the *Divine Comedy*. He found himself midway in the journey of his life, in a dark forest. He was about to enter hell. Two years earlier, Marco Polo had recorded his adventures in another hell, a Genoese jail. Both men were Italian; they would both share a single era. Chronology here is rigorously mathematical: Dante lived from 1265 to 1321, Marco Polo from 1254 to 1325. Something even more important: the synchrony that marks both the composition of their fabulous adventures and their impact.

Dante's allegory transported his readers to the center of

themselves: to sin, doubt, faith. It was a work of a believer for believers. News from China proved to be even more surprising than reports from the Inferno or Paradise. More than anything, it awakened suspicion and disbelief. The tale of the sixteen years Marco Polo spent traveling through the Far East seemed highly exaggerated to his fellow countrymen, and it earned him the nickname of *Marco Milione*. The fact is, however, that both Dante and Marco Polo followed the path on which the European imagination had affirmed its roots. The confused waters that seemed to be parting opened right from the pages of Homer: voyagers seeking the unknown set out for mythic, or fabled, or geographical regions without distinguishing between them. The adventures of Ulysses birthed maps and novels, measurement and boundlessness. Both tales can be conceived of as "travel literature"; one because of its occasionally scabrous geography of the soul, the other because of the legendary geography of the Orient. We can grant them equal importance: Marco Polo's journey was as significant for navigation as the *Divine Comedy* was for poetry. But some important differences cannot be ignored. Dante's journey was Gothic, vertical; Marco Polo's, a portent of the discovery of America and the European renaissance, was horizontal, worldly, modern. The two crossings were not parallel. They represented the intersection of reason's horizontal line and Gothic's vertical. The latter closed an era, the former opened one. Theology and its language were left behind. In this sense, the *Divine* but vernacular *Comedy* anticipates the liturgy of today's Mass, where the lessening of Rome's influence has resulted in the disappearance of Latin and genuflection. The plurality of life styles and milieus stimulated an interest in history and geography, and this plurality was recounted in turn in a plurality of languages: Spanish, Portuguese, English, French. Already aroused when Homer gathered and organized the strange events narrated by the warriors of his time, as now by tourists no less barbarous, European curiosity inclined decisively toward the sailor rather than the soul. Apparently one could go further with navigation than with theology. Which is why not Charon but Vespucci, Columbus, Cartier, Cook, and Magellan were sought for passage to the other shore. The sky itself ceased to be a dimension of the soul and became an object of study. Saints were less interesting than astronomers. Proof of this: astronomers not saints were now burned.

In 1600, inflamed *About the Infinite and Its Limits*, Bruno found himself among the many victims of the Inquisition and its bonfires. Having been fired up by the Reformation he was fried by the Counter–Reformation. Just a few years later, once again over hot astronomical issues, a pair of reluctant characters from the Spanish baroque, that aesthetics of Counter–Reformation, got "more than a little scorched." These new victims of fire were burnt mostly as a joke. The world was becoming more worldly: bulls were turning to bull. Nevertheless, when Don Quixote and Sancho mounted Clavileño they became instruments of criticism. A scathing, double criticism, of both literature and society. In the adventure of Clavileño, Cervantes not only parodied classical literature but also made a clear allusion to astronomy, a hot issue in those days. He was parodying Cicero's *Somnium Scipionis*, one of the models for Dante's journey to the otherworld. He also made it possible for the nightmare of his own era to be reflected in the mirrors of irony. This adventure is a further example of what I have called a *style of appetite*, but one that is very typical of a particular moment, since we intuit in it very obvious signs of loosening and disillusion. The entropy of a style.

In 1584 Bruno had published "Ash Wednesday Supper," an important "metaphysical dialogue," which is what discussions about astronomy were called at the time. An appetite for spices and space: the title of that dialogue, which unfortunately proved to be prophetic, recalls infinite conversations about the infinite that Bruno held with hosts eager for theory. Amid so much sermonizing about narrow, closed heavens he was truly a lover of the infinite. His pulpits: the book, the head of a table. An appetite repeated in the adventure with Clavileño. In his name, and almost always in his behavior, Sancho crudely embodies one of the hungers implicit in this style. He is first of all Panza, paunch. Later, in adventures like that of Clavileño, he overcomes his own limitations and shows he is capable of sublimating his primary appetite in risk and fascination, in the journey. *Style of appetite* is eventually manifested in him with such intensity that in this adventure we find him more receptive than his master to the world of fantasy: he turns out to be more quixotic than Quixote himself.

Don Quixote has by now lost faith:

Since all these things and all these events fall outside the natural order, it is not surprising that Sancho would say what he does. For my part, I can say that I moved my blindfold neither up nor down, nor did I see either heaven or earth, sea or sands. It is true that I felt I was passing through the region of air, and even that I was touching fire; but I cannot believe we went beyond that, because there is a region of fire between the firmament of the moon and the furthest region of air, and we could not have reached heaven, where Sancho says he saw the seven nanny goats, without being roasted alive. Since we were not burned to a crisp, either Sancho is lying or Sancho is dreaming.

Sancho believes, or believes he believes, or pretends he believes, to have gotten "so close to heaven" that between them there was only a "palm and a half."

My lady, I felt that we were flying through the region of fire, just as my master told me, and I wanted to uncover my eyes just a little bit; but when I asked his permission, my master would not consent. Since I'm always bursting with curiosity, though, and want to know whatever's impossible or forbidden to me, carefully and without letting anyone see me, right around my nose I loosened the cloth covering my eyes. That let me look down at the Earth, and it seemed to me that it was no bigger than a grain of mustard, and the men walking on it weren't much bigger than hazelnuts; so you can see how high up we must have been.

Let's go back to two of Sancho's comments: the Earth was no bigger than a grain of mustard, men looked like hazelnuts. The paradox is clear to us: the part is bigger than the whole. Millions of hazelnuts will fit on a grain of mustard: they are angels on the head of a pin. Distance, in any case, is measured by proportion. This is what Cicero had done in *Somnium Scipionis*:

As I looked at everything from up there, all the things I saw seemed marvelous and wonderful. There were stars we have never seen from our world, of a magnitude we would never suspect. . . . The starry spheres were much larger than the Earth, and the Earth itself looked so small I almost pitied our empire, which was no bigger than a dot.

From the Milky Way, young Scipio has watched Earth grow smaller. So much smaller that his own empire moves him to pity, since "it was no bigger than a dot." Proportions here are expressed in geometric, almost abstract terms, without paradox. Magnitude, spheres, then a planet, and on it a dot, like the center of a circumference that has almost run out. An enormous reduction. Sancho has also soared toward the heavens, has seen his own, meager world from their vastness, has known proportions. But to express them, Panza—parody incarnate—substitutes a gastronomic reference for a geometric one. He substitutes the dot with a grain of mustard or with hazelnuts. This substitution, in addition to its parodic connotation, has another, equally modern. It is there that Sancho, far from being a vulgarity, constitutes a style.

Centuries later, when the baroque is powerfully reborn in the figure of Lezama Lima, proportions place us before the same mirror. Hazelnuts reappear, fleetingly, in the fugue of size. "Candies that left hazelnuts like panes of glass, translucent when held to the light; pineapples with sparkling facets, reduced to the size of an index finger; coconuts from Brazil, reduced until they resembled grains of rice, which flaunted their bushy heads again when dipped in orchid wine." It would seem that the play of proportions here does not go beyond the framework of the delicacies themselves. The comparisons refer dishes to transparencies, to the body, or to other dishes. But earlier, with a bundle of needles, Lezama had hinted at the extreme elasticity of this framework. A sum of distant threads, achieved by using the palate to allude to a double distance of era and landscape. Time and time again, as these comparisons are pursued, the excursion on Clavileño winds up in the ruins of Carthage. "It was the day with no day," Lezama says, "one unmarked by any saint or event. He worked silently, gathering delicacies of preserves and almonds, Salamancan hams, fruits in season, Viennese pastries, liqueurs pulled from the ruins of Pompey, which had by now turned into syrup, or wines aged so long that pouring one drop on a handkerchief made it assume the characteristics of the handkerchief Mario had used to wipe his persperation in the ruins of Carthage."

The above comparisons have linked Sancho with the lineages of Scipio and Cemí. A third comparison will prove less risky because it will deal with a character closer to Sancho in the illusory *metron* of chronology. Like Sancho, the Admiral was a prevaricator of language. One could say that in his case the problem was one of translation, since his blunders occured when he tried to repeat Taíno expressions in his Italian Spanish. *Cubanacán* became *Gran Khan. Caribe* would become *caniba*, which as the Admiral wrote in his logbook on December 11, 1492, "is nothing other than the people of the Gran Khan," hence *cannibal*. We could also say, in Sancho's defense, that he translates into Spanish from Greek, or from what to him is Greek or Chinese. For example, in the well–known dialogue of *the famous Adventure of the Enchanted Boat:*

"A long way," answered Don Quixote, "for when we come to the line I mentioned we will have covered half of the water and land of the 360 degrees that are on this globe, according to the computations of Ptolemy, the greatest geographer and astronomer ever known.

"By God," Sancho said, "I don't care how tall he is, your worship should be able to round up a more gentile witness than that strong ass with his copulations."

Columbus and Sancho are victims of an enchantment. Constantly misciting and missighting, they turn even common places into missed sites. They sail in enchanted boats, lose their bearings in a landscape, in language, on the palate. For Columbus, *naná* was *piña* and *carib cannibal*. Faced with anthropophagy, that spellbinding limit on the European *style of appetite*, the panic of the Caribs felt by the Taínos seemed to graze an identical panic in the European unconscious. Just as centuries before, the European bristled again with a premonition of Carthage: Hannibal was approaching.

Like inversely symmetrical figures of a single style, neither Columbus nor Sancho could manage without his dreams and visions. One way or another, they each made a pact based on illusions and lies. In 1494, the Admiral's companions swore that Cuba was "the beginning of the Indies." To retract that oath would cost ten thousand maravedis, one hundred lashes, or one tongue. At the beginning of the seventeenth century, master proposes to servant a silence no less moving. In one of the most human moments of the novel, and perhaps for this reason one of the saddest, Don Quixote searches for a formula for avoiding the Latin for *retraction*:

Sancho, since you want me to believe what you saw in the sky, I want you to believe what I saw in the cave of Montesinos. I'll say no more.

About the Rebellion Against the Gothic

Copernicus, Bruno, Galileo, and Kepler rebelled against an ideal heaven. The hunger for spatial frontiers, both those of the planet's land masses and those of its relation with other worlds in an *infinite universe* such as Bruno's, creates an immensity inconceivable except in mathematical terms: neither geocentric nor theological but heliocentric, astronomical. Without a doubt, this involved, albeit implicitly, a profound rebellion against the Gothic, as the Inquisition was well aware. Hence the fires and the Index. This was a rebellion against the Gothic as profound as the Reformation's rebellion against Rome. The new martyrs were scientists who advanced the laws of motion against the fixity of dogma. *Stasis* was ardently defended by the religious world, Catholic and Protestant alike. Galileo was threatened and gagged by the Inquisition, Calvin had Miguel Servet burnt at the stake. What they were trying to wipe out at the core was a highly revolutionary thesis: circulation.

Stars and blood circulated; in this way geometry reached a dynamic, vital dimension and confirmed what philosophers had known intuitively: the circle embodied the possibility of perfect motion. For the religious fanatic, however, the perfect and the true were notions of necessity linked to the static. True, protestantism would promote the accumulation of money through incipient capitalism, but—*stasis* of interest—money would circulate only to become more stagnant. The polemic caused by Darwin's theory of evolution would prove that, even centuries later, the religious world found it difficult, almost repugnant, to dissociate its notions of the true and the static. *Eppur, si muove!* Neither Calvin nor Torquemada could eradicate the novel and dangerous scientific theories. It would have been necessary to burn not only men and books but also the roundness of Earth itself. It would have been necessary to burn America. To argue that they tried to do so would be an exaggeration. But the clear brutality of the conquest of the New World, whether of the south by the Catholics or the north by the Protestants, seems, at least in part, to have been the product of confusion and resentment. In any case, America was part of this sudden elasticity and expansion of limits. And a decisive part, to be sure. One example is the change that occurred between 1491 and 1493 in anatomical studies. Chronology neither lies nor exaggerates. Nor does chance. 1491: the first edition of *Fasciculus Medicinae* was published in Venice. It included not a single naturalistic representation of an internal organ of the human body. This should not surprise us since no such representation had ever appeared in any printed book. 1492: half the world was born. 1493: when the second edition of *Fasciculus medicinae* was published things had changed. In this edition a naturalistic representation of an internal organ appeared for the first time. The fact proved to be so singular that we could speak without any exaggeration of two books rather than two editions. The difference between them was that radical, and this was because chronology itself was radical. That chance probably intervened in chronology is undeniable. Nor would there be reason to deny it, but whatever chance intervened was highly objective. Soon after America was dis/covered the anatomy book included an internal organ.

Did one event have nothing to do with the other? Half the world had been born. Did this not influence the second edition of *Fasciculus Medicinae*, which was characterized precisely by its reproduction of the female reproductive organs? Beginning with 1492, Europe would undertake inner and outer explorations simultaneously. Expedition and dissection would be its instruments of cognition and recognition. There is a deep mirror in the new lands and in that other recently discovered and conquered landscape, the corpse.

The duality journey/dissection is implicit in the Jesuits' vow of obedience. The Soldiers of Jesus were obliged to abolish every trace of individual free will. According to Sedgwick, they let themselves be led like soldiers and moved like corpses. The same duality was synthesized in the case of Laurentius Frisius, a Dutchman. Frisius was a teacher of Mercator, but he was a doctor as well as a geographer, and the author of *Spiegel der Arztny* (1518), which contained important anatomical illustrations. Frisius belongs, then, to a Flemish tradition that includes maps—among them one made by Mercator in 1538, where the name of America is first given to the entire continent—and also paintings like Rembrandt's *Dr. Tulp's Anatomy Lesson.*

That tradition is not only maintained thematically by presenting territories and tissues as visual signs; it is also affirmed in a primary, immediate way with the material on which these signs appear, the actual support of their representation: the canvas. In this respect, a very provocative definition of "map" is offered in the famous *Tesoro de la lengua castellana o española* (Treasure of the Castilian or Spanish language), published by Sebastián de Covarrubias Orozco in Madrid in 1611:

MAPA. Name given to the board, cloth, or paper on which the Earth is drawn in a manner either universal or particular. It may derive from "mappa," which means cloth or napkin, especially that thrown down by the praetors in the circus as a signal for the games to begin; and it was bleached or chalked, similar to what we would call starched. Because the cloth or canvas on which the world and its parts were drawn was prepared in this way, it was called map and "mappa mundi." For this reason we also call these things canvases, since they are found on canvas.

History, anatomy, grammar, geography, painting, all manifestations of culture were in the process of being synthesized. The fact is proved as much by a collective vow of obedience as by one indiviual. Or by one word.

Pioneers of Hell

Frontiers as we know them today were born in 1492. From that date there would be goals rather than unreachable points in space or in consciousness. Suspension points . . . that would culminate in Einstein's theory about the curvature of space. Man was ready to know and traverse the infinite and the infinitesimal, and for this he multiplied and sharpened his senses. The telescope and the microscope would permit an exhaustive cartography of the vast and the barely perceptible. The heavens and the cell would become challenges rather than mysteries or taboos. From the world created by sailors, explorers, and astronomers arose a radically modern figure: the pioneer. Swamps, deserts, jungles, mountain ranges: from Alaska to the Amazon the difficult, inhospitable, the unknown were no longer impenetrable. Instead, they became irresistible temptations. Synthesis of medieval man, Dante was also a pioneer of pioneers: the first pioneer of hell. Despite the frightful inscription read over a gate—*lasciate ogni speranza, voi ch'entrate!*—he explored hell and plotted its map in *terza*, and terse *rima*.

Given the new, seemingly inexhaustible frontiers, theologians abandoned their calculations about the exact number of angels pinioned on the head of a pin. At the center of the pineapple there is only one, Wallace Stevens would say, alluding no doubt to taste. Loyola, with his Spiritual Exercises, created an army that served as the tip of a penetration into the soul and the new landscapes. The Jesuits reached India, Japan, Paraguay, sowing Rome, which grew in an also-growing world. Only at the end of the eighteenth century, when European society exhausted its territorial frontiers and was forced, through revolution, to look within itself for a new dimension, was there a reappearance of the head of a pin and the pinioning of angels. The head of a pin was the Earth's capacity to produce food, and the angels were the planet's population. Food, as Malthus would observe in 1798, grows in arithmetic proportion; population, in geometric proportion. The Earth, as poor Sancho found out dreaming Scipio's dream, was no longer either the center of the universe or a goddess or infinite possibility, but a rigorous and inevitable contraction. A nightmare. Something like an ache in the head of a pin.

Toward 1300, having traversed hell, man traveled to Paradise. And again in 1492. No further trips to hell would be necessary until the frontiers of space had been exhausted. Milton was one of the first symptoms of that exhaustion and of a permanent, insatiable appetite for depth. Jules Verne, a key symptom. As were Baudelaire, Lautréamont, and Rimbaud. Another key and contemporary symptom: Michaux. Hence *Flowers of Evil, The Chants of Maldoror,* and *A Season in Hell.* Or the miserable miracle of mescaline and those fabulous beings invented by Michaux, which seem to have been resurrected from the chronicles: Emanglons, Hivinizikis, Gaurs, Meidosems. Science fiction and poetry foreshadow an imperative to return to the other shore, the unknown, but it would be a scientist who undertook that perilous descent. An indication that Marco Polo continued to be more influential than Dante, it would be Freud who traveled to hell, to the farthest Orient, to return, like Dante, full of nightmares and allegories. After Freud we know—we believe—that hell is the unconscious and its circles are dreams.

With Dante and Marco Polo, humanity's appetite for frontiers was renewed. And man needs not only paradises but also hells from his frontiers. America was both, as the unconscious and the atom have been. With language that seemed trapped in hyperbole, the descriptions of Columbus and the first chroniclers revealed a new Edenic world. The explorers had recovered paradise. Using the same hyperbolic language, Bartolomé de las Casas would narrate the hell that was also America. Through discovery, new myths and yearnings were awakened: Atlantis, utopia. There was a possibility that geometrical perfection would become incarnate in man. Unfortunately, those yearnings for perfection were not realized. A tropical version of the *gulag* has flourished in America, but Europe has proved incapable of achieving the utopia promised by the New World. It was not More who prevailed but his contemporary Machiavelli. Today man's life is ruled by a law of terror as rigorous as the laws of gases or gravitation. This no exaggeration: when the state does not practice terrorism, the people do. Hitler and Stalin succeeded in inventing a science as precise as Newton's and Boyle's, and they left us a world that grows less hospitable every day. A new unlivable life, which we all live, since we all live under the threat of some manifestation of the gulag: locked in jail or in fear by the state or imprisoned in our homes for fear of the street and its new masters, the terrorist and the thug.

Public space, no longer for everyone, is for no one. The street has new masters, as does thought: the censor and its obverse, the propagandist. Neither ideologies nor consumer products are given to thought; they live from submissiveness and sales. Their poetics is the prosaic. Carnivals of faith, when the ancient metamorphoses were revived by Christians disguised as grotesque figures and devils, have been replaced by the carnage of political parties. When hell comes out into the streets, it no longer entertains nor is entertained by outwitting prohibitions; rather it imposes prohibitions. Hell comes out to kill, to prohibit life.

The Geodesic Pineapple

The fall of Constantinople to the Turks toward the middle of the fifteenth century was one of the events that made way for the surprise of the discovery. Centuries before, the city had become an important commercial center, through which Europe received the products of the Orient. Among those products, spices were particularly important. To the Orient, Western culture owes not only its religions but also its art of cooking. If it is impossible to conceive of *deus absconditus* without the image of Varuna hidden in a drop of water, it is equally imposible to conceive of desserts made without cinnamon, ginger, or that *zukkar* the Arabs found in India and the crusaders tasted in Antioch. Thanks to the Conquest of Constantinople by the Venetians, the luxuries of the eleventh century had become necessities. What is more, Marco Polo was born in Constantinople, to a family engaged in Byzantine commerce.

In 1453 recipes created the need for maps. Culinary art provided navigation with a strong impetus, literally orientating it. As plates began to seem incomplete, the roundness of the planet became complete. The Earth was ditched as a plate so that plates could once more be dishes. Savvy and savor spring from the same zest, just as spices and space arose from the same appetite. Latin still says this: appetite is from *pĕtĕre*, to head for a place. There's a dessert that says the same thing, and says it even better: the heavenly "bacon" known as *tocino del cielo.*

The Admiral's persistent belief that Cubanacán was the kingdom of the Gran Khan was not mere coincidence. On June 12, 1494, barely two years after Nebrija published the first map in the Castilian language, Columbus made his captains and crew swear that Cuba was "the start of the Indies." Possible punishments for withdrawing this oath included a very literal, radical withdrawal: the tongue. Nor was the wealth of details mere coincidence as the first explorers told of savoring surprising new tastes: chocolate, tobacco, tomatoes. How could it seem strange, then, that Oviedo devotes so much space to that most unusual flavor "they call pine although it is not"? Recipes, maps, grammars everything referred to the palate, the tongue. America as cornucopia. The New World was called to replace an ancient city. The exotic supplanted the urban. Or better, an exotic market supplanted a Byzantine one. "And after looking carefully and considering everything we had seen," Bernal Díaz says, "we turned to look at the immense plaza with its hordes of people, some buying and others selling; the murmur and hum of their voices and words alone could be heard for more than a league, and there were some soldiers in our group who had traveled to many parts of the world, to Constantinople, all of Italy, and Rome, and they said they had never seen a plaza so well proportioned and designed, nor such a crowded one." A market that is a hum, a gigantic hummingbird. How not to believe it? When, with Bello, the pineapple proves to be as appetizing as ambrosia? And how to doubt it when, with Zequeira, the pineapple proves to be even more appetizing than ambrosia? And how to deny it when the pineapple's rare and exquisite flavor could cause such loss? Tongue tried: tongue tied. A leap from savor to surprise places the pineapple on Olympus. Makes it sacred, petrified.

This same context also allows us to approach a poem like "Someone Puts a Pineapple Together," Wallace Stevens's striking ode to the pineapple. The pineapple as puzzle. In his "Notes Toward a Supreme Fiction," a poetics of abstraction, Stevens had mentioned the pineapple. With it he had synthesized a landscape and a season: "There was an island beyond him on which rested,/An island to the South, on which rested like/A mountain, a pineapple pungent as Cuban summer." In "Someone Puts a Pineapple Together," he stresses this miniature. Fruit turned into landscape. "The momentary footing of a climb/Up the pineapple, a table Alp and yet/An Alp, a purple Southern mountain bisqued/With molten rings of related things . . ."

According to Stevens that small, purple south is a totally artificial nature. His description, like Oviedo's, will be highly visual. Once again, text and drawing occur as illustration, almost literally. Except that Stevens will carry plasticity to an extreme abstraction. He paints nature as "still" life, but in order to get beyond the frame of the immediate: from the object on the table and the small reality conceived as a proportioned, reasonable chain of objects, he departs in search of total reality, in search of his longed-for "supreme fiction." His poem, which in all aspects is out of the ordinary, begins with a paradox, one that deals more with great Christian metaphors like the Trinity or the Resurrection than with Eleatic thought. On this "husk of Cuba," everything is possible: "The profusion of metaphor has been increased." Fruit is telescope and kaleidoscope. The poet is once again astronomer, and he refutes Copernicus, Kepler, Bruno, Galileo: "It is as if there were three planets: the sun,/The moon and the imagination, or say/Day, night and man and his endless effigies." Stevens goes further than Bello or Zequeira, he goes further than a mythology that deep down is only ornamental. Moving from mythology to theology, from paradoxes to miracles, he encounters greater mysteries. Oviedo and Zequeira are left far behind. Here the metaphor, above all the metaphor of the infinite, is not rational, is not a labyrinth of appearances and numbers. Truth, profound reason, is much closer to Origen, Tertullian. And at the beginning of the poem, a landscape of mental corners, the following dimension is suggested: "The angel at the centre of this rind,/This husk of Cuba, tufted emerald,/Himself, may be, the irreducible X/At the bottom of imagined artifice." Later in the poem Stevens risks even more:

He had not to be told

Of the incredible subjects of poetry.
He was willing they should remain incredible,
Because the incredible, also, had its truth,

Its tuft of emerald that is real, for all
Its invitation to false metaphor.
The incredible gave him a purpose to believe.

Shadows, horses, knives cut through the mind. On the edge of metaphors, Zequeira runs toward invisibility, toward transparency. Tertullian holds on to his faith in spite of his reason; he bases it on the irrational, on desire, on blind sources. A savage, magic, tribal thought to explain miracles and mysteries. No, not to explain: to accept, believe. The very syntax of his famous argument seems impossible. His conjunctions must form a chain of antecedents and consequences from what cannot be related. The unconnected connected: reason is thrown out of orbit, but faith holds on, gravitates. In Stevens's poem there is something like a periphrasis of *prorsus credibile, quia ineptum*. The world of poetry, illuminated almost geometrically from the center of the pineapple, from the angel or the mind, is believable because it is absurd, is certain precisely because of its impossibility. We are standing in Tertullian's shadow and in Mallarmé's as well. The pineapple turns in the poem and the poem also turns. Its axis is the mind, the number between sensation and grammar, between the immediate and geometry. The vast conjunction of the sideral and the syntactic recalls Igitur, who *literally* embodies "the infinite chance of conjunctions." So as, as, consequently, then; as such, I repeat; in short: in the pineapple total artifice is shown to be total reality. The fruit is the sum of all its complications: the dimension of incredibility—absurd, necessary—that makes belief possible.

In Which the Telling of This Bromeliaceous and Brometological Tale Is Brought to a Close

On Gallé's vases, a voluptuous, exotic flora brims with overly full, fleshy leaves that recall the animal kingdom and thus suggest yet another facet of the androgyny so evident in such transparency. Glass as aesthetics against nature, as an inversion of proportions, a displacement of primary by secondary characteristics, or open deviation. Exactly what will appear in Lezama's enumeration of delicacies. Like books, the pineapple can end up on the Index: ". . . Candies that left hazlenuts like panes of glass, translucent when held to the light, pineapples with sparkling facets, reduced to the size of an index finger; coconuts from Brazil, reduced until they resembled grains of rice, which flaunted their bushy heads again when dipped in orchid wine."

The prose of a drop of water: in the pineapple's flesh, its pulp, we see the light of the tropics, our landscape lit from within the center of that other, more intimate solar system that is appetite. Gastronomy as astronomy. Griddles, riddles. Incorporated through poetry, like anything that thrives by casting category aside, the pineapple, according to the playful exaltation of our poets, is finally triumphant, the centerpiece on the table of the gods. There we have had to study, contemplate it, like a truth greater than ambrosia, in order to see it on our own tables later, humble, ordinary, but—like bread—also capable of linking the palatal roof with the slow, almost permanent construction of the cathedral. Anything that has truly been touched by poetry makes possible a communion, an appetite capable of transforming stones, land, into a landscape, an address. Dressed by Zequeira's invisible knife, the pineapple is a world that goes through the mirror, a breath that creates images, an energy that crosses the nonexistent frontier between say and savor.

Let's recall the first verse of "*Peso del sabor*"(Weight of taste): "Seated inside my mouth," Lezama says, "I am present at the landscape." Also a dictum of Claudel that Lezama recalled frequently: "the poet is the man who without speaking senses the sense of words by their taste." Poetry as a savvy of saying through savor. Poetry as the language that speaks through man, through man's appetite. An arrow heading toward Saint Sebastian that reaches heaven. Between malediction and miracle, the poet, opening infinite doors: metaphor, image, octopus, spider. Alchemy of the verb: "bite into a crab and exhale it through the tips of your fingers as you play the piano." From claw to finger, pineapple to index, tune to tip-off.

I see the poet eating a claw of Moorish crab and returning it, now perfectly grafted, assimilated, in the weight of a hand on a high C. Crab or pineapple, a grafted hand weaves paradise from the worst threads of hell. A spark of Lezama, guffaw of words, lightning flashing in that heavenly *tocino del cielo*. Poetry as the ultimate metaphor, flesh as a taste for transubstantiation. Eight-breasted women, giants, dwarves, androgynes, at times the poem seems like a circus figure that violates all forms in order to invent the body crumbling in statues. Man in marble and ash moistens his fingers in the light of the pineapple, grabs the flesh from the crab's watchful pincers, and plays the piano.

Infinity and I

Up the ladder of smoke
I approach the gods.
Opening the window like a book,
I follow the steps of animals lent to light.
Bears, fish betting their scales as they swim,
scorpions inflamed slowly,
the trace of a blind geometer
in the vastness we now find less confusing.
Assembled points become signs, clues, hints.
Thread becomes soul, which covers us.
A world shaken by its prey.
A world whose walls the spider peruses,
the spider watching us with her skimpy needle's eye.

The dead gods talk of infinity,
I show them the enameled wafer
stuck in my childhood on the roof of my mouth.
With that clapper like wafer,
in words foreign as a matchbox, I repeat
that I still believe in them.
Repeating each name that was mine through the years,
I dance and die once again in each name
until a lone ant carries off our voices
and only an ant like silence remains.
I am the son of all families.
I am no one, I tell them,
I look like everyone.
My saliva is mercury.
My tongue sprinkles without moistening until thirst is
quenched.
My words are round, perfect mirrors
where images boil and slide.
The gods do not believe me, the gods believe in no one.
Nothing, never, no one: the loftiest altar of zero.
A pyramid of swift negations.

Dust here is snow for the poor
and wild boars are less feared than the buzz of a humming-
bird.
In each *yagrumo* a river empties.
The water flowing unobserved through its branches
finds me perched on a raindrop.
I wish Botticelli could see me.

At the head of a rectangle
Bruno postulates infinity.
The table is in London, but it could have been anywhere.
The table is a window opening on the sky,
a telescope extending its cluster of fingerprints.
Such confident error
follows the sting of infinity.
Bruno died like a bolt of lightning.
My tobacco also added a firefly to the night.
Fire reaches the points of the star
and fate, laying stones over the cradle,
looks like a cat splintering as it miaows,
a dog of silken cinders that licks us.

Today I watched the birth of a cloud.
We will always need a piece of moon.
Let's set limits, fix a center,
raise our house in all dimensions.
Beams of air and doors of fire,
walls of water, windows of earth.
Our welcome must not bristle like the *jabillo*.
Nothing in the vastness of the house
oppresses like the drop of water
that separates plowed ocean from ocean yet to be plowed.

Horace opens Book Three of the *Odes*
by clipping a rabbit's wings:
"As pilings were lowered,
the fish felt their ocean grow smaller."
Outrageously multiplied,
size remains a docile quantity,

an ox that plows the master's field twice.
But the image
—slippery, untamed, pursued—
leaps between two numbers
bearing us to the corner where the wounded animal
picks up what bones it has left.
"As pilings were lowered
the fish felt their ocean grow smaller."
A pin pierces the stag's ear;
holds it in the air, geometric, sharpened,
like the highest point of a star.
The hyperbole is an ellipsis.

Fish do not feel
the heavy birth of a pier
but the snip of navigation.
Mapped, porous, paradoxical: the world grows and ends.
Once again men and gods
kill themselves debating the size of the immeasurable.
How and how long to debate
the size of the immeasurable.
The struggle between finite and infinite,
limited and unlimited,
gods and men.
José, a peasant, told me:
"The *ceiba* has four roots, like a rocket."
The emperor believes in extension
as in the weight of an *aureus*.
There is nothing alien, he thinks,
there is nothing your phalanxes
cannot bring to the staircase outside the palace.
Borders too are an enemy army you can destroy.
Dreamed like infinity, the city
is a geometry adrift, an endless pier.
"Rome has condensed that world into the name of a city.
No matter where you were born, you live at its center."
The image of condensation
is not a raindrop but the highest tide.
A circle, whose center is everywhere,
run awry, its circumference growing wild

but always from the same center, like a streamer
uncoiled in all directions at once.

With the possible map of Aristides
Pascal will make a possible model of infinity.
Another circle, another hell, an enormous cage for God.
The image leaps, repcats itself
in the many-eyed face of Ezekiel.
City, circle, god: countless centers and none at all.
Empires where the sun never sets
end in flames.
For Caesar borders are an enemy army,
a quantity owed him by the gods.
For us expansion is the death of space.
As we cross boundaries
we do not savor the taste of growth
but the aftertaste of reduction.
That was Horace's warning.
It was Bruno's hunch
when he suggested mud as a model for infinity.
Our spheres collapse,
the gods enter their long exile.
Horace celebrates the Empire
yearning for Grecian limits.
Such nostalgia pleases me
more than a perfectly round sun.
Among infinite conversations about infinity
Bruno leaves an image of nature as ruins.
Neither earth nor water: mud.
The spot, the obscurity of guilt,
marks the step from deduction to the inductive.
I am part of that night.
Infinity and I are alike
in just a few small ways.

A Mouthful of Infinity

In Memory of Juan Antonio Vasco

Despite being mineral, the mollusc's protective shell obeys the same law as rings of xylem or the soft loose matter inside a caterpillar. Secreted from a hard center, a calcareous substance propels a logarithmic spiral, the simplest and most economical of modular progressions. *Here dynamic symmetry is invented.*

—Roger Caillois, *Esthétique Géneralisée*

A Few Questions

Reading the unreadable. Translating the indecipherable. Don't these tasks as well fall to poetry? Although it proves futile, doesn't it, or even absurd, to contemplate possibilities or impossibilities that at first glance seem downright laughable? A reading of some poems by Luis Justo collected in *El libro del fumador* (The smoker's book) leads me to raise these questions again. I raise them with a vague sense of doing something useless, autistic, and therefore exquisite. Nowadays both the questions and their possible although nonexistent answers are incapable of arousing anyone's curiosity—much less anyone's passion. Or almost incapable. *Forms of absence* have always obsessed me, though—ever since I was a boy, when my country came easy to me, until this moment when I sit down to write in a city that will never be mine. In the easy country of childhood, as I began to probe those forms, I was preparing myself for a long exile. Obviously optimism is not something unknown to me: if that were the case, I would use the experience of exile itself as just one more tool of the trade. There would be such a thing as fate.

The Invention of Stone

The Apocrypha offers a clue, which of course cannot be verified, for a suitable translation of the Phaistos Disk. Translation requires the creation of an analogy between random but absolutely definitive events and a series of signs pointing decisively toward an elusive and perhaps enigmatic meaning. That analogy proves no less difficult than inventing stone so as to then place a stone in just the right position for signs and events to converge on it like layers of possible relations. A Rosetta Stone invented rather than discovered. A Rosetta Stone engraved not only with the sense of signs but also the nonsense of acts. So that history and language would be strictly geological formations. Let's suppose that clay was a first attempt to invent stone. Let's suppose that we intuit a pulse, a nerve twitching, a moving shadow in a fossilized knowledge or feeling. Let's suppose we can look at an incrustation and discover in it the flight of a pterodactyl. That sudden interstice, which would allow us to relate unrelatable things and add up impossibilities until we got a figure, let's name that the philosophy of the arrow. Or of the shot.

Smoke and Geology

As a child I wasted hour after hour on endless handwriting exercises. It would have been better for me to do breathing exercises. Hoyle's rules appeal to me more than Boyle's laws, perhaps because they are rules rather than laws. What's certain, though, is that, like Justo, I've been bothered more than once by a "question mark big as hydrogen." On trains I sit facing backwards. I slip blindly into one landscape with my eyes peeled on another that slides quickly into the distance. On airplanes I spend hours looking at the clouds, discerning here and there fleeting forms, signs, even the outline of a syntax. For the same reason I started to smoke cigars. My first one was an H. Upmann 5 presented to me by Harry Matthews, a strange novelist and an even stranger character; I smoked it in honor of José Lezama Lima. Ever since then I've smoked in order to feel myself surrounded by absences, as if the smoke could tack me miraculously to heaven and to the island no less distant. A fumin' being. This is why I can never get free of those large but barely perceptible, diffuse, bubbly questions we can only pursue with breath. Breathing is the soul's way of keeping in step with the stars. I should have smoked my first H. Upmann 5 when I was five years old.

Ascendent, levitative, smoke perverts the laws of gravity. It's one of the two ladders for climbing to heaven. The big ladder, as the song says. Apparently Justo also glimpsed this. "I should weigh a ton," he writes, "but thinking of your eyes transports me,/it's such a strange thing to walk above ground."

With smoke we approach the gods. Smoking is a method for reading St. John of the Cross and Saint Teresa. How might history have been written if Newton had been a smoker instead of a health nut who insisted on his daily apple? When we smoke we feel the whey as opposed to the weight of existence. A sensation really no less terrible. Like opium eaters—I'm thinking of De Quincey—we know that "All is finite in the present; and even that finite is infinite in its velocity of flight towards death."

This sensation, along with the aversion I've felt for history ever since I was an adolescent, awakened in me what might be a morbid attraction for archaeology. I replace roots torn from me by the present—infinite in its velocity of flight toward death—with others that are deeper and literally pulled from the ground. Ultimately, geology attracts me more than archaeology. If there is no escaping history, I prefer to be part of a history that is truly domineering and slow.

Biblical Gossip

In the appendices of the Acts of Pilate we read that when Tiberius learned of Christ's healing miracles he sentenced to death those responsible for the crucifixion. How could you have let him be crucified? It should have been clear, the emperor wrote to the governor of Judea, that if Christ was not a god he was at least an extraordinary doctor. The crucifixion was a huge crime and an even greater stupidity. As punishment for such a monstruous error, Roman soldiers killed all the male Jews in Jerusalem. Pilate, Archelaus, Annas, and Caiaphas were arrested and taken to Rome. According to this version of events, Caiaphas died on the way, in Crete. Annas was sewn inside the skin of a newly sacrificed bull; the skin shrank as it dried, killing him slowly. Archelaus and Philip were crucified. The fate of Pontius Pilate is engraved on very wide, disconcerting spirals: they seem to wind with exquisite precision toward a single point, which was of course the governor's death. The facts are apparently chaotic, but it would be impossible to escape them. Justice, it follows from this most curious parable, is a branch of geometry.

A Library for Alexandria

"He emits an axiomatic library of spirals." An unmatched image of that reader and smoker who is Just(o). Problem: how can one be a just smoker if smoke is so imprecise? The game will permit no dodging of an issue fundamental—axiomatic—to the philosophy of smoke. A step at a time, I tell myself. Let's adopt one of Ortega y Gasset's tactics. I look in Corominas's *Diccionario etimológico* (Dictionary of etymology) under A: ATALAYA-ATLAS, ATLETA-ATRIBUIR, ATRIBULAR-AURA, AURIGA-AVAL, AVALANCHA-AVILANTEZ, AVION-AZALEA until I come to

AXIOMA, 1607. Tom. del lat. *axioma,* éste del gr. *axíoma* 'lo que parece justo,' 'proposición (en lógica),' deriv. de *axióo* 'yo estimo justo,' y éste de *axios* 'digno, justo'.

AXIOMA, 1607. Fr. L. *Axioma*, which is from Gk. *Axioma*, 'that which seems just,' 'proposition (in logic),' deriv. from *axióo* 'I consider just,' and this from *áxios* 'worthy, just.'

There's the answer: the axiomatic is just, *Justo*. We can walk unafraid into this burning "axiomatic library of spirals."

Smoke suggests a different approach to certain sensations. Sensations that call for a sufficiently inexact, sufficiently imprecise language. Another possible ambush of reality. Or irreality: let's remember that Kafka is the architect of the library and Borges its director. Smoke teaches that certain things, Ilse Aichinger would say, must be left in their "improper perspective." I find this necessary imprecision in *El libro del fumador.* "On that day"—reads a line from in "*A lo largo de una pared*" (Along a wall)—"we resemble them more if we are seen in profile." Illusions and betrayals of similarity. Does this same smoker not translate quite imperfectly and inconstantly the sensation of flight confessed by the opium eater? Does he not assert that "No one gets lost slowly, nor is there anything patient about ideas"? Justo is a translator, and he knows perfectly well that inexactness and imprecision prove useful as well as inevitable.

How effectively Magritte's humor works when he uses a pipe of words that is not a pipe to poke fun at the illusion of representation. Where doubt pipes up, we repeat, thinking of that terrible Attila, smoke, illusions will never grow again. Did Mallarmé not learn from the cigar that "Too accurate a meaning's sure/to rub out your vague literature"? Do his patches of words, his constellations, not arise from that experience, like abolishments? Can we not imagine him holding the paper ring from the cigar close to the flame and glimpsing, suddenly, the relation between the word and the blank page? Is Aichinger not looking for "inferior," which is to say inexact, imprecise words as a result of another spiral apprenticeship, this time the terrible smoke of the crematoriums?

Baudelaire, De Quincey, Michaux, Artaud, even that acid-soaked poet Timothy Leary have a place in my "axiomatic library of spirals." A labyrinth where there will always be infinitely more questions than answers.

The Return of the Statue and the Phantom

In Caracas, on Christmas Eve 1979, I was presented with 65,000,000 years. An English geologist showed me his fascinating collection of fossils and stones. I picked up a fossil and began to tell him about the Phaistos Disk. It's a round clay tablet with signs pressed in the clay. One of the signs is a man's head wearing a tuft of feathers. Isn't the unfolding and folding curious? I told him how the tuft was part of a spiral written toward the center. That ancient writing intrigued me, I explained; even though it wraps us in mystery and, like boustrophedon, tempts us to risk a brush with the labyrinth, it always leads to a center and therefore spares us any chance of a missed encounter, like spirals from a cigar when they are part of silence or good conversation. The whorls of the conch, I told him, always carry us to the sea. You touch them and a door opens. Which is why a spiral drawn toward the center suggests the idea of movement, fate. It can be the propellers on an airplane or the hands on a clock, a record by Billie Holiday or Pachelbel at 33 rpm. I did not think he understood. It can be a scratched record, I told him, or an uninterrupted thought, or memory. I spoke very quickly, as if I were running and my own breathing were wind, resistance. It can be one of Calder's *mobiles* or a Venezuelan child repeating "Six plus two are eight/ minus five are three,/I count straight ahead/backwards too you see." I lowered my voice until I did not say a dog with a mouthful of letters. I was silent when he asked what I had said. I repeated: it can, also, be this ammonite.

It embarrassed me, the enthusiasm, spiral, and hurried catalogue that I assumed was rapidly turning into a geologist's confusion. I moved to return the ammonite to its place, not on the shelf but in its deepest center, as St. John might have said of a fossil. The geologist would not let me. Take it, it's yours, I heard him say, and he put it in my pocket. I repeated no, why, what for. But I was lying. As the *cornu Ammonis* fell into my pocket, I was in Cubanacán, I was Daedalus, or Dante, I entered and emerged from the labyrinth, from hell, as if they were no more than thresholds, or letters in the mouth of a dog. In the weight of the ammonite I felt something resembling the exact center of a space I had always looked for in vain. Falling at the center of its spirals, Newton's apple and the final period of a perfect sonnet. I remembered the Phaistos Disk and my Phaistos Disk about the Phaistos Disk. I remembered Newton's disk and I turned it around and around until it became a blank page. I remembered the kaleidoscope I had bought for Oana, the beautiful symmetries of fire over sea sparked and multiplied by light and glass. I remembered the Castillo de la Fuerza, one of the points from which Havana casts its spell, and Kandinsky drawing a dot that was time. I realized again that the final period is a dot that invariably points both ways. All a round.

Pilate Dies Again

Who has not felt it? Pontius Pilate soiled his hands by washing them. Who has not considered Pilate's death a well-deserved punishment? The victim of his own guilt or of the vengeance wrought by God knows how many people during these last two thousand years, the governor of Judea died—has died—many times. That should surprise no one. Most likely he will continue to die for at least another century or two. Or forever. In my memory he is buried as a suicide, beheaded, banned. Of his many deaths, the most impressive—perhaps I should say my favorite?—awards him the dubious eternity of geometry.

According to ancient law, any condemned man who managed to see the face of the emperor was pardoned. The grandson of Apuis the Blind did not want to see Pilate, which is to say he did not want to be seen by Pilate. He did not want to pardon him. Pilate's sentence was absolutely unappealable. The doomed governor would be locked away in a cave on the outskirts of the city. There he would await his final punishment, far from the emperor's sight.

The facts are never simple. One day Tiberius set out hunting and followed a doe to the door of the prison. Although briefly, the condemned man knew what it means to experience great happiness. I imagine he could not believe his eyes or what they were about to see. He glimpsed the figure of the emperor. Immediately he pressed closer to the window, straining to see the emperor's face. His desperation did not last long. At that instant Tiberius shot the arrow. He missed the doe but not his true—albeit hidden—target.

The arrow entered the small window and killed the crucifier. Perhaps Pilate even saw the face of the terrible master of Ilyria. Paradoxically, that was exactly what brought about the completion of his sentence. For him there would be no salvation.

A Gift of Infinity

I dream that I'm making a Möbius strip with the smoke from my tobacco. Or a flattened figure eight. In the meantime, especially when I have nothing to smoke, or when I must refrain from smoking lest I spark the certain enmity of inadequately civilized noses, I draw the miraculous sign on a slip of paper and put it in my pocket. An infinity for Borges and for Hegel. Literally a pocket infinity I can take with me anywhere. It is pressed to my flesh as I walk. If I run into a close friend, I give it to him. Some of my friends understand. Others do not know how to interpret this absolute, geometric generosity. Maybe they're afraid they can't reciprocate, which is absurd, because there is no need to reciprocate. Besides it would be infinitely easy to do.

One way: give out handmade readings for smokers. Suggest that Quevedo owed one of his most famous lines to frequent puffs of Cuban tobacco: "they will be ash, but it will retain sense." Or suggest that smoke rising in the Gongoran chain toward nothingness is from the Cuban province of Vuelta Abajo.

More? Let's draw again on that smoke from Góngora: Our lives are the smoke/that will empty into the nothingness/of the fumy gate.

In addition to perverse readings of classical verse, certain poems can be given as presents, like boxes of H. Upmanns and Montecristos. For example, a poem by Mallarmé, expertly translated—smoked—by Alfonso Reyes ("*El cigarro*") or by Frederick Morgan.

The Whole Soul Summed Up

The whole soul summed up
when slow we breathe it out
in several rings of smoke
giving place to other rings

vouches for a cigar that burns
sagely all the while
the ash keeps itself clear of
its bright kiss of fire

So a choir of ballads
flies to the lip
Once you begin you must exclude
the real because it's cheap

Too accurate a meaning's sure
to rub out your vague literature

Tobacco and poetry are versions of a single fire. This sonnet has to be opened like a box of cigars. Or, to reverse that: a box of *Romeo and Juliet*s must be read. The poet, the poetics of smoke tells us, is like the smoker. A conjunction of the precise and the imprecise.

The Spiral as Translation

On the Phaistos Disk signs plot a spiral aimed at something hidden and still unattainable: a reader, the shot of an arrow whose randomness renders it no less effective. The version of Pilate's death taken from the Apocrypha, that vast medieval soap opera, is also a spiral written toward the center, which is always open, or always opens. In any case, its opening prefigures the shot of the arrow. Uncertain facts translated as indecipherable signs. Acts translated to stone by a lithic impulse in the whirling path of a spiral. Pilate peers from a stone window at a blank space that is brimmed with meaning as the arrow hums and approaches. He reads, maybe he understands, he dies. A last, fatal reading. Definitive.

The space formed by the stone is, becomes, a page. The Phaistos Disk is a clay stone and is also the blank space framed by the window of the cave. In other words, another page. Or perhaps the same one. An Eleatic language in the making, an arrow stopped in flight, a meetingplace between things headed toward death, things escaping death, and things that come and go again and again from death toward life. In order to reach that place and manage to decipher it, you must attempt the impossible. First, tighten the spiral like a screw. Next: turn into the spiral and sneak toward the center until you have it occupied. Beyond that: be both the commander releasing the arrow and the condemned man waiting for it at the window. Above all: be the arrow.

Wand, Wind, Wind

Absurd? Impossible? Let's blur the spirals made by the arrow and the disk by using spirals of something else. Hashish, opium, tobacco. Spirals identical to the ones offered by clay and legend, except for the reverse way in which they become visible. No sentence is being carried out through them. They are not moving toward something predestined, like the spiral described by Tiberius and Pilate. They are not unusual events linking one with another until they fashion a syntax, and they are not oriented toward an enigmatic center in quest of the marble of meaning. On the contrary, they are born from the center of the body, from breath, so as to seek distance on increasingly wide, increasingly diffuse waves, like geometry falling to pieces. Since their growth starts from a center, spirals of smoke are related most closely to the shells of moluscs. They too invent what Caillois would call "dynamic symmetry." Except in their case the symmetry is too dynamic: it goes up in smoke.

According to the experiences Baudelaire recounts in *Paradis Artificiels* (Artificial paradise), smoking would provide another key to that possible translation of the indecipherable glimpsed in the appendices of the acts of Pilate and on the Phaistos Disk.

"I imagine you seated and smoking. Your attention"—Baudelaire writes—"will rest a little too long on the bluish clouds rising from your pipe. The notion of a slow, successive, eternal evaporation will take hold of your spirit, and you will quickly relate that notion to your own thoughts, your own gray matter. Thanks to an extraordinary equivocation, to a kind of transposition or intellectual *quid pro quo* you will feel yourself evaporate and you will credit your pipe (in which you seem to be crouched and scrunched up like tobacco) with the strange ability to *smoke you.*"

From smoking to being smoked to going up in smoke. From making spirals to being spirals. Smoke becomes a profound link between body and mind. It plays a role analogous to that of the sacred syllable repeated obsessively in certain meditations for the precise purpose of emptying the body and making it approach an emptied mind. In the emptiness of spirals one finds equivocation, transposition, *quid pro quo*, translation of the indecipherable. A cloud of smoke will never abolish chance.

No doubt Baudelaire had this meaning in mind when he risked his quite daring and equally apt characterization of Thomas De Quincey, although De Quincey was not so much a smoker as an opium eater: "De Quincey's thought is not only tortuous; that word is not sufficiently expressive: it is naturally spiral." I would underline two words: "naturally spiral." Something like the calcareous substance secreted by molluscs to form their shells.

The link between the bluish clouds and this type of thought will never be found in *The Origin of the Species*. This link is live, burning. Rather than Darwin, then, Freud, or Mallarmé. Syntax: a spot of words. Humorous and fumous: the Apocalypsis of St. John, the Geologist. By smoking—burning ourselves—we go back to forms that are more and more elemental until we reach the amorphous, the inorganic. It is worth recalling one of Lezama's obsessions: the hypertelic. Thanatotic desire is realized to the extent that death holds meaning, in other words in an unforeseen way, as an apogee of the obscure, teleological will.

We become molluscs, then ammonites, and finally earth, smoke, dust, nothing. We feel our blood turn to ash. Ash shooting through us like the shot of an arrow: the Quevedian convergence in *sense* of feeling and signification. As we smoke, the vertigo of the finite that is infinite in its velocity of flight toward death lets us escape from the circumstantial and enter atavistically a time out of time. We are no longer segments of that tapeworm called history. We are now, finally, an instant in stone, geology.

A Memory

When my father's friend smoked he discharged the smoke from his fabulous H. Upmann as he might have discharged overly nosy servants. He made small circles of white, gray, blue. They were perfect. Or they seemed perfect to me. A circus of infinite rings. Acrobats, beasts, diabolically circular clowns. I could not take my eyes from them. I could not even blink. They were as precise and round as if they rushed through his mouth straight from Euclid's hand. Yes, they were perfect. As I followed them, my vision blurred. It blurred again—forever, I feared at one moment—when the deceptive firmness of their form was erased while I watched them grow wider and wider. Using my shyness to overcome a fear of ridicule, more than once I dared to attempt the impossible. I tried to grab one of those circles with my hand. No luck. They were like rings of ghosts. I was destroying the form that rose perfectly toward its own destruction, and when I opened my fist it would be always empty. This was like taking apart a toy and not knowing how to put it back together. Except that here the strange toy came apart by itself. I was very young. My father's friend must have laughed at me. Of course he laughed at me.

That man will never know how grateful I am to him for this game. My father's friend was my Prometheus: he gave me fire. Or at least smoke. Today I see those small adventures and misadventures as one of my earliest apprenticeships in the deep. My vocation was born there, perhaps entirely. My search for exact although evanescent, useless, perfect, imprecise, easy, difficult forms. Through the years, as I have met with exile and fleetingness not only in time but also in landscape itself, recalling those spirals has enabled me to discover the possibility—the necessity—of becoming a conch. I too am a builder of ruins.

The Tomb of Senmut

Beneath the sky in Turgua
you imagine the tomb of Senmut,
greatest among the great.
Constellations and gods in profile
are engraved on the walls, the ceiling.
Lines, shapes, colors:
signs that burst on stone and create four frontiers.
Orion, in the south, turns his face toward Sothis.
You are buried, as told by the heavens
placed by hand within hand's reach.
Light is mineral and hard and totally black.
A river that slowly prods its coils.
A lode in the startled ninth bed of the eye.
To see so far light must be totally black.
Stars watch you from the fish.
Scales, blazes of flesh, gills that cannot die.
Everything sparkles, everything is, everything breathes.
Not enough, the water you drank with your name
or the day smeared on the wall.
Not enough, the voices promising more ash,
discrete ice baptizing the gaze of beasts.
A transparent eyetooth tears your flesh made of night,
and exposes the god hidden in a drop of water.
Squander of infinities: the gaze
rests on a firefly
that never rests.
The soul, you remember, wanders among trees.
Absence is contagious.
So much sky waiting to be sunset.
You reach orbs, fruits;
darkness offers you billions of seeds.
A parade, all creation accompanies a dead man.
Celestial bodies pass in procession.
Cycles, celebrations, seasons:
Senmut's gods were born from such routine,
like Senmut himself. You also are born from time to time.
Your image is drawn on a calendar of ash.

Above all is order.
Below all is stone.
Body, soul, ka.
Once more, a passing firefly.

Essay in Smoke

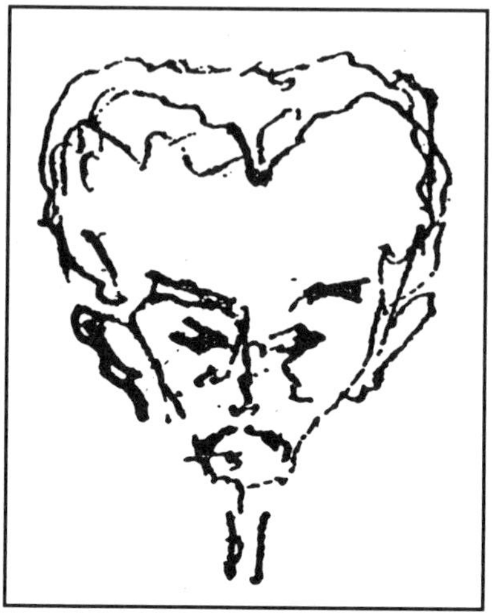

The gods will not appear to everyone.
—*The Odyssey*, Book 16

Latin for Taking It Back

One of the nicknames given to Croniamantal, the assassinated poet, is in Latin: Quoniam. According to Apollinaire's not at all Apollonian narrator, this frequently refers to the off color parts in the popular tales of the Middle Ages. But in Latin, *quoniam* is a conjunction meaning *since*, *because*, *now that*, *after*. Croniamantal, then, is another incarnation of that race whose belief in the absolute prompts the search for an Orphic interpretation of the universe and the hope of fixing or reducing chance to infinity. His immediate antecedent is Igitur, whose name derives from another Latin conjunction that means *and so, well, therefore, then*; *well then, I repeat*; *in short.* Other antecedents vanish on the walls of time. Croniamantal is a cross of two fossils: the Cro-Magnon and the Neanderthal.

There is nothing remarkable about the fact that these two figures are embodied as syntactic figures and specifically as conjunctions. An orphic autism as the reverse of surrealist automatism: Igitur and Quoniam are anachronisms, pure, perfect links, ghosts of a lost relationship between man and the cosmos. Born of words, words themselves, and words that exist only as functions dependent on other words, they both seem to disappear in the tangle of mechanical, obligatory relations:

conjunction. (from L. coniunctio, onis) Gram. Uninflected part of a sentence that denotes the relationship between two sentences or between the members or words of sentences. It always joins or links those members or parts grammatically, although at times it might indicate an opposition or difference in meaning between them.

Igitur and Quoniam, however, represent yet another of the forces inherent in language. Its ultimate root, in fact: the intuition of a possible order and a possible relation binding everything that exists. Hence their names in Latin, root of roots, source of etymologies: thanks to the ritual prepared by St. John's du(m)b act, they are purified—perfect(os).

"Everything that exists," at last we read a sufficiently imprecise definition of the desired conjunction, "owes to its race having been pure, perfect; to its purity, its perfection having been torn, for Being, from the Absolute, leaving only an Idea that borders on Necessity; to this Act proving perfectly absurd, except as a (personal) movement restored to Infinity; and to Infinity having been *fixed*, finally."

Visible appearances of the invisible, Igitur and Quoniam are embodied in words that are conjunctions. Instead of conjugating, however, or conjoining, as it was once called, they conjure words and vanish in silence and nothingness. Through them, if only for an instant, we manage to avoid the presumptuous cage of language and submit to a larger order, a higher truth. We are connected to the void, then, not through grammatical but astrological or astronomical conjunctions. For an instant you and I and everyone inhabit a single celestial house.

In *Le Poète assassiné* (The assassinated poet), a modern version of the Orphic legend, Tograth's guffaws condemn Croniamantal to death when, like a cloud, the impassioned Croniamantal turns into a mediator between history and eternity, the high and the low, God and man:

I am Croniamantal, the greatest of living poets. I have often seen God face to face. I have withstood the divine glare, which my eyes tempered. I have lived eternity. But the hour having arrived, I have come to stand before you.

Tograth, the assassin of this Orpheus, is an infernal manifestation of Orpheus himself. Torn to bits by the Maenads, it is Orpheus who tears Orpheus to bits. The poet whose song calms the winds is conquered by Tograth, who scatters the clouds or unleashes the storm and carries it where he wills. Sermon seems to triumph over song, prose seems to conquer poetry. But we know that by letting himself be torn to bits Orpheus succeeds in traversing the world of the living and the dead and thus becomes an even more marvelous, perfectly pure song. Both Quoniam and Igitur attain nothingness, or less, so that song can always start from scratch.

It is possible to "follow the burial" of these conjunctions, to participate in the Orphic funeral rites at their root. Igitur lies down in the tomb: "on the ashes of stars, the undivided family ashes, the unfortunate figure was lying, after having drunk the drop of nothingness lacked by the sea. (The empty flask—madness—is this all that remains of the castle?) With nothingness gone, what remains is the castle of purity." Croniamantal's tomb is his own statue in nothingness, the void:

In the clearing, the bird of Benin set to work. In a few hours he dug a hole about half a meter wide and two meters deep. . . .

The bird of Benin spent the afternoon sculpting the interior of the monument in the likeness of Croniamantal.

The following day the sculptor returned with some workmen who lined the well with a wall of reinforced concrete . . . so that the void was shaped like Croniamantal, and the hole was filled with his ghost.

Two days later, the bird of Benin, Tristousse, the prince of poets, and his lady friend returned to the monument, which was filled with the dirt that had been removed, and there, once night had fallen, they planted a beautiful poet's laurel. . . .

Igitur ends up on the ashes of stars, Quoniam underground beneath a laurel—in the statue in nothingness that holds his ghost. Castles of purity at each end of the vertical.

Another example: disguised as Icarus, Orpheus writes a marvelous cloud poem in the sky. He is Altazor with his parashoot. Acrobat and pilot. A master of Skywriting. Of course the clouds scatter; words break apart; the spectacular flight ends up a fall. A failure? In *Altazor* Orpheus is language itself, which has been torn to bits at the end of the poem. But as this happens, another song springs forth like a redemption, intoned by the wind, pure and orphic:

Campanudio lalalí
Auriciento auronida
Lalaí
Io ia
i i i o
Ai a i ai a i i i i o ia

As he dies, Altazor turns into an *auronida*, a son of the aura. The final exclamation is song itself as a miraculous conversion of essences. Pain will be eased, will be joy. It will be a soft, gentle wind. One capable of dispelling complaints and representing, as symbol, the poet's vague craft. A wind also capable of letting the poet cagily pronounce his beloved's name forever without ever saying it. "L'aur'amara fa'ls bruoills brancutz/ clarzir . . . " "Ieu sui Arnaut qu'amas l'aura." Arnaut Daniel shouts to the four winds a name hidden in the wind. His pronunciation shelters and protects it. When pronunciation successfully mimics the wind—an orphic miracle—it can veil a complaint while repeating it infinitely.

According to an unpublished essay from 1980 that no one is ever found "Reading Reading"—such is its title—this is exactly what Shakespeare, that unexpected precursor of mariachis, achieves in Sonnet 104. To quote Shakespeare, or Shakspere—Whitman's spelling tries to pronounce air, wind: "To me, fair friend, you can never be old,/For as you were when first your eye I ey'd,/Such seems your beauty still . . ." Eye I ey'd: the pronunciation leads inexorably from English to Spanish. The meeting of gazes, flip of the biblical eye for an eye, is reduced to a mirage in the mirror of language. Rings of smoke abolished by later rings. Gaze disappears, pronoun disappears, as the beauty of the beloved will no doubt disappear as well. But the lament, the lyric is left. In miniature, and as a tribute to love, the miracle of tongues is repeated. A petite, very pagan Pentecost: Eye I ey'd: ay, ay, ay. High in an English whose roots are lost in the howling of wolves, the exclamation of our Romantic poets and our popular music beats and echoes powerfully. Jorge Negrete and Fosforito would see eye to eye with me.

Poetics of Smoke

Tobacco and syphilis were two of America's first gifts to Europe. A holy vice and a venereal disease. It happens that syphilitics were the most frequent users of tobacco among the sixteenth-century colonists: "I know that some Christians already use it," Gonzalo Fernández de Oviedo says, "especially those afflicted with sores." The disease was to become rampant in Europe—particularly in France—the vice as well. "The great pox" came to be known as the "French disease": "syphilis" is derived from the name of a character in Hieronymus Fracastorius's poem *Syphilus, sive Morbus Gallicus*. Tobacco was not transmitted by blood but by poetry. Flower of evil and artificial paradise, as it passed from Baudelaire to Mallarmé it became a poetics, another French disease.

Free verse and prose poem, a fresh experiment and above all a passionate poetics of reading, a star chart, drawing, song, musical score, theater of the spirit where even paper has a role—as if for an instant ancient papyrus awakened the gods in order to announce the challenge posed by this nascent, radical hieroglyphic—hypothesis and alchemy, prism, symphony, laboratory for the subdivisions of the Idea, *Un coup de dés* (A throw of the dice) has not ceased to disquiet and astonish since it was published in the journal *Cosmopolis* in 1897.

The poem seems both to evoke the theology and science of distant centuries and to anticipate twentieth-century physics. On the one hand, it is impossible not to feel the ancient music of the spheres in the conjunction of musical score and star chart embodied in the poem. On the other hand, the idea of spacing reading so as to accelerate or diminish movement—a method of scanning lines that for some readers have neither feet nor head—links the notions of space and time so closely that it fuses them, creating a spacetime for poetry through the *simultaneous vision of the page*. Finally, *Un coup de dés* places thought in an orbit very close to Heisenberg's principle of uncertainty. Thought fits, or, rather falls, in the cage of chance; it is impossible to escape chance, despite an heroic effort to place a limit on infinity. The fundamental phrase, which is the title, "A throw of dice will never abolish chance," continues until the very last line, "All Thought is a roll of dice."

Typography underscores the idea that in essence we are reading a single, irrevocable, interminable, abysmal phrase. Scattered throughout the poem—on its only page—and mounted in the largest of the types used, the title is foregrounded continuously. The last verse, in the smallest type, occupies the background. This is doubly true in both instances: because of the order of reading and because of the spatial expansion or contraction implicit in working with different types. The throw of dice ends in another throw of dice that is the same one and the same as always. Dice, words, ideas, types run across the page until they are lost in the mind. Poem of blank spaces, music of silences. We see, read, hear the forms of absence. Verbal phrase and musical phrase tend toward extreme purity: they expand in silence and they express it. Drowning out, drowning in quiet. The idea empties in an abyss of infinite possibilities, as does the poem. Poem? Drawing? Score? The poem seems to embody the uncertainty of a throw of dice. It is a genre of genres. *Un coup d'ideés* that combines and generates genres.

A writing of abolishments, vague literature, tobacco smoke appears among Mallarmé's poems like a small, fleeting constellation. Another throw of dice, another fall into chance. In his poem to the cigar, the soul is slowly exhaled "in several rings of smoke/Abolished by later rings." Evanescence suggests a perfect—sufficiently imperfect—syntax for language that is articulated beyond all possible conjunctions, in impossible abolishment. On the blank page, a single word shines, wiping out that blank page and wiping out itself. It is the word *abolish*. Everything is emptied of meaning in order to draw us closer to meaning: to write is to erase the blank page with words that erase themselves. More than text: tissue, writing laces, lace is. Signs that dissipate and therefore make visible the invisible and the inaudible audible. Perpetual dissipation of meaning, that form so precarious and so human for drawing us close to infinity as the reverse, emptiness, or negation of form.

Smoking and writing blend in an extreme, strict poetics in which meaning blossoms because words are silenced. Conceived in terms of painting, as an absence of words, writing will be an apogee of intentions and sensation. Toward the end of 1864, Mallarmé wrote: "Inventing a language that of necessity must spring from an absolutely new poetics which could be defined in a few words: *Don't paint the thing, but the effect it produces*. Verse should not, then, be composed of words but intentions, and all words should be snuffed out in the presence of sensation." A poetics implosive for writing and explosive for reading. A poetics of the reader. Also, of course, a poetics of the smoker. Words will be "Rings of smoke/abolished by later rings": they will be drawn in and puffed—snuffed—out, until if only for an instant the poem becomes pure sensation.

Kasimir's Cloth

There is a page in *Paradiso* that faithfully translates the poetics of smoke: *Don't paint the thing, but the effect it produces*. What is more, this involves a translation of the blank page into Latin's din and the excessive ease of phrases' false faces.

Another phrase that when referring to Señora Augusta, Grandma Cambita, doña Carmen Alate, had about it something of a Druidic embossment, the most untouchable familial distance, where faces seemed to dissolve as if we were looking at them under water or they were always incomplete and nascent, marked the Pontus Euxinus of the family line, and when she was said to be the daughter of an oidor *or "hearer" in the High Court of Puerto Rico, it was that word* oidor, *heard and savored by José Cemí like the impossible key to an unknown world that recalled the Empress Plotina's stone face in the Palazzo Capitolino, where, because of its peeling paint, the rocky cowl that forms her nose creates the impression of an Egyptian face from the Dipylon Age, which reveals the youthful condition of its skin as the strips of linen are torn off, thus causing a novel effect where time intervenes like blind but precise artifice, abolishing the principal qualities achieved by the artist and adding others he would have found humbling since they devised for that face in stone the new solution he could not even envision. To us time seems to mock time there, since, even as it pounces fiercely on the stone face and wins a first momentary victory by peeling the paint from its nose, that same nose reappears, rhyming or conversing with the face that has remained unchanged. The word* oidor *thus marked a boundary, the limit of the family where no further definitions in blood or surnames could be established, although at the same time it filled that horizon with Greek dolphins and salmon, with lotus-bearing tortoises like those found in Hindu mythologies. It was in this way, that when the phrase* the oidor's daughter *popped up in family conversations, doña Cambita assumed the stature of a dual divinity; one manifestation was old and gnarled, barely reconstructible, its obverse was a maiden returning from exile, who emerged from the forest accompanied by a young nobleman invariably asleep in her arms and a startled antilope that looks with endless distrust at the phlegmatic king who comes forward to embrace his daughter.*

The word *oidor* echoes until it is eclipsed by wave after wave of impressions. Words take on prefixes that abolish one meaning to impose another. That undermine and provoke. That empty and multiply words like abolishments of words: an untouchable, unending, unchanging, unfinished peeling. Prefixes are deceptive: they peel words by adding syllables. Nevertheless, they reflect the throng of sensations perfectly. An infinite stumble. A true labyrinth of the ear for the ear: the present of the hearer of the *oidor* is lost in the distance. It spirals within the center of a conch. Vanishes, like smoke.

Virgilio Piñera has also fallen on spirals of smoke into Cubanacán. It happened, we read in *La isla en peso* (Shouldering an island), when he explored certain key words—mantras of the Cuban world:

I pause on certain traditional words:
downpour, siesta, plantation, tobacco.
With a simple gesture, hardly even onomatopoetically,
I pass titanically over their music.
And say: water, midday, sugar, smoke.
I combine:
the downpour beats on the backs of the horses,
the siesta tied to the tail of the horse,
the plantation devouring horses,

the horses disappearing stealthily into the dusky emanation of tobacco.

The last wave of the Siboneyes while the smoke passes through the pipe
like the cart of death.
The last gesture of the Siboneyes
and I dig in this earth for idols to make myself a history.

Words as archaeology: digging like a prefix in the familial mantra, Lezama found an idol to make himself a history. José Cemí, literally, is the ancient *cemí*, the God. He hears the word *oidor* and, like one of the pack, joins the chorus of howls seeking each other in the night. Eyetooth of origins, rings of smoke abolished by later rings: he speaks, he speaks to us in dizzying associations. Porous prose, tobacco leaves the leaves of books, the images catch fire and cross our gazes like the constellations in Senmut's tomb. Juan de Zabaleta, in an image that would perhaps have drawn a loud guffaw from Lezama, says even the cleanest of hands have pores and pores emit smoke. Lezama felt tropical heat as the birth of constellations on his skin. The suns were closer to that sensual mulatto Mallarmé than they were to Senmut.

We fall in love with skin, he says in the first paragraph of the "*Coloquio con Juan Ramón Jiménez*" (Colloquium with Juan Ramón Jiménez), *we gaze invariably at the same skin that covers us like a star chart. Skin, gaze, sidereal cartography. Later it turns out that skin does not correspond to body, which should answer for skin and gaze. The crystal snake proceeds, pursues itself, leaving behind its skin, which has become shadow, an arrow passing over the shadow, a wall that collapses on the inflated back. The crystal snake is atop another skin now and we are convinced only slowly that what was skin is now role, roll, that paper falls with the elegance of a leaf crumpling. When we were expecting the green leaf, the electric, purple leaf appears, the leaf that grows on backs and foreheads like a head of hair seen under water, like a cluster of fish revolving on a very fine, eternal crystal. Afterwards, skin, blood from smoke. A strong hand squeezes, strangles a lemon, defines a throat.*

Stages: skin, the skin of a glove, skin stuffed. A crystal snake: style, manner, the convention of sensibility. One day we mock the first of them. Lives multiplied by thrones, authority, devils and angels could perhaps not achieve the second, so as to answer for everyone once and for all but remain definitively in failure, collapse, silence.

Blazing on skin, the star chart springs from neither a page of the Zohar nor a French poem. It springs from blood. Light and darkness conjugated miraculously in the astronomical order are summoned as a possible, desired order for the chaos of being mulatto. I remember one of Lezama's very astute observations, told to me by Lorenzo García Vega: "The fullest—purest—expression of mulatto poetry is summed up in a line by Andrés Nuñez Olano: 'I synthesize an unbroken will to asceticism.'" Like Nuñez Olano, not like Guillén—with his mulattoes á la Broadway musicals. This is how the body speaks as it dissolves in bodilessness. This is how blood speaks when transubstantiated in smoke. Soul and will to asceticism: the synthesis of being mulatto erases body. More precisely, that synthesis is a superposition of two colors. The tormented mulatto soul develops an unbroken, suprematist will: it searches, always in vain, for Kasimir Malevich's white on white. But Malevich's elusive, treacherous suprematism is no hideaway. Cashmere is usually a black fabric and it is made with merino wool, in other words from sheep and ewes that have big wide snouts and bodies covered with short curly hair.

A synthesis or superposition of Lezama's two paragraphs suggests how mulatto suprematism creates Kasimir's cloth: "peeling, tearing off strips of linen until reaching skin that did not match a body, since an Egyptian face appears in the face of the Empress Plotina, sloughs of the crystal snake, the paper falls, and the green, purple, electric leaf like heads of hair or faces seen under water, incomplete, dissolved, skin underwater, skin of a glove, skin mounted under glass, blood of smoke that reveals its youthful condition and soars to the boundary, the limit where it was no longer possible to establish definitions in blood and surnames, we fall in love with skin, hardly reconstructible, endless, gnarled, untouchable." Abolishments: the body dissolves in bodilessness. Beyond Grandma Cambita, the *oidor*: white. Beyond the Empress Plotina, the Egyptian woman: black. Chess board and checkmate. Cemí is a god disinterred only to remain definitively in failure, in collapse, in silence. But words have managed to transubstantiate his blood into rings of smoke.

Spirals of Smoke and the Letter S

The intuition—concealed and one could say secularized—of a sacred language in spirals of tobacco passed from the indigenous to the colonial world and survives to this day. In the first place, as ritualism developed, it extended progressively from smoking to the minute, often exorbitant care lavished on the cultivation and production of tobacco. To see the miracle through from seed to smoke, involves a craftsmanship capable of raising cathedrals or pyramids. A craft that will sink a man's ship, according to today's wise men.

The spirals of our Gothic rise from a liturgy. A liturgy where the invisible is playfully and furtively manifest as gospel in the reading of newspaper serials. Among us, smoke, rather than fire, searches out the library. In *Paradiso*, recalling how her father raised tobacco, Grandma Munda says that "he worked with the care shown by someone deciphering an ancient writing." As they sowed, watered, raised, and harvested tobacco, the parents of her grandfathers deciphered hieroglyphics. Lineage protects its origins; it reads and rereads our genesis of smoke; copyist and librarian, it preserves the fleeting, winding writing that will also be deciphered by the smoker. The fathers of the grandfathers and the sons of the grandsons feel blood in their smoke. We are all carriers: it's a gene in our symbolic world. The race known by its pronunciation and breathing—because of how it inhales S's and smoke—possesses a sacred alphabet that conjugates heaven and earth in infinite spirals. This laborious and miraculous collaboration in blood and smoke is reflected in the quality of tobacco. The anonymous grower and the anonymous craftsman make possible the great brands: *Partagás, Upmann, Montecristo, Romeo y Julieta*. There is nothing remarkable about this: in every language the great creations are made possible by anonymous growers and craftsmen.

The second and singular step with which the ritualism of smoking is concealed in the craft stresses the survival of the ancient language, of the origin: the *lector* or reader in a tobacco factory is an atavism; he is the Taíno grandfather who still relays the word of our ancient *cemiés*.

There are three factors that contribute to the magical richness of the soil in Vuelta Abajo: its volcanic origin; its chocolate color, which suggests another sacred product of the American world; and its great depth. But neither the soil of Vuelta Abajo, nor the centuries-old care in the selection of leaves and seeds, nor the indisputable skill of its craftsmen can fully explain the quality of Cuban tobacco: it is the *lector* who bestows that strange and unchanging aristocracy. To leaves being rolled meticulously he transfers the spell of voice and texts. Gutenberg and Mallarmé dissolved in an oral, oracular world: texts printed by the voice on leaves of tobacco. Words that will literally be smoke rings. The leaf of tobacco is a more austere, more pure blank page.

The craftsman's hands follow the tale: this *oidor* even has an ear in his hands. The sirens call him and he makes a conch with their voices. He rolls the tobacco, filling it gradually with phrases and characters, tones, accents that will later be revived by fire. Smoke makes visible these invisible presences. With a *Montecristo* or a *Romeo y Julieta*, the courtship of reading and tobacco will advance from the craftsmanship of production to the exquisite and ultimate craftsmanship of smoking. Not ultimate, penultimate: tobacco and ashes are read in the world of witchcraft. Reading as book burning: we are consumate decadents whose vice lets us reduce Dumas and Shakespeare to rings of smoke. Apocalyptic, as if we were even more Wilde than Oscar, we sleep with Igitur on the ashes of stars. We leave the ruined ivory tower. We aspire to a tower of smoke. No: we aspire to live in a tower of smoke. The rest is only literature.

Cuban to the hilt, the spell cast by the word *oidor* lets us advance another of our pieces on the board. In Cuban tobacco factories the figure of the *lector* is traditional. In the nineteenth century, serialized novels, news items, and poems were read to the workers. Sometimes an orator replaced the figure of the reader. Cuban oratory thus reached some of its greatest moments. It is enough to recall one of them: Martí addressing the tobacco workers in Tampa. Rings of smoke abolished by later rings: at the present time there are still readers in the Socialist Republic of Cuba. These readers are of course influenced by the latest technology in addition to a strict ideology. Nevertheless, the curious tradition continues.

Magic and machine: demeaned, mechanized, industrialized, the *behíque*, lord of the sacred word, survives in the figure of the reader, the man heard in silence by the participants in the rite of the *cohoba*. The *behíque* who finally lifts his face toward heaven and relays what the *cemí* has told him, can be Martí, someone who reads selections from *The Count of Montecristo*, or an impersonal microphone, distant, cold and capable of reducing the world to slogans. Or it could easily be José Cemí narrating—we are the reader's readers—his trip bark and froth to paradise. A symbol of the universality of things Cuban, J. C. is Jesus Christ, but his first name is from a *mambí* apostle, and his surname belongs to a Taíno god.

The craftsmen listen quietly. They listen in silence, as they have for centuries. Facing them is one under a spell, and they beg him to tell everything he has seen and heard. The *behíque* speaks then with astonishing speed. Speed is what authenticates his word. It is the rush of blood bursting with light and faith. Speed exposes his effort to translate the word of the gods, and it is the hurricane unleashed: it is god himself. We are truly face to face with the *cemí*.

Cuba filled with *oidores* as the production of tobacco became a craft. The figure of the reader—*cacique* or *behíque*, José Martí or José Cemí—makes of tobacco workers and by extension all Cubans a tribe of *oidores*. That tribe, according to an old, sad song, wants to unearth a voice: "It's a voice we need, friends,/yes, a voice,/the voice of that Cuban mockingbird,/the voice of that martyred brother,/oh Martí was his name,/yes, Martí." What was heard in Martí was the deepest spiral of the sacred conch. The voice of the fossil. The spell that rouses the orator in our history or the singer in our everyday life is profoundly tribal. Here we have already followed two burials, those of Igitur and Quoniam. Let's follow two more, variations of the Orphic funeral rites. When we recall the crowds that accompanied Eddy Chibás and Rita Montaner to the cemetery we cannot help feeling a certain strangeness. We recognize an atavistic rite in a people that takes to the streets and follows its dead to the center of the Earth: the tribe gathers to bury the voice of the *cacique* and the reader, the voice of the smoker and the magician. The force unleashed by Chibás's last shot owes to that root. So does the quality of Cuban tobacco.

Anatomy of Inspiration

Anatomy as history: both the cabalist Luzzatto and Harvey the physiologist are from the seventeenth century. But long before, starting from the thirteenth century, Jewish cabalists were thoroughly familiar with both circulation and its bond with the sacred. Luzzatto was heir to this age-old tradition; Harvey's work was based on his immediate past, especially on Servet. In other words, before being discovered by physiologists and appearing in medical texts, circulation had left its traces in prophetic writing: it appeared in sacred language, as a propellent.

In 1553 Calvin was responsible for the death at the stake of Miguel Servet, the Spanish theologian who had discovered pulmonary circulation and the conversion of venous to arterial blood. Without intending to, in a form that was certainly rough and still blurred, Calvin was taking back to Geneva an inkling of the newly discovered American world: the mysterious relation between fire and blood, between quickened, magical circulation and magic circles of smoke. While Servet was discovering circulation in Europe, other Spaniards were discovering it in America. And they were discovering it in the rite of the *cohoba*, in other words, in a function both theological and physiological. No doubt the detail would have been of enormous interest to the author of *Christianismi Restitutio*. Nor should we lose sight of it when referring to the technique of automatism among the Taínos: in Europe circulation was discovered by a theologian. In America as well: head bowed, hands on his knees, the *behíque* had turned it into an instrument of sacred language. He translated it, spilled it forth in prayers and prophecy.

According to the indigenous Cubans, tobacco smoke made invisible power visible. It was writing and the abolishment of writing: fleeting, imprecise, in each mouthful a minimal, almost imperceptible Milky Way rose from the roof of a mouth until it smudged that other roof the sky, carrying the imperfect but silenced word of men to the gods. Breath blended with the vastness of the landscape; limits between the night of the lung and the constellations were dissolved.

All of the senses participated in the rite, at first one by one, then all together until they were exhausted in the distance of sensation. While the tobacco was being lit, the dominant sense was touch, which drew the flame like a trapped firefly toward the bunch of leaves, turning them round and round so as to make a perfectly burned geometry from its tip. Hearing recognized the firefly's intermittent advance; breath met fire in the barely perceptible crackling of leaves. Hearing foretold the ashes. Then palate, hearing, sight, joined the dance. Scent traced its invisible circle around the smoker; smoke repeated that circle in a hundred mandalas, and language became visible in its seeds: initials, syllables, letters. An alphabet of sensations: hearsee confusing senses, meaning explained by heresay. Since that instant, men no longer speak: the gods speak. Men listen, look, touch, savor, sniff. Senses on the lookout for sense: translating it.

When the caciques *want to consult with the* cemí *about the outcome of a war, or concerning their harvest, or their health,* wrote Pedro Mártir de Anglería, basing himself on earlier accounts, *they enter the* bohío *or hut sacred to the god and take* cohoba *through their nostrils,* cohoba *being their name for the plant that makes them instantly delirous. They rant and shriek so much that both the hut and the objects it contains are set spinning, and the men walk with their heads turned around and their feet going in opposite directions. The strength of that powdered* cohoba *is so great that taking it immediately wipes out every faculty and every sensation. Once the passing madness has disappeared, they are left stunned, with heads bowed and hands on their knees, and they remain a short while in that position, until finally they raise their heads lethargically, as if they were awakening from a heavy, deep sleep, and lifting their eyes to heaven, they recount what the* cemí *has told them.*

From the first accounts—of Columbus, Pané, las Casas, López de Gómara—we know of the relationship between sacred language and tobacco, whether taken as powder, chewed, or smoked. What stands out in this primitive Cuban cabala is not only the existence of that language prompted by smoke and translated by the lord to his companions but also a technique practiced simultaneously in one of the oldest traditions of automatic writing.

Let me emphasize a few words: "they are left stunned, with heads bowed and hands on their knees, and they remain a short while in that position, until finally they raise their heads lethargically, as if they were awakening from a heavy, deep sleep, and, lifting their eyes to heaven, they recount what the *cemí* has told them." When he described the rite in Chapter CLXVI of his *Apologética historia* (In defense of the Indians), Bartolomé de las Casas noted other details: "And I saw them celebrate their *cohoba*, and it was something to see how they took it and what they said. . . . The one who began was the lord, and until he was finished everyone remained silent; once he had taken his *cohoba* (which involves inhaling those powders through the nose, as I have explained, and is done seated on some low but beautifully carved benches called *duhos*, the first vowel being long), he held his head to one side for awhile with his arms placed on his knees, and then he raised his face toward heaven speaking certain words, which must have been a prayer to the true God, or to the one they believed was god. . . ."

The smoker's posture, as described by the chroniclers, is always the same. This is not coincidental. The rite of the *cohoba* demanded that invariable posture which is at once symbolic and practical. The body is seen from without, its gestures deeply expressive: the man lifts his face and turns his eyes toward heaven. The body as conjunction: that gesture is a bridge between god and the soul. But gesturing also has its anatomy, and in it a technical process is being carried out. The body as precipice: posture unleashes verbal extravagance. An automatic writing literally *avant la lettre*.

In the *Zohar*, Rabbi Simeon places his head between his knees and remains that way an entire night transcribing what he heard. The Rabbi Moses Hayim Luzzatto, author of *The Second Zohar*, sat with his head pressed between his knees to wait for the dictation of the holy secrets. In that position Luzzatto entered a hypnotic state that let him write at a rate four times faster than normal. The *Zohar* is from the thirteenth century and *The Second Zohar* from the seventeenth: two centuries before the discovery of America and two centuries after Jewish cabalistic tradition linked writing and the circulation of blood. Writing accelerated by accelerating and augmenting the accumulation of blood in the brain. As the Spanish proverb says, *la letra con sangre entra* (learning the alphabet is bloody work): an artificial paradise that foreshadows Harvey, Baudelaire, and the abnormal normal-school masters who will teach reading and writing, ruler in hand. Evidently the Taínos also associated sacred language and circulation. But they consumed tobacco as well, in other words they very specifically related that language to breathing. This is logical: through breath, made deeper and deeper, they prepared the voice, a bodiless writing that, like tobacco smoke, returned the visible to the invisible, blanked the page.

Translations of Light

The mirror on the head of the enchanted crane revealed the end of Montezuma's empire: in broad daylight, the reflection of a sky filled with stars. The sun and all the constellations were present, as on the roof and the walls in Senmut's tomb. They were also present when Simeon ben Yohai was about to reveal the mysteries. A flame passed over the Earth and his disciples began to tremble. And with good reason. A mad throng had been heard in the sky. Thunder, lightning, and immediately before, this: "the sun was setting," we read, "but the sky was full of signs and marvels. The sun got brighter and brighter, and it stopped in its course without setting. The moon appeared in all its glory and the stars in all their splendor. . . ." As the master spoke, the roof of his mouth became the roof over the world. His word: light.

Religions of light, of the sun, of the hurricane are an embryonic physics, astronomy, and meteorology. Also, and above all, they are exaltations of and insults to the body: anatomy. The cabalist master, the Aztec priest, and the Taíno *behíque* communicate—stage—a profound knowledge of the body and its ties to all creation. Anatomy has a hidden, plural meaning: the body is filled with wind and fire. The sun circulates in its veins; there is ether in the darkness of its lungs and its soul merges with the immense distances of the night.

The *Zohar* is a book in flames. There, all the mysteries are translated to blazing lights. "Every part of the holy name is light." Light is born from the word of God: "And it happened, in the beginning, that the sound of the word collided in the void and formed an imperceptible point, the origin of light." The master is the one who can approach light through the word. He is also the translator of light. "And the breath that leaves our lips forms curtains through which the supreme light becomes visible." This could have been said by a *behíque* of tobacco. The supreme light, call it hurricane in the case of the *behíque*, becomes visible: breath, spirals of smoke; and it can be translated by a stream of words.

Before it became a branch of medicine, a subject of study, anatomy was a religious rite; and in extreme cases this rite was vivisection and dissection. Remember, for example, the blood-curdling last supper of the temporary kings. Divided or multiplied, the body is an extravagance of energy that links the human and the cosmic. Anatomy as exaltation of and insult to the body: gape, rape: mutilations, orgies. In the cult of Ancient Mexico streams of blood translate—and maintain—the sun's energy. An anatomy lesson that would no doubt have horrified Dr. Tulp and Rembrandt, perhaps even Jack the Ripper, but one that literally lays bare the roots of ritual canibalism and the Eucharist. As Thales said, everything is filled with gods. The force and beauty of the divine is sought in the ancient *tlacamictiliztli* and in today's plastic surgery, in the millennial pyramid and the ultramodern operating room. Because even a thing so despicable as the human body is filled with gods. Even with hunchbacks, lepers, and albinos it is possible to enact a sacrifice.

A reading of the *Zohar* as an anatomy textbook would shed considerable light on the relation between tobacco, blood, and words. For example, in "Revelations Concerning Man" we read:

Don't believe that man is no more than flesh! What really makes man is his soul. And just as God forms the hidden point of which all the heavenly hosts and all the higher regions form the cover, so too is man represented by his innermost soul, of which all the parts of his body form the wrapping. Flesh, skin, bones, and the rest are only clothing, a cloak. They are not man. And when man leaves this world, he sheds all the cloaks that cover him. In spite of all this, we should not disdain our bodies, since the various parts of the body conform to the secrets of divine wisdom. *The skin represents the firmament, which is spread over everything and covers everything like a garment. Skin recalls the evil side of the universe, which is to say the element that is only external and perceptible. The bones and veins are like the heavenly chariot: the forces that exist internally, and which we consider the servants of God. Even so, all this is still clothing because only in his inner being will we find the mystery of celestial man. Thus, within, celestial man is exactly the same as terrestrial man. Since everything that takes place here below is only the image of what takes place above. It is in this sense that we understand God to have made man in his own image. But just as in the firmament we see different figures formed by the stars and planets, which tell us about deep, hidden mysteries, so also on the skin covering our bodies there are lines and forms that can be seen as the stars and planets of the body. And all of them have hidden meaning.*

The words of Simeon ben Yohai are from a a medical consultation—one of his young disciples "was painfully afflicted with maladies of the flesh"—and they constitute a diagnosis and a treatment. Reading that *skin represents the firmament, the evil side of the universe*, we recall with trepidation the star chart Lezama felt over his skin, or the page Mallarmé raised to the power of a sky filled with stars, or the firmament placed within the reach of Senmut's hand. Here the issue is different, however. Bones and veins, the master says, *are like the heavenly chariot: the forces that exist internally, and which we consider the servants of God.* Heavenly chariot: forces that exist internally: servants of God. A poetics born from the gut: anatomy as style. The physical posture assumed by the master—head between the knees—allowed him to receive the dictation of the holy spirits. If the cranium is placed near the femur, the tibia, the astragalus, and the fibula, blood accumulates in the brain. Head and heart meet in this anatomy of inspiration. Which is why bones and veins are servants of God. In a certain posture they make it possible for automatic writing, writing of revelation, to come spurting out: the stream of words.

In their rites the Mexica and the Taíno start from the same intuition and from identical elements, except that one of them establishes a different sequence between blood and word, and they both add a substance—hallucinogens, tobacco, chocolate—as an ingredient of ecstasy to sharpen the senses and accelerate circulation.

Among cabalists the stream of words follows the concentration and acceleration of blood; among the Taínos that stream also arises from an artificial and ritual circulation complemented by the consumption of tobacco. In the Mexica world, the sequence was inverted. Chanting—supervised by *tlapizcatzin*, priests devoted exclusively to this task—and hallucinogens excited the victim's body and prepared it for bloodshedding. No doubt this involved a particularly cruel ritual. But in fact there is nothing unusual about it: the mass is always a conjunction of blood and word. In certain traditions, to be effective, that conjunction demands from blood or word the speed of light. A Christian variant synthesizes all those elements—speed, blood, word—in the miracle of transubstantiation. The word of the priest transforms bread and wine into the body and word of Christ. In this way the Gospel is kept alive through the Eucharist. Sacrifice is a permanent source of energy for words, and words in turn lead to that outpouring of energy. In the miracle, the word cuts bread and bleeds it. And for an instant that broken, bled bread—could one not think of Orpheus?—brings the word of Christ back to life on the priest's lips. Light is suddenly present; time almost ceases to exist.

Occasionally, light substitutes speed as evidence of the strange, divine presence or speed is harnessed in a way that allows it to become manifest inescapably and intelligibly. Many tongues are then demanded of the tongue. In the *Zohar*, the master studies and analyzes light. Light both arises from and reveals the name of God. It has to be translated. "The sacred Point," says the master, "projects a light in four directions, so brilliant no one can bear it. Only the rays emanating from it can be viewed." Having said that, he looks at and describes the flame of a lamp. It is Valle-Inclán's *La lámpara maravillosa* (The lamp of marvels) and the Aztec *quincunce*. First he sees two lights. Then in the dark blue light he identifies many *hues*. The master as prism: not the speed of light but its composition. Its anatomy. Vivisection and decomposition of light: more lights. The name of god shines in every letter of every word of every tongue. The phenomenon had been known in the Christian world. The miracle of Pentecost as a prism: flames that are tongues and more tongues. The spectrum of light as a tongue: from infrared Elamite to ultraviolet Mede. Everything is filled with gods, and through miracles the gods will appear to everyone.

Acts of the Apostles

And when the day of Pentecost was fully come, they were all with one accord in one place. And suddenly there came a sound from heaven as of a rushing mighty wind, and it filled all the house where they were sitting. And there appeared unto them cloven tongues like as of fire, and it sat upon each of them. And they were all filled with the Holy Ghost, and began to speak with other tongues, as the Spirit gave them utterance. And there were dwelling at Jerusalem Jews, devout men, out of every nation under heaven. Now when this was noised abroad, the multitude came together, and were confounded, because that every man heard them speak in his own language. And they were all amazed and marvelled, sayng one to another, Behold, are not all these which speak Galieans? And how hear we every man in our own tongue, wherein we were born? Parthians, and Medes, and Elamites, and the dwellers in Mesopotamia, and in Judaea, and Cappadocia, in Pontus, and Asia, Phrygia, and Pamphylia, in Egypt, and in the parts of Libya about Cyrone, and strangers of Rome, Jews and proselytes, Cretes and Arabians, we do hear them speak in our tongues the wonderful works of God.

Cum complerentur dies Pentecostes, erant omnes pariter in eodem loco: et factus est repente de caelo sonus, tamquam advenientis spiritus vehementis; et replevit totam domum ubi erant sedentes. Et apparuerunt illis dispertitae linguae tamquam ignis, sedítque supra singulos eorum: et repleti sunt omnes Spiritu Sancto, et coeperunt loqui variis linguis, prout Spiritus Sanctus dabat eloqui illis. Erant autem in Jerusalem habitantes Judaei, viri religiosi ex omni natione quae sub caelo est. Facta autem hac voce, convenit multitudo, et mente confusa est, quoniam audiebat unusquisque lingua sua illos loquentes. Stupebant autem omnes et mirabantur, dicentes: Nonne ecce omnes isti, qui loquuntur, Galilaei sunt? Et quomodo nos audivimus unusquisque linguam nostram, in qua nati sumus? Parthi et Medi et Aelamitae, et qui habitant Mesopotamiam Judaeam, et Cappadociam, Pontum et Asiam, Phrygiam et Pamphyliam, Aegyptum et partes Libyae, quae est circa Cyrenen, et advenae Romani, Judaei quoque et Proselyti, Cretes et Arabes audivimus eos loquentes nostris linguis magnalia Dei.

But Peter, standing up with the eleven, lifted up his voice, and said unto them, Ye men of Jerusalem, be this known unto you and hearken to my words: For these are not drunken, as ye suppose, seeing it is but the third hour of the day. But this is that which was spoken by the prophet Joel; And it shall come to pass in the last days, saith God, I will pour out of my Spirit upon all flesh: and your sons and your daughters shall prophesy, and your young men shall see visions, and your old men shall dream dreams: And on my servants and on my handmaidens I will pour out in those days of my Spirit; and they shall prophesy: And I will show wonders in heaven above, and signs in the earth beneath; blood, and fire, and vapour of smoke . . .

Stans autem Petrus cum undecim, levavit vocem suam, et locutus est eis: Viri Judaei, et qui habitatis Jerusalem universi, hoc vobis notum sit, et auribus percipite verba mea. Non enim, sicut vos aestimatis, hi ebrii sunt, cum sit hora diei tertia: sed hoc est, quod dictum est per prophetam Joël: Et erit in novissimis diebus (dicit Dominus) effundam de Spiritu meo super omnem carnem, et prophetatbunt filii vestri, et filiae vestrae, et juvenes vestri visiones videbunt, et seniores vestri somnia somniabunt. Et quidem super servos meos et super ancillas meas, in diebus illis effundam de Spiritu meo, et prophetabunt: et dabo prodigia in caelo sursum, et signa in terra deorsum, sanguinem et ignem, et vaporem fumi. . .

—Acts 2:1-11 and 14-19

Day broke as we were en
Caballeros to La Vega, and
blessing for our souls. In the
surrounded us on both sides
side thick with flowers, bor-
tance, where thick sugar cane
mango, the horses stepped
were in bloom and the orange
palm tree still held to earth by
coconut bent, from its weight,
ceibo, *spreading its strong*
the royal palm. The tobacco
and caimitos *and* guanábanos
One's breast fills with author-
tion is courageous and affec-

route from Santiago de los
its clarity was a deep, gentle
faint light, American nature
of the road. In that country-
dered by mountains in the dis-
grows at the foot of the leafy
more gracefully: the mangoes
trees ripe; there was a fallen
its mass of wiry roots, and the
with its uneven tuft, and the
arms high in the heavens, and
was bursting through a fence,
had sprouted beside a stream.
ity and faith. The conversa-
tionate.—We dismounted at

a roadhouse to have our coffee and some bitters.—Surrounded by listeners, seated on a tree stump, there is a ragged old Haitian with fiery gray eyes, a worthless bundle at his feet, and worn-out sandals. I talk to him, my words streaming out in a French he finds bewildering, and he looks at me half-threateningly, half-mockingly. He fell silent, then, that pilgrim who had entranced everyone with his disjointed droning. People began to laugh at him: "And so another speaks the saint's language better than the saint?—"Look at him now, and there he was like a god in a banana grove."—"We were like yucca, and he was like the grater." The old man picks up his bundle and sets out to resume his wandering, biting his lips: wandering onto the holy hill . . .

—Martí, *Diario de campaña* (Field Diary), 16 February

Smoke Album

In three of the few surviving photographs of Martí—there is a total of forty–two—he is surrounded by tobacco-factory workers whom he has clearly just addressed or is just about to address. All three of the photos are from 1892, a year of intense revolutionary propaganda and fund–raising.

In one we see him at the entrance of the tobacco factory owned by Vicente Martínez Ybor, in Ybor City, Tampa. Next to Martí, General Serafín Sánchez, José Dolores Poyo, Esteban Candau, and Eligio Carbonell. The other two photos were taken in October, at Temple Hall, a tobacco plantation near Kingston, Jamaica.

In a fourth photo, taken in Key West in 1893, Martí appears with a group of Cuban emigrants who were holding shooting practice at Martello Tower, the old fort located on land belonging to Eduardo Hidalgo Gato, the tobacco manufacturer.

The last portrait made of Martí when he was still alive is quite grotesque. I cannot refrain from mentioning it, though, in this brief summary of his image and smoke. It is the account of Juan Trujillo, medic of the Second Peninsular Batallion, who was present at the combat in Dos Ríos. Today it would be called an oral portrait.

The aforementioned companies observed no details other than that they had seen two "rebels" fall, and they advanced, firing heavily; but Antonio Oliva (mulatto), the guide who was with them, went to the men he had seen fall, and when he got to where José Martí had fallen and he recognized him, he asked "What might bring you here, Martí?" but since Martí was so badly wounded, he did not answer, making instead only a contorted gesture, throwing his head back; and then Oliva finished him off with a shot from his Remington. It seems that Martí took out his revolver as he fell, since I saw him lying on the ground with his arms outstretched and the revolver on his right. After he died, I noticed that his tongue was bitten and his teeth were literally piercing it. . . .

The last speech: biting one's tongue. Chewing on it like tobacco. Silent as smoke.

It should come as no surprise that quite a few of Martí's portraits are framed in smoke. In fact it can be argued that Cuban independence was won by dint of smoke. This may explain why, rings of smoke abolished by later rings, it was immediately lost in a fake republic and a false revolution. One thing is certain: achieving independence demanded the clash of two economies, tobacco and sugar. The nomadic, literally ethereal economy of exile, and the deep-rooted baroque sugar economy of the ever-faithful island of Cuba. Tobacco was used to fight sugar cane. In order to burn sugar cane, tobacco was smoked first. A battle of heaven against earth where fire was the only victor. "The horses are disappearing stealthily," Virgilio Piñera's poem says, "in the dusky emanation of tobacco." Smoke on horseback, as in Carlos Enríquez's painting. A smoky scene screening the swarm that brought us Attila.

Let's look at the photographs again. Next to Martí at the entrance to Vicente Martínez Ybor's establishment is José Dolores Poyo. Poyo was a reader in a tobacco factory and editor of *El Yara,* a Key West newspaper. Poet and tobacconist, reader and writer meet, as in a poem by Alvaro de Campos—ring of Pessoa abolished by a later ring. The *behíques* meet, organize the rite, prepare the sacrifice. "I am nothing," says Alvaro de Campos, speaking like smoke in "Tabaquería" (Tobacconist's shop). "I will never be but nothing./I can only wish to be nothing./Except for that, within me I have all the dreams in the world." This may have been exactly how Martí felt when he posed for the photograph in Ybor City. "All action," we read in a letter from writer to reader, "enacts suffering."

Sacrifice was an obsessive theme for Martí, especially in the last years of his life. He prepared to enact something sacred: a homeland, smoke. His entire life—forty–two years, forty–two photographs—was a preparation for death. A sacrifice. "You grieve," he wrote on 25 May 1895 in a farewell letter to his mother, "in the rage of your love, because my life is sacrificed: and why was I born from you with a life that loves sacrifice?" "A homeland is an altar, an Ara, not a pedestal," he said. Cubans, it is true, prefer to recall him as marble, statue, rather than ashes. It is easier. Martí died like ashes, but "he who serves a revolution"—to conterfeit a phrase by Bolívar—"thrashes against statues in vain": during the last thirty years Cuba has been the pedestal of someone who dreamed he was Martí reincarnated.

"I know how to disappear," he assures Manuel Mercado a day before going up in smoke and entering the light. He is going to die like a good man. He is going to die like he wanted, facing the altar, the *téchcatl*, like a sacrificed warrior. "And for the cruel one ripping out/the heart to which I owe my life . . ." How can one lose sight of the *téchcatl*? The simplest reading of *Versos sencillos* (Simple verses) places him on that stone, an altar, not a pedestal. Oliva the guide, the mulatto priest is approaching. But for now the man next to Martí in the photo is José Dolores Poyo, the reader. One who knows the squeamish monster. You yourself, hypocrite reader—my likeness, my brother!

In the photographs from Temple Hall—we are still in a temple—the flag with the single star is flying. No, it is not flying: the wind has reduced it to the red triangle with the white

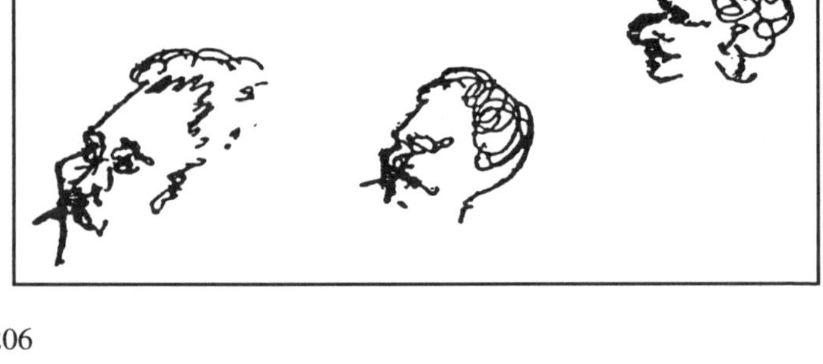

star. But the triangle is not yet red, not really. The three-colored flag appears in black and white and Martí has not yet died. In one of those two photographs there is a little girl dressed in white toward the center of the foreground. Barely visible. She seems to be hiding in her father's body; he is also wearing white. On the other side, to the right, two little boys. In the back, at the far right of one of the two groups occupying the middle distance, the group on the right, someone is holding the flag on its pole. Projected from the middle distance to the foreground, and exactly in the center of the field of vision, the flag marks the true center of the image. The flag as parallax: the star is on the horizon. Optical illusion and prophecy: the tricolor in two colors, which seems to be made of smoke and on which only the star stands out, is placed above Martí. Placed like a constellation—Ara, the homeland—above the head of the tribe, the one-man tribe. The star under a star will see stars; like smoke, he is a conjunction of two planes, two worlds. Martí is about to grab hold of the star's closest point, he is at the point of getting burnt. "Give me the yoke, oh mother," he asks in one of his *Versos libres* (Free verses), "so that/when I stand, on my brow will shine/Brighter the star that sheds light and kills." It is the Pythagorean star medieval magicians used against witchcraft. The five points that suggest the five wounds of Christ on the cross also suggest the five priests holding down the victim in the *téchcatl*: "All action enacts suffering."

Gato Got Your Tongue?

The workmen at Eduardo Gato's tobacco factory in Key West, we read in Felipe Núñez Gallardo's biography of Martí as we look again at the photograph taken at Martello Tower, *pre-*

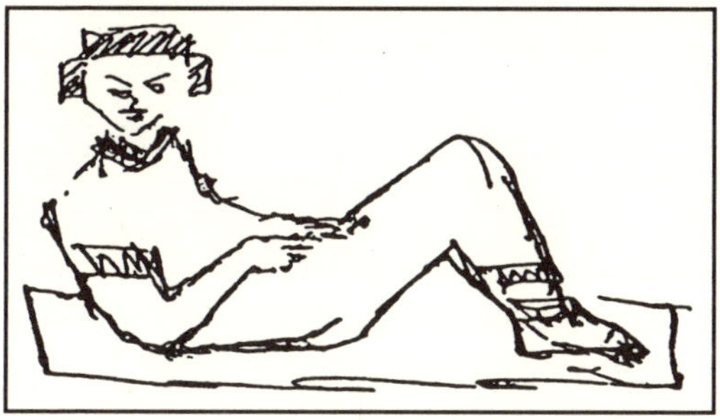

sented Martí with a silver amphora, and the women who worked there gave him a cross of shells a half a meter high, as if they had a premonition of his tragic end. A sad omen! The cross of the martyr. The chalice suggested the chalice he would drain in the midst of the singular landscape he found in the Cuban bush.

Gato was one of the most generous contributors to the cause of independence. As were his workers. "I saw you on that gorgeous Key," Martí wrote to Juan Fraga in July of 1894, "when, pounding the blades of their *chavetas* so hard it touched the heartstrings, the six hundred souls of the house of Gato greeted with affectionate madness the thin, pitiful man who had just asked them for another contribution, which they gave because of the faith in their souls, and they gave more than he asked for; I saw you at Ibor's factory, which was rather stingy the first day, because the Spaniards had the time I was sick to worm their way into the workers' hearts, but the next day the workers avenged themselves, lifting up their hearts with enthusiasm, and, like Gato's people, gave more than they were asked for; in my most anguished hours, when I don't think I'll have enough time—because, given time, there will always be enough virtue in our people—I have seen you at my side like a brother whose sympathetic gaze follows me and continually gives me strength to leave behind what strength I have left."

There is something ominous in the pounding of those knife blades that touches the heartstrings. Even happiness is expressed through a hint of pain. Another detail: it is important not to forget that Martello Tower is located on Gato's property. Martello: martel: martyr: Martí. Yes, a pounding of knife blades . . . And yet I would dare to say that we owe the only instant of levity in Martí to tobacco—specifically to Gato—perhaps because in the factories he found enthusiastic support from the owners as well as the workers and experienced moments nearly resembling happiness. I do not doubt that this levity was involuntary, which would only prove there is a bit of hot air smoking unconsciously in any Cuban.

As a Cuban not conscious of that bit of hot air, or in any case as the Cuban unconscious, on January 18, 1894, Martí wrote to General Serafín Sánchez, one of the men beside him at the entrance to *V. Martínez Ybor & Co. Cigar Factory.* "Don't let Gato peter out. Keep him hot for me." Despite

Gato's feline name, there is no question here of cat's-paw nor of keeping something in the bag. The metonymy could not be more precise: it's a question of Gato being hot for Martí. The tobacco manufacturer is hot, like one of his Havanas. And it's important not to let the flame die out. The general must have laughed aloud. And if that laughter reached Martí's ears, he must have bitten his tongue as he did one year, four months, and a day later when he faced the sarcasm of Oliva the mulatto. But maybe Martí said it with intent?

That possibility cannot be entirely discounted. Not if one has seen the zincograph made in 1879, where he appears seated on the floor with his son between his legs. He is smiling in that photo and there is a mischievous look in his eye. We could say he slipped out of focus there since he slipped out of marble. That look in his eye allows us to dream another Martí, feel his story rather than his history. For an instant the man of marble has the lightness of ash. It is an instant best kept in mind by all Cubans who sculpt—and scalp—him.

Martí and the Chac-Mol

Almost all of Martí's self-portraits look like puffs of smoke. Four of the six that have survived could be described that way. One very small drawing, not even an inch high, looks like a spiral of smoke that has just left the lips. His neck, two lines, a smoke still dense, almost tubular, disintegrates to form his face. His face is a heart. The phrase *Por América* (For America), repeated several times accompanies this drawing. *Sursum corda* and *tlacamictiliztli*: a rising of spirits and a ritual death. "They lifted up their hearts with enthusiasm," "pounding the blades of their *chavetas* so hard it touched the heartstrings," he wrote in a letter to Juan Fraga.

But one of the six self-portraits is in stone rather than smoke. To make it, Martí used as his model the Chac-Mol, the stone on which, still beating, hearts were placed after the sacrifice: a reclining man, his torso elevated and his legs arched, holds in his hand the tray on which hearts will be laid.

His head is turned to one side, his gaze lost in the distance. It would not be difficult to link the gestures represented in this stone, which passed from Tula to the Mayan and Aztec world, with that of the tobacco rite among the Taínos. His head to one side, arms on his knees, the *behíque* accumulates and accelerates blood—the beating heart—until his lethargy breaks and he lifts his head to speak.

Martí as Chac-Mol: the gestures and rites of the sacrifice are present at the hour of death. According to the account of the medic Juan Trujillo, Martí did not answer Oliva the guide. It was not possible: he was too badly wounded. But he made *a contortion, throwing his head back.* The orator nicknamed Dr. Torrent by the Guatemalans; the man whose streams of words held Cubans spellbound in Spanish and Haitians spellbound in French could not speak. He had been knocked from his horse by two shots, one of which passed through his neck: "bullet wound in the neck"—reads the description of the exhumed cadaver—"whose point of entry was below the chin by some 15 centimeters, and whose point of exit was located above the upper jaw, right side, so that his lip was destroyed." This shot replaced the *collera*, the wooden ring that during the *tlacamictiliztli* one of the priests placed around the victim's neck so he would not scream. Martí's last speech: a grimace, a *collera.* His neck and lip were destroyed.

A second shot caused the most serious wound. "A bullet wound penetrating the chest whose point of entry seems to correspond to the front of the chest, on a line with the manubrium sterni, which had been fractured, the wound's point of exit apparently lying in the rear part of the thorax, in the fourth right intercostal space, at about 10 centimeters from the spinal column." The flint blade would open the breast with just one cut under the ribs in the second intercostal space. Through it, the priest—the cruel one ripping out the heart to which he owes his life—extracted the heart.

The third shot—the one that killed Martí—was fired by Oliva the guide. It is important not to forget the mulatto's scorn: "What might bring you here, Martí?" He was rubbing salt in the wound. The Cubans had accused Martí of being Captain Araña, a cowardly "spider." Oliva, Cuban to the hilt—ay, such a sense of humor—was joking with the dying man. He was pinching him, reproaching him. Torture was his game. Hence the inexplicable, final wound in the thigh: "Another wound, also from a bullet, in the lower third of his right thigh towards the inside." He was trying to humiliate Martí, and he dealt him a finishing joke instead of a finishing stroke. Oliva is Tograth before Croniamantal, his shot a guffaw.

Deconsecration, the final part of the Mexica rite, was being carried out unwittingly. The victim's body, where a god had become flesh through sacrifice, was loaded with mana and could not be handled like just another cadaver. Depending on circumstances, it was flayed, beheaded, rolled down the stairs of the temple, eaten, thrown to the garbage collectors. Sometimes it fed Montezuma's reptiles and wild animals. Almost a century ago, Oliva the guide began the final, chilling ceremony. But the deconsecration of the Apostle continues. The veritable cult surrounding Martí reduces everything to rhetoric and statuary. Shots in marble.

((((((Parenthesis with More Smoke))))))

As I write *shots in marble,* I feel that I want to make amends to Martí. A Cuban rite capable of inverting the terms: instead of a merciless, growing desecration disguised in marble, an apparent profanation that in essence will restore the original mystery. Let the vocation of sacrifice be fulfilled in smoke and ashes.

I take a blank page, a piece of marble, and cover it with prose even more profane than this. On it I copy the report of Dr. Pablo A. Valencia, the surgeon who performed the autopsy on Martí. I now have the cadaver before me exhumed in a few phrases replete with anatomy. Fumous humus: we do not pull the *behíque* from the Earth but from the word, and we will not return him to Earth but to air. To nothingness. We erase the Latin root from our exhumation with a Taíno breath. After all, our land has gone up in smoke. Which is no doubt the reason we write so many words in exile. Exile is the homeland we have enacted so we can suffer.

I also have in front of me a book by Giovanni Papini. A few pages about recent sculpture. It pleases me to know that the first page of *Gog* is dated *Cuba, November 7*. For Matiegka, the unknown young Czech sculptor, all masterpieces die, disappear. For this reason, and also perhaps because as an albino he has an aversion to marble, Matiegka makes statues in smoke: "What difference does it make with respect to eternity if a statue lasts ten years or ten seconds, what difference if both that one in marble and this one in smoke must disappear in the end?"

I recall Igitur lying on the ashes of stars. I recall Croniamantal and the statue in nothingness made by the bird of Benin. I decide that the rite must be carried out exactly as Matiegka orders. So I repeat it precisely. Except that instead of a blackish paste as my point of departure I use a blank page stained with the description of a cadaver. Also, in order to light it, I light a cigar. I have no Cuban cigars. I use a *Cañón Rayado*, from Venezuela. I place a bit of crumpled leaf on the cadaver of words before crushing it in my hand. With the lit tobacco, I light the wad of paper. I think of Gato and laugh. But I laugh, like Darío, "saddened by fiestas." One last detail: I try to make a small heart-shaped face. No luck. I console myself with a line from Góngora that for Matiegka would summarize the history of sculpture: "in earth, in smoke, in dust, in shadow, in nothing."

))

Conch

I look at the sky: the rectangle of the window generates a tumult of forms. Capricious, unstable, unrepeatable forms that nevertheless turn an infinite profile toward resemblance. By lending itself to a spontaneous brush with the geometrical, to the seductiveness of the inflexible frame and to transparency inflexibly denied, heaven's population shows its invisible face in the greatest possible jumble of visibility. The clouds are angels. Messengers. Mediators between heaven and earth, matter and spirit. In this way the sky becomes the pure space of creation: an immense fresco by Michelangelo; the ceiling of the Sistine Chapel. As painting and architecture, heaven places itself within hand's reach, a sympathetic response to the latent Gothic impulse. A painted sky, the ceiling vaporizes architecture, erases matter, draws us closer to the creative hand of God. We fall to heaven on the spiral of a gaze that has become a prayer: in the clouds we make out the marble of cathedrals and the wooden carvings of Latin American colonial art. For centuries the Archangel Raphael has been standing on a mahogany cloud. An altar rests on cedar angels. The gaze breaks loose and passes from form to the unformed, from the heights to the highest; space turns until we feel the gravitation of the stars more strongly than the gravity of Earth; marble returns to cloud, scatters at the pinnacle of appearances and metamorphoses until it again describes the geometry of nothingness, the empty rectangle of a window, the transparency where, meticulously, as in a tiny box of primavera, the gaze places the shreds of its adventure, the sea of sight: of smoke abolished by later rings abolished by later rings abolished by later rings abolished by later rings abolished by later rings

Diamond of Wood

Neither day is day
Nor night is night
Lights and names
Halfway through time
Time is born
Motherwell says
My generation
Had no faith in the deceit of lines
In his German Cage reads
Kafka's German
I must be crazy
His German seems clear
Which ear?
A metamorphosis of language
For the metamorphosis of Samsa
Gregorian chant in this ear
Gregorian Samsa
Gregor samsara
Tune and tale
Music
          Histrionics
Nix?
        Nix
We are in Cagecoslovakia
We are and are not
Chin over shoulder
Said *German* Mateo Alemán
In his Spanish Spanish
How do you spell
Kageka?
              Cafka?
Locked in his name
Cage writhes like Samsa
Locked in his name
Cage is Samsa
                        Samsara
You
      Me
No one

Above all no one
Prague is a capital
But Czechoslovakia is not a country
I forget who said that
But it's true
In El Rocco
Westphalen spoke of his life
In other words
Of the past to be lived
As he spoke
He had only eyes
There was no gaze
Or vice versa
There was a gaze
The eyes
Were left in his face
As if by chance
I listened
Like the empty seashell listens
Waves
          More and more distant
Or like a child peering
Into a shell broken
Torn
Perfect
          Turn
Neither day is day
Nor night is night
Blanca has a translator
Named Snow
In El Rocco
Life spoke of Westphalen
As it spoke there was only voice
There were no words
Or vice versa
There were words
Voice mouth air
Belonging to someone barely remembered
The Count of Villamediana
Relinquishes diamonds
Rather than break his stride

Everything is movement
Gregor samsara
Gregorian Samsa
Neither diamond is day
Nor stride is night
The diamond is movement
I turn time broken
The broken shell spills its halves
Night and day
Lights names
On the tip of the tongue
Dore realized
I was talking about painting
My words were painting
In one of Cornell's boxes
She told me
There is no room for rumination
It's true
If he thought
Cornell thought with his eyes
With touch
Thought as object
He did not think it
He boxed it
How would one box
Villamediana's stride?
In a diamond of wood
The box bounds
Movement is a stone
Perfectly cut
Cage: *jaula*
Cornell: *caja*
Outside in the distance: Villamediana
Blood flows through here
Like the swiftest mirror
From country to city
From city to home
From home to room
From one cage
It escapes forever
To another smaller cage

Neither day is day
Nor night is night
Blood flows
Halfway through time
In these lines
Time is born
It would make a beautiful seashell

Kafka's Living Room

1

I've been thinking for several days about which of two options would be worse for an occasion like this one: say a lot in a few words or say nothing. I will do my best to say nothing.

It's too much, isn't it? I thought, hoped, you would laugh. Your laughter allows me to summarize briefly and thus point out one of the dilemmas of contemporary literature. A dilemma that Kafka's work, perhaps more than any other, dared to embody.

2

There is a man running and another chasing him. A third—witness, reader—watches without knowing what to do. Is the man in flight running because he is guilty of some crime or because he is the victim of a criminal? We don't know, so it's best not to interfere. Their race is paralyzing, like that of Achilles and the tortoise. At times inadequate and confused, at times exacerbated, logic always heads us toward failure. Failure is something we are really good at.

3

I walk upstairs and reach the basement. I walk downstairs and reach the attic. I have entered one of Escher's castles, one of Borges's labyrinths, one of Kafka's parables. I'm trapped outside of all possible thought. I'm trapped in a Möbius strip. I know how to fail.

4

"Let's have on this summit just one instant," we read in *Las firmezas de Isabela* (The constancy of Isabela), a play dated 1610, "peace for the eyes and respite from toil./That mountain which, precipitant,/ has collapsed now for centuries. . . ." In just one instant our gaze can take in a whole landscape that—and here the rhyme emphasizes how much vertigo there is in this sensation—"precipitant,/has collapsed now for centuries. . . ."

Curiously, paradox within paradox, what Galeazo and Emilio longed for was "peace for the eyes." The baroque gaze, as Velázquez's work testifies, never rests. That gaze, here, keeps the landscape of Toledo in the tension of its double movement: downward, from gravity, and upward, rising, ascendant.

The city is like Zeno's arrow: even when in motion, in reality it remains stationary. It is not a question, in this case, of a capricious—or sophistic, as Aristotle would say—negation of movement. Rather it reflects the terrible spiritual tension of an era. The baroque gaze translates paradoxes—"death that gives life," "that I die because I do not die"—from its own religious undercurrent. Those paradoxes were perspectives contributed by Spanish Renaissance and mystic poetry to the emergence of a gaze that, considering the extent of its distortion, owed infinitely more to an exclamation by Saint John of the Cross than to one of Tintoretto's vanishing points.

5

In many of Escher's lithographs—I'm thinking, for example, of "Waterfall," "Ascending and Descending," "Relativity," "Print Gallery"—it is possible to glimpse visual translations of Kafka's parables and paradoxes. This brings us no closer to an understanding of them, but it will enable us to bring the uneasiness provoked by our reading to an even more atrocious and revealing halt.

It is not at all surprising that Escher and Kafka share an interest in certain themes: the Tower of Babel, metamorphoses, perfect stagnation within apparently incessant change. By pointing out the nonexistence or the futility of movement, both suggest a common origin: Eleatic thought. Faced with the immobility of Zeno's arrow, Escher proposes his variations: characters who walk neither up nor down stairs as they walk up or down stairs; birds that fill precisely that small frame that they never abandon in spite of a perpetual flutter of wings: stationary flights in an equally stationary space that is other—those same—birds.

Kafka paralyzes his characters—and his readers—with processes that are meticulously reasoned but also insistent on never achieving any other end than the unreasonableness of their existence: to approach half of the half of an infinitely elastic goal. Which is why there are those curious stairways suspended between two floors but not touching either one; or that messenger who tries vainly for thousands of years to leave infinitely concentric rooms in infinitely concentric palaces surrounded by enormous crowds, in order to hand to us personally the message from an emperor who is dead and certainly forgotten. Neither his effort nor his message makes sense. The only thing that might make a bit of sense is the nightmare of imagining it. Imagining it is almost as disastrous as waiting for it. After all, in several thousand years could we decipher the message from a dead man? Would it not be even more difficult to dream our own immortality this way than to face all the obstacles confronted by the stubborn messenger?

In *The Trial*, where there is also an infinite and concentric series of obstacles—increasingly imposing doorkeepers block passage from one room to another—the priest warns K. that he should not hurry to reach any conclusions: they must first be put to the test. But the possible interpretations of the Law, the proofs necessary for arriving at every possible conclusion, paralyze thought. Like the man who wanted admittance to the Law, like K., the reader reaches, or is at the point of reaching, a melancholy conclusion: lies must be accepted as a universal principle.

It is, of course, the race between Achilles and the tortoise. Only now Achilles is convinced of the uselessness of his effort. Thanks to Zeno, he knows he will never reach the half of the half that will always separate him from the very slow tortoise. Perhaps the only way of reaching it—I say this thinking about the builders of the Tower of Babel dreamt by Kafka, who knew for a fact that it was not possible to build too slowly—would be to run as slowly as possible, in such a way that little by little the halves he needed to run were less and greater, until who knows, the tortoise would have to traverse multiples of an infinite and useless distance. Thus, within another possible paradox, the impossibility—which is also dreamt—of occupying a single space, both he and the tortoise would always arrive first at the true goal: their definitive separation.

6

The city of Toledo, seen by Góngora or El Greco, is a magic mountain. I allude to Thomas Mann's novel, thinking about those characters who preferred not to recover but to stay in a sanatorium, taking part in small rituals and activities that necessarily ended in absolute paralysis. Tuberculosis as privilege, as caste: sickness and death were accepted, provided that one was, and continued to be, part of a closed circle where boredom could be dreamt as an activity.

The strange relation between anatomy, architecture, and nature that we find in Mann also becomes evident in a starker way in the drawings of Vesalius. By the sixteenth century, skeletons and cadavers in different states of dissection—predecessors of the tubercular patients of *The Magic Mountain*—had posed in the middle of architecture, of landscapes and rituals that conferred on them a not unsurprising singularity.

Toledo also seems like an enchanted landscape to us. In an era obsessed by theological themes—sixteenth- and seventeenth-century Spain discussed, perhaps more than ever, the Fall and the Ascension, as if by so doing it could, albeit paradoxically, of course, ease the way for Isaac Newton—the city painted by El Greco and described by Góngora rests not in perfect but tense equilibrium. Nature, architecture, humanity, tossed between the Fall and the Ascension: if it were not for the grace of God, we gather, Toledo would come crashing down.

7

Rereading some lines by Góngora, we draw back our gaze a little. We are in 1588, 1596, 1621. The English have defeated Philip II's Grand Armada, they have taken and burned Cadiz, and Philip IV is riding through a park, on horseback. An empire is crumbling and no one notices. Or those who notice can say nothing about it. It is the era of the great deception. It is also, not so strangely, the era of a stubborn, blind faith. Perhaps the city described by Góngora in 1610 and painted by El Greco, probably in that same year, expresses the tension of the moment: Toledo is a precipitant summit but it will not crumble, it will fall on its peak eternally. If the empire seems to be at its zenith when it has really hit rock bottom, the city that seems to be falling remains fixed on a mountain. Appearances deceive: the only thing that matters, as an anecdote about the Count of Villamediana suggests, is impulse, or passion, unleashed precisely by the growing schism between appearance and reality.

As I think about the negation or futility of movement proposed by the Eleatics and noted by Escher and Kafka, I am reminded of an anecdote from the seventeenth century that, for me, synthesizes the entire Spanish baroque. Philip IV, the new king, enters the park at three in the afternoon followed by thirty-six knights. Among them is the Count of Villamediana. "Villamediana made quite an impression," we read in Góngora's letters, "at his own expense as usual, and this because while he was running he dropped a diamond badge valued at six hundred *escudos*, which he relinquished rather than seem petty or break his stride." Horsemanship is more important than jewels: stature depends on a gallop not a diamond. Only movement exists.

It is the era of deception. Hyperbatons and paradoxes in poetry. In painting, images that leave the canvas and remain suggested, suspended indistinctly in a mirror. The mirror, a contradictory mimesis, is painting itself, poetry, politics: a world of illusions. Thus, in *Las Meninas*: the mirror where the royal couple's portrait casually appears occupies the center of the canvas. But of the canvas where the king and queen are actually portrayed we see only the stretcher. The mirror robs us of a possible center, a possible image, a possible gaze. The center decenters: we don't see anything. Our gaze is thrown off balance, squandered around an indistinct target, erased. The imperial gaze, which appears in the mirror and which is also ours, is blinded by distance.

A paradox: Velázquez's gaze includes us in the painting and our own gaze excludes us, since from our position behind the royal couple, we should also appear in the mirror. Uneasiness: we are neither in the background nor on the surface of the painting. There is no background: what appears there in the mirror is right here, close to us. Nor is there a surface: we see only the reverse of the painting's true surface, which is the canvas where Velázquez is still painting the canvas we see.

Uneasiness and paradox as multiplication: by denying us a regal image, the painter gives us true images. We stand before his gaze and he before ours: painting itself, the act of painting is the image.

8

We return to Góngora's verses with the surprise provoked by Velázquez's painting. Where are we? "In this occident east, in this orient. . . ." The beginning of a sonnet seems to place us on a capricious cardinal point. As in *Las Meninas*, where our gaze puts us behind the royal couple, we are here but here is there. Where? Vertigo, suspension, fall: an Occident East.

But where is this Occident East? It is an illusion, it does not exist: it is an appearance underlined in order to better deceive. A syntactic mirage: the substantive lacks substance: it is an adjective. There is no East, period. In the sonnet, Góngora meditates on the sixty-three years he has just reached. It is, then, a question of an approaching sunset, the end of a life. "In this occident, in this, oh Licio,/climacteric lustrum of your life. . . ." In Góngora's time, as in Velázquez's space, we can glimpse a spectacular, shattering architecture. For that reason, reading itself, like our gaze as we look at Velázquez's painting, becomes a trap: "each uncertain foot is a fall," within a trap: "each easy fall is a precipice."

"The unified earth is breaking apart," the poet tells us, commenting not only on old age but on the hesitation of his reader faced with a duplicit, perhaps treacherous, meaning: a meaningless meaning. The poem as trap: talking is tempting, an attempt to trick us or a tempting because we are tricked. There is not necessarily a meaning in what you read here, what you see here, it seems to tell us; not even your own senses can make sense of it: the more you persist in a possible order, the more fall there will be for your always uncertain foot, the more precipice for your easy fall.

Baroque painting and poetry oppose a disconcerting symmetry to Renaissance perspective: whatever is central gets pushed to the margin. In paintings the image jumps, bounces, hides between gazes that look for it; in poems the syntax is contorted, grows in the elasticity of distant relations, throws, through hyperbaton, the in-no-way linear accumulation of meaning out of focus. The Occident East, like the mirror of *Las Meninas*, is a false point of convergence: there the semblance of an order splits and, our uneasiness, between one word and another, between the gaze and what it sees, grows.

9

I promised to do my best to say nothing. It would be, I thought, my homage to Kafka. For that reason I have referred in these pages, perhaps to your confusion, since I have intentionally done it very obliquely, to a shattering, uninhabitable architecture: Borges's labyrinths, Escher's castles, Góngora's Occident East, Kafka's tower of Babel. In all these constructions, as in the Count of Villamediana's ride, there appears that always contradictory and at times counterfunctional inner space, which occurs within each word and between one word and another. A sudden interstice of meaning that some, Kafka among them, have conceived statically. In that interstice, between concentric walls that can no longer be deemed merely symbolic, Kafka awaits our message. When he receives it—but never, never could that happen—we will be dead and forgotten. It does not matter. The important thing is the idea that when evening falls, as he sits by his window, he dreams that our messenger will arrive at any moment.

Invisible Blue

1

Trace it in the depth
of the very last sphere.
Keep suspended the bull of death
and let go in the light of death.
Music should be one single bird.
Only one.
Do not waver.
If you have learned the nature of the abyss,
deepen its darkness.

2

On a grain of sand
you anticipate the highest tide.
Clinging to your *jabillo*,
you press its thorns
toward the dormant center
of seashells.
Yours, the most fragile perfection
of the remote.
The best ocean, you know this,
departure, not return
to these repeated, ruined islands.
The words where you live
are distant,
always more distant.
Cling to that tree, press harder.

Poetry as *Eruv*

Ruins are better for defense than intact buildings.
—General Frido von Senger und Etterlin

1

There is one dossier I will never forget. It belonged to a Latin American who applied for a teaching position in a Venezuelan university. Among his professional qualifications he had included two that were totally, absolutely new to me: Torture, Exile. Their presence seemed to offer my vision a physical challenge, daring me to join the blackness of a few letters and form those two words on a predictable, boring page. My eyes slid on the letters and could not connect with them, as if the words had been left there like the banana skin that turns up in so many sitcoms. But this was not a case of carelessness; this was a serious joke. The two words blazed like the colophon of a carefully prepared document. I felt sad, amused, sick to my stomach.

For me, exile had always been a decentering experience. I looked desperately for an elusive center that perhaps had been hopelessly lost. As if they were pieces of a puzzle, I joined bits of landscape, tastes, phrases, instants that might permit a semblance of continuity. A possible history. I was determined to construct ruins, and I looked for everything, saw everything in the rearview mirror that was Cuba. People who know me well know that those efforts—those failures—were part of an increasing bitterness.

Exile isolated me not only from the island but from the isolated Cuba-in-exile, and the cowardly aggression and pettiness I encountered increased my solitude. There were, and there are, people who persecute those exiles who do not fit easily into their particular image of the American diaspora. I have a *curriculum* too, of course. Wasn't it Darío who said that everyone among the living has a *vita*? Mine, however, excluded me automatically, because it indicated my date and place of birth. As a Cuban exile, the only discipline available to me was bitterness. Others did not suffer what for many years I have been calling a double exile. This is why some people underline the supposed condition of "tortured," "exiled" when they apply for jobs. But how can a decentered being dare to approach the center so boldly? The torture victims I have known do not usually talk about their tortures. Maybe they never learned how to capitalize on them? We are certainly living in pathetic times if to the profession of torturer we can add the no-less-terrible profession of tortured. Exile has also become a profession. After all, here I am, momentarily but absolutely centered, to repeat once again *et campos ubi Troja fuit, etiam periere ruinae, et in Arcadia ego!* I will not do it. I am probably going to disappoint you, but today I want to speak of an appealing illusion: the adventures and advantages of exile. Exile as Arcadia.

2

When I speak of poetry as *eruv*, I realize that I am building castles in the air, for it would certainly be no easy task to undo the work of heavenly bodies and politicians with a poetics. Nevertheless, this must be tried. Poetry could be a cure for some of the ills that afflict our planet. And since we are talking about castles, even though they are in the air, I want to recall a curious therapy whose roots go back to the days when castles were built. This so-called cure was healing by sympathy, also known as magnetic transfer, transplanting, or translation. It was only applicable to movable diseases. Movable or transplantable. Some years ago I spoke to several groups of translators about the five types of cure by *translatio*, since I believed and I still believe, that language—being a movable disease—is susceptible to this treatment. Evidently exile is an even more *movable disease* than language. Consequently I feel obliged to list once more the various types of sympathetic therapies, all of which involve the transference or transportation of an illness from the affected body to another body: *inseminatio, implantatio, impositio, inoratio, inescatio.* According to this doctrine, it is believed that a patient will be cured if the body used as the object of transference falls ill or dies. On the other hand, if the body rejects the illness, there is no hope. For example, in the treatment by *inseminatio*, a seed is sown and watered with a liquid distilled from *magnes mumia*, the remains of a mummy; its growth determines whether or not a cure will be possible. Healing by *impositio* is no less dramatic: a piece of skin from the affected part of the body or some of the patient's excrement is inserted between the bark and the trunk of a tree and then covered with mud. In *inescatio*, a third type of healing by *traslatio, magnes mumia* is fed to an animal. A variation of *inescatio* is of particular interest with respect to the theme of exile, of transposition: nail clippings from the patient are tied to a crab that is then thrown to the current. In this case, there is a literal effort to distance the illness. Perhaps we exiles are crustaceans thrown to the current by the millions in order to cure or remove the ailments of our peoples. If this is true, the sacrifice may well be worthwhile.

3

To read Valle-Inclán's *esperpentos* and Joyce's English after he put so much English on it is to consider the possibility of a tribal revenge: the use of intense caricature, a billiard prose to counter the linguistic models imposed by the metropolis. Grimaces, deformations, defects as effects produced by a rigorous sequence of disrespectful caroms all throw language out of whack, provoking an eccentricity that can sneak Galician into Castilian and Gaelic into English. Exiles are very sensitive to this kind of eccentricity. The distance and time that gradually separate them from their landscapes and their people threaten to ruin their languages, rip their last ties away from them. Language is seen, felt, and traversed as territory. Excess and word play are methods for keeping it alive. The fascination awakened by the mechanisms and mysteries of a language reveal a fear of losing it. Exiles turn into Champollions not to interpret hieroglyphics but to create them. Every day they risk burying or disinterring their own tongues. Finally, there comes a moment when they themselves do not know if they are speaking a dead tongue, since exile is a shadowy zone where languages can die, become petrified, pulverized. Exiles fight, play with their languages to keep them from turning into Latin in the hands—and handling—of power. This gives them the advantage of knowing danger in the flesh, of feeling the immediacy of its painful reality. People who have not experienced such an apprenticeship live in a hypnotic state: ideological and commercial propagandas are the poetics of pawnbrokers and jailers. In truth there is no longer a free world.

4

Recently, we have seen literature, language itself as a living image of human experience, become a clandestine activity. Through the erasures of censorship and self-censorship, which are very routine phenomena for a large part of humanity, we are made aware that what gets expressed barely hints at expression itself, and that expression, which is at times hidden, oblique, latent, is based on simulation, on silence, and on an emphasis dismantled and dissolved by discreet irony. The abyss between what we say we mean and what we mean to say, between the meaning of a particular expression and the meaning it expresses, has perhaps never been greater. That abyss reveals one of the state's most radical encroachments, perpetuated on behalf of a new man who has already been duly mummified. As an added insult, the same state that strips words imposes abundant and monstrous catchwords. You must learn to silence what you feel and you must also learn to proclaim what you do not feel.

Exiles enjoy a freedom inconceivable in the landscapes they left behind. They are trapped like the rest of their compatriots, but they are outside the cage and can therefore take notes for an unofficial, heterodox history. This is one of the decided advantages of exile. People in exile are living documents, their very language is a document. Thus the obsession, which grips some as if they were notaries, with fixing an image, a moment. Certain aspects of things Cuban, even of Cuban speech, have been frozen in Miami, Paris, London, New York: as living fossils, they may survive mutations, mutilations, and many deaths. In this sense the literature of exile has the ghostly, poignant presence of a daguerreotype. Remember, for example, how Spain has been remembered in the Sephardic tradition, which is still alive. Archaic, conservative like the earth, like language and motherhood, the tradition of the diaspora recovers what history and time itself erase, forget. In 1981 a collection of ballads by Spanish Jews living in New York was published in the United States. Recited in New York and published in Los Angeles, these ballads carry us back from both coasts of English America to the Spain of the Catholic Kings. When we hear or read them, we are in 1492 and Spain is descending on America. Perhaps those of us now in exile were then conquistadors, *encomenderos*, and slaves. Or Jews. History repeats itself.

We no longer enjoy an easy homeland. The millions of Latin Americans in exile are the Sephardics of Spanish America. I recognize the exaggeration: it is hard to compare an experience of years or decades with one of centuries. Nevertheless, I feel as though we were living in 1492, a year of discovery and expulsion. The discovery of America proved that Earth was not a dish. But we twentieth-century Americans have insisted on refuting geography with history, which is certainly not round. We are falling from our landscapes into the abyss of exile. At least for us the Earth is a dish. Which is why some of us are gathered here in Colorado, an English-speaking land with a Spanish name. A new language, a new world.

We have repeatedly emphasized the tragedy of expulsion, but we have not dared to throw ourselves into the adventure of discovery, because we are so weighed down by an intense, painful fidelity to the past. In a radical way, however, exile forces us to espouse a difficult but rich and unexpected new humanism. When we encounter new languages, we have no choice but to discover new worlds. A chain of changes and transpositions, the deepest meaning of *uprooting*, recalls translation and its original sense of transfer or removal. For us, the word *translation* still has that flavor, which is why some of us are bilingual, why most of us are a bit schizophrenic. Whether we like it or not, expulsion has made us cosmopolitan in the stoic sense of the word, that is, in the best sense. We can testify to the fragility of borders between peoples and nations; we can testify to the traitorous expiration of documents and papers, those friends of fire; we must submit to laws that are infinitely more human, since at times we are undocumented and we are always outcasts; we know that language itself, the only territory we have left, permits no complacency, that language has meaning only if we are willing to grant it meaning, if necessary placing it again and again on the stone of Sisyphus. After it falls a thousand times, maybe everyone will be able to glimpse the stereotype of the absurd in the lapidary cooing of dogmas.

5

Exile is not only alienation. It can also be a cosmopolitanism, albeit an involuntary and painful one. The experience of transposition, which is deeply related to translation, implies the possible convergence of two unpaired spheres, that of the exile and that of the host. People in exile are never completely dispossessed; like snails, they always carry along their homes: the languages, customs, traditions of their countries. They transpose and translate: they live between two shores. Their homes and landscapes live within them, although they are no longer places of physical dwelling. Seen in this way, exile becomes a staggering enlargement of a landscape's four walls. When people are uprooted, those walls become windows. The exile's very existence represents an endless challenge to immensity and formlessness. A permanent construction and reconstruction of what has been lost, and at the same time a cautious, laborious appropriation of what is discovered, in other words, what is different. Because of the very circumstances of this uprooting, the pressing need to overcome or sublimate helplessness, the poetry of exile could take on, and perhaps fully carry out, a task that Heidegger set for poetry in his essay about Hölderlin: the creation of poetic dwelling.

Heidegger bases his thoughts on the expression *dichtersich wohnet der Mensch*: man dwells poetically. I suggest a different one: *eruv*. In the Mishnah there is a list of the thirty–nine principal types of chores affected by ritual restrictions that absolutely forbid any kind of work on the Sabbath. For example, tying a knot, untying a knot, twisting two threads, separating two threads, sewing two stitches, making a tear so as to sew two stitches, lighting a fire, putting out a fire, writing two letters, erasing in order to write two letters. Another restriction that is perhaps no less surprising to Gentiles forbids the transportation or conveyance of things from one sphere to another, in other words from the private sphere to the public sphere or vice versa. Among Orthodox Jews there is a legal fiction—denoted by the word *eruv*—that permits the conveyance of certain things—a house key, for example—without breaking the laws of the Sabbath. On Saturdays, Orthodox Jews designate an area of their neighborhood as a private sphere by encircling it with a piece of wire. An *eruv* is this wire rampart that enlarges the house and suspends the Sabbath restriction by converting the house into a walled city, into Jerusalem. When I return to Cuba, that is if I return to Cuba, I will ask Christo to surround the entire island with an *eruv*. I want him to wrap it like a present so that it finally belongs to everyone. In the meantime, the poetry of exile could serve as a rampart. Wire, architecture, dwelling, walled city: J*eruv*salem. Perhaps we can make a sphere of translation itself. At least we can try.

Other titles from Lumen Books

Deconstructing the Kimbell: An Essay on Meaning and Architecture
Michael Benedikt
ISBN: 0-930829-16-6

For an Architecture of Reality
Michael Benedikt
ISBN: 0-930829-05-0

The Architecture of Enric Miralles & Carme Pinos
Peter Buchanan, Dennis Dollens, Josep Maria Montaner, Lauren Kogod
ISBN: 0-930829-14-X

ANGST: Cartography
Moji Baratloo & Clif Balch
ISBN: 0-930829-10-7

Independent Projects: Experimental Architecture, Design + Research in New York
Anne Van Ingen & Dennis Dollens
ISBN: 0-930829-18-2

SITES Architecture 25
ISBN: 0-930829-33-6

Josep Maria Jujol: Five Major Buildings 1913-1923
Dennis Dollens
ISBN: 0-930829-35-2

The Narrow Act: Borges' Art of Allusion
Ronald Christ
ISBN: 0-930829-34-4

Written on a Body
Severo Sarduy
Translated by Carol Maier
ISBN: 0-930829-04-2

Borges in/and/on Film
Edgardo Cozarinsky
Translated by Gloria Waldman & Ronald Christ
ISBN: 0-930829-08-5

Transparent Cities
Brian McGrath
ISBN: 0-930829-17-4

Space in Motion
Juan Goytisolo
Translated by Helen Lane
ISBN: 0-930829-03-4

Reverse Thunder, A Dramatic Poem
Diane Ackerman
ISBN: 0-930829-09-3

Sor Juana's Dream
Edited & Translated by Luis Harss
ISBN: 0-930829-07-7

Culture & Politics in Nicaragua: Testimonies of Poets & Writers
Steven White
ISBN: 0-930829-02-6

Dialogue in the Void: Beckett & Giacometti
Matti Megged
ISBN: 0-930829-01-8

The Animal That Never Was In Search of the Unicorn
Matti Megged
ISBN: 0-930829-20-4

Byron and the Spoiler's Art
Paul West
ISBN: 0-930829-13-1

Urban Voodoo
Edgardo Cozarinsky
ISBN: 0-930829-15-8

Under a Mantle of Stars
Manuel Puig
Translated by Ronald Christ
ISBN: 0-930829-00-X

SITES/Lumen Inc.
446 West 20 Street
New York, NY 10011
Phone/Fax 212-989-7944